The Changing Face of Representation

The number of women in the U.S. Senate, while still small, is growing and, consequently, so is the number of citizens represented by female senators. Kim Leslie Fridkin and Patrick J. Kenney evaluate the information presented by senators to constituents, news media portrayals of senators, and citizens' attitudes about senators in order to identify the role of gender in representational communications. Focusing on the 2006 congressional election year, in which 14 of the 100 U.S. senators were women, they chose a sample group of 32 senators collectively representing 17 states. They conducted detailed content analysis of senators' official websites, examined almost 2,000 press releases and nearly 4,000 stories in local newspapers, and analyzed surveys of 18,000 citizens in the 17 states to discern their attitudes about their senators.

The authors conclude that gender-role expectations do indeed constrain the types of representational and campaign messages disseminated by senators. Gender stereotypes also influence news coverage of both candidates and elected senators, with the media often reinforcing stereotypes even when politicians' own messages challenge gender expectations. Interestingly, while citizens appear to be less influenced by entrenched stereotypes, they pay more attention to female senators' messages and become more knowledgeable about them, in comparison to male senators.

Kim L. Fridkin is Professor of Political Science at Arizona State University.

Patrick J. Kenney is the Dean of Social Sciences in the College of Liberal Arts and Sciences, Associate Vice President of Research, and Professor of Political Science at Arizona State University.

CAWP Series in Gender and American Politics

SERIES EDITORS:
Susan J. Carroll, Rutgers University
Kira Sanbonmatsu, Rutgers University

Center for American Women and Politics
Eagleton Institute of Politics
Rutgers University
www.cawp.rutgers.edu

The Changing Face of Representation

THE GENDER OF U.S. SENATORS AND CONSTITUENT COMMUNICATIONS

Kim L. Fridkin and Patrick J. Kenney

University of Michigan Press
Ann Arbor

Published in the United States of America by
The University of Michigan Press
Manufactured in the United States of America
⊖ Printed on acid-free paper

2017   2016   2015   2014   4   3   2   1

A CIP catalog record for this book is available from the British Library.

ISBN 978-0-472-11923-3 (cloth: alk. paper)
ISBN 978-0-472-12008-5 (e-book)

Contents

Acknowledgments

WE HAVE BEEN working together for more than 20 years. On most days, it seems impossible that so much time has gone by; yet, here we are completing another project. This book marries Kim's long-standing interest in the role gender plays in American politics and our mutual interest in studying elections, voters, candidates, the media, and U.S. senators. Thanks to the founders of the Republic and the 17th Amendment, the U.S. Senate is an ideal laboratory to study the effects of campaigns and representation. The distinct characteristics of the states and the number of senatorial elections provide critical variance on many fundamental concepts linking elections and representation. Specifically, in this project we were motivated to explore whether the gender of a U.S. senator influences the nature and consequences of representational messages emanating from Capitol Hill and flowing to citizens.

This project, like all of our previous undertakings, was extremely labor intensive. We began collecting data for this project six years ago. We content analyzed press releases, newspaper articles, political advertisements, and official senate websites. We linked these communications to citizens in a number of states. We needed to rely on a large and dedicated group of undergraduate and graduate students in order to undertake this large data collection. We are especially grateful to a number of our graduate students, many of whom are now running their own research agendas: Sarah Gershon, Robert Bond, Hyun Jin Choi, Jessica Leiser, Kantara Sakuwa, Matthew Bergman, Brian Blanchard, Jill Carle, Yong Ouk Cho, Shannon Conley, Samantha Gassie, Christopher Hale, Nicole Havens, Julianne Hill, David Muchlinski, Jeffrey Popowski, and Travis Timmerman. A number of undergraduate students worked with us as part of the very successful Junior Fellows program at Arizona State University. We owe a debt of gratitude to James Baumer,

Alyssa Bisanz, Elizabeth Bixby, Jesse Burke, Michael Daniels, Lisa Fernandez, Devon Gan, Bryan Garcia, James Grier, Matthew Hamilton, Russell Hoober, Douglas Lowden, David Madden, Tim McDonald, Edward Morgan, Bobby Ochoa, Jessica Potter, Ralph Robles, Katie Sachs, Jesse Snook, Daniel Stedman, Scott Tippett, Geoffrey Vetter, Ben Whaley, Nick Wearne, Brianna Wright, and Wendy Zupac.

We would also like to thank Professor Jamie Druckman for letting us use his campaign website data; we also appreciate his enthusiastic support of the project. We presented some of the preliminary results in this book at the annual conferences of the American Political Science Association and received helpful feedback from other panelists and members of the audience. The survey portion of this project was supported by a grant from the Institute of Social Science Research at Arizona State University. We received careful and efficient editorial support from Kacie Cannon at Arizona State University.

We are pleased to be associated with the University of Michigan Press ("Go Blue"). Kim holds three degrees from the University of Michigan and somehow thought she was going home when Michigan was interested in the manuscript. We have been lucky to work with Melody Herr, who has guided us efficiently through the editorial process. We, too, want to thank Professors Susan Carroll and Kira Sanbonmatsu for their feedback on the manuscript. Also, Professor Jan Box-Steffensmeier helped guide us to Michigan. The entire experience at the University of Michigan Press has been delightful.

We dedicate this book to our families. Kim is grateful to her husband Bob for his support, patience, and love, and to her teenage daughters, Jennifer and Melissa, who always inspire her, but sometimes challenge her, as she attempts to balance work and life. Pat is thankful and owes everything to his wife, Sally, of 33 years, and his grown children, Jessica, Sean, Michael, and Mary.

CHAPTER 1

The Senator's Gender and
Representational Messages

"I have always felt the special concern and the unique responsibility to single out those issues that are so important and critical to the future of women, and to make those changes, because [women's] voices can't be heard otherwise . . . But I think that women in Congress, in both the House and the Senate as well, will give special attention to those issues. We tend to carve them out as priorities, and that's important, because so often women have been overlooked as a priority in some of the issues, or the role they play in our society."[1]

SENATOR OLYMPIA SNOWE (R–MAINE, 1995–2012)

IN THE WAKE OF THE historic presidential and congressional elections of 2008, it was clear that President Obama and the Democratic majority in Congress were focused on passing the most far-reaching and significant piece of health-care legislation since Medicare and Medicaid were signed into law on July 30, 1965. President Obama urged Congress to pass health-care reform during numerous speeches, including his State of the Union address in 2009. Republican and Democratic representatives introduced 133 bills related to health care during the first year of the 111th Congress (Jan. 2009–Dec. 2009).[2]

Senators and House members spent the spring, summer, and fall of 2009 communicating with constituents about the health-care proposals churning through committees in Congress. They posted messages on their websites, they sent press releases to the national and local press; they canvassed their states and districts, appearing at town-hall meetings, in school gymnasiums, at picnics; and they met with members of interest groups and with professional lobbyists. Conversations between legislators and constituents were characterized by a back-and-forth, sometimes combustible, mixture of listening, explaining, emphasizing, and justifying views about the government's role in health-care coverage at the start of the 21st century.

In Maryland, where citizens live in the shadow of Capitol Hill, Democratic senator Barbara Mikulski and Senator Ben Cardin were busy discussing their views of health-care reform to over 5.7 million constituents. For 73-year-old Senator Mikulski, born and educated in Baltimore, health care has been a central feature of her life's work. Before politics, Mikulski cut her teeth working with people who slipped through the health-care system in jobs with Catholic charities and Baltimore's Department of Social Services. Elected to the Baltimore City Council in 1971, Mikulski captured a seat in the U.S. House of Representatives in 1977 representing Maryland's 3rd Congressional District; in 1987 she began representing every Maryland citizen as U.S. senator when she defeated Republican Linda Chavez by nearly 20 points in the 1986 U.S. Senate race.[3]

As the details of the health-care-reform legislation began to take shape in the winter of 2009, Senator Mikulski issued a series of public statements to her constituents in late November and early December. She posted 11 press releases on her Senate website; 6 of these statements focused directly on health care, including "Mikulski puts Women First in Health Care Reform Debate" (11/30/09), "Mikulski Applauds Senate Passage of Bill to Support the Caregivers of our Wounded Veterans" (11/20/09), "Mikulski to Introduce Amendment Guaranteeing Mammogram Coverage for Women Beginning at Age 40" (11/19/09), and "Mikulski Troubled by New Mammogram Recommendations" (11/18/11).[4]

On December 3, 2009, the Senate approved Senator Mikulski's amendment safeguarding coverage of mammograms and preventive screening tests for women under the newly revised health-care system. The Mikulski Amendment gave the Health and Human Services secretary authority to require health plans to cover these additional preventive services for women. The amendment passed the Senate on a vote of 61–39.[5]

Senator Mikulski highlighted her legislative achievement in press releases posted on her official senate website. She explained, "Without this amendment, there would be no guarantee that women under 50 would be covered for mammograms, no guarantee of an annual women's health exam that would include screenings for heart disease, and no guarantee that women would have access to this preventive care at no cost. . . . Insurance companies have used every trick in the book to deny coverage to women. This amendment makes sure that the insurance companies must cover the basic preventive care that women need at no cost. . . . Women can count on me to keep fighting for them on the Senate floor and all the way to the White House to end punitive insurance company practices that treat simply being a woman as a pre-existing condition."[6]

Senator Mikulski's junior colleague from Maryland, Senator Ben Cardin, was also busy discussing his legislative priorities with constituents in November 2009. Senator Cardin had been in the U.S. Congress for over 25 years. He, too, was born in Baltimore. Senator Cardin began his career in politics by winning a seat in the Maryland state legislature in 1967 and he became Speaker of the Maryland House in 1979. In 1986, as Mikulski ran for U.S. Senator, Senator Cardin was elected to Maryland's 3rd Congressional District in the U.S. House of Representatives, Mikulski's former seat. Senator Cardin was elected nine times to the House before deciding to run for the U.S. Senate in 2006. He was elected to the Senate by defeating Republican Michael Steele by approximately eight points. Both as a House member and as a senator, Senator Cardin has voted consistently with other Democrats in Congress, especially on matters of health care. He voted for the Mikulski Amendment in late 2009.

Yet, in the weeks leading up to the vote on the Mikulski Amendment, Senator Cardin issued 11 press releases, of which only two dealt with health-related issues.[7] In contrast to the messages sent by Senator Mikulski, neither of his press releases dealt specifically with women's health care; instead, Senator Cardin covered a more diverse set of communications, such as warning against cyberterrorism, praising the EPA for its decision to continue testing ethanol blends, and championing human rights in Asia.[8]

By the summer and fall of 2009, the health-care discussion had become deeply partisan, with Democrats in Congress, by and large, supporting President Obama and Republicans on Capitol Hill, more or less, opposing the reforms. The two Republican senators from Texas, Senators Kay Bailey Hutchison and John Cornyn, epitomized the GOP opposition to the health-care reform. As had the senators from Maryland, Senators Hutchison and Cornyn communicated with their 25 million constituents about how they felt toward President Obama's proposed reforms. Senators Hutchison and Cornyn have deep roots in Texas and are adept at relating with fellow Texans about their attitudes and actions regarding local and national politics. Senator Kay Bailey Hutchison, born in Galveston, earned a law degree from the University of Texas at Austin. She entered politics in 1972, capturing a seat in the Texas legislature. She lost an attempt to capture a seat in the U.S. House of Representatives in 1982 and remained out of elected office until she won a U.S. Senate race in 1992. She has won four consecutive terms since 1992, never securing less than 61% of the statewide vote. Senator John Cornyn, born in Houston, entered the U.S. Senate in 2003 after a distinguished legal career. He served as a district judge in Bexar County, Texas, sat on the Texas Supreme Court for nearly a decade, and won a statewide election to be the attorney general of Texas in 1997.

As the Mikulski Amendment was gaining momentum in the U.S. Senate in late November and in early December of 2009, Senator Cornyn issued a series of press releases lambasting all aspects of the proposed health-care reforms. His communications included the following: "CBO Analysis Indicates Reid Bill Will Increase Family Premiums by $2,100 a Year" (11/30/09) and "Report: Texans' Premiums Would Skyrocket Under Reid Health Care Bill" (12/3/09).[9] These messages about the proposed health-care legislation were uniformly negative, focusing on the projected costs of the legislation both nationally and for Texans, far too expensive for Senator Cornyn to support.

Senator Hutchison, on the other hand, was conflicted, at least on the subject of women's health care. In general, she could not support key elements of the reform, including the increased role of the federal government and the proposed cost of the program. However, Senator Hutchison rose to the floor of the U.S. Senate on the night of December 1, 2009, to talk about the Mikulski Amendment. She began her speech by noting her previous partnership with Senator Mikulski on women's health care, including preventative mammograms. She noted, "Senator Mikulski and I have worked together on women's health issues for a long time in this body. Two years ago, we championed the reauthorization of the national breast and cervical cancer early detection program which provides screening and diagnostic services. So, we know how important it is to address women's health care issues. And, I was in complete agreement with this new taskforce recommendation on mammograms and the need for mammograms under the age of 50."[10] She went on to explain, however, that the Mikulski Amendment allowed the government to play a central role in medical decisions she believed were best left to women and their doctors. Two days later, both Texas senators voted against the Mikulski Amendment.

To be sure, the health-care debate raged for nearly six more months, but on May 23, 2010, President Obama announced: "Today, after all the votes have been tallied, health insurance reform becomes law in the United States of America. The bill I'm signing will set in motion reforms that generations of Americans have fought for."[11] As expected, the votes in Congress fell essentially along party lines, with Democrats supporting the president and Republicans opposing the president. The debate over health-care reform did not end with the passage of the Patient Protection and Affordable Care Act. Indeed, an intense and often acrimonious partisan discussion focused on the legislation, pejoratively termed "Obamacare," during the 2010 federal midterm elections and health-care-reform legislation remained a key issue in the 2012 presidential election. Senators Mikulski and Cardin, across various mediums, continue to send messages to the citizens of Maryland explaining their support for the reforms, while Senators Hutchison and Cornyn steadfastly communicate to Texans their desire to repeal the legislation.[12]

Against this backdrop of entrenched positions, however, Senator Hutchison on July 19, 2011, issued a press release supporting an increase in funding for breast-cancer research: "Feinstein, Hutchison: Majority of U.S. Senate Sponsors Breast Cancer Research Stamp Renewal." The press release read, "Legislation introduced by U.S. Senators Dianne Feinstein (D-CA) and Kay Bailey Hutchison (R-TX) to extend the sale of the highly successful Breast Cancer Research Stamp has the support of a majority of the United States Senate, the senators announced today. The sale of each 55-cent stamp designates 11 cents to breast cancer research. Since its introduction in 1998, more than 915 million breast cancer research stamps have been sold-raising $73 million for breast cancer research. The legislation would renew the popular Breast Cancer Research Stamp for an additional four years. Without Congressional action, the stamp will expire on December 31."[13]

During the same week in July 2011, Senator Mikulski continued to highlight her commitment to women's preventive health care in press releases posted on her senate website. For example, on July 19, 2011, she wrote, "Mikulski Applauds Institute of Medicine's Comprehensive Recommendations for Women's Preventive Screenings And Care To Be Covered Under The Affordable Care Act." Again, on July 22, 2011, the following message was posted: "Mikulski, Senate Colleagues Urge Secretary Sebelius to Swiftly Adopt IOM's New Recommendations on Women's Preventive Health."

In contrast, Senator Cornyn and Senator Cardin were completely silent on the topic of women's health care during this same period. Instead, both senators released statements on the extended debt-ceiling debate, with Senator Cardin arguing for a "balanced approach" in a July 22, 2011, statement, while Senator Cornyn explained his views in a press release entitled "The Challenge is Not the Debt Ceiling—It's the Debt." The two senators also discussed other issues, including Senator Cardin's praise for the repeal of Don't Ask, Don't Tell, and Senator Cornyn's criticisms of EPA regulations.

The arc of the story following health-care reform and the communications of four U.S. senators from the fall of 2009 through the summer of 2011 reveals a puzzle at the intersection of gender and representation. Do male and female senators send different messages to citizens, even when these senators share the same party and the same constituency? Democratic senators Mikulski and Cardin have represented the exact same constituents from Maryland in the U.S. House and U.S. Senate for the better part of three decades. They are both advocates of a strong government role in health care. They both vote together on legislation focused on women's health care and on preventive care related to mammograms, specifically. Yet, on the crucial days surrounding an important amendment focused on women's health and on the renewal of legislation related to continuing breast-cancer research, they were communicating with constituents on different topics and issues altogether.

Likewise, Republican senators Hutchison and Cornyn are loyal conservatives from Texas, one of the key states forming the foundation of the GOP's power base nationwide. They know well what Texans, especially Republican Texans, want regarding health care: less government involvement, fewer government regulations, and lower costs. Senator Cornyn's messages about health reform are uniformly negative, emphasizing the costs of medical reform. Senator Hutchison's messages, in stark contrast, are more nuanced. Although she is steadfastly against the health-care reform authored by President Obama and the Democrats in Congress, Senator Hutchison felt the need to communicate and explain to her constituents why she voted against the Mikulski Amendment and why she partnered with Senator Feinstein directing federal dollars for breast-cancer research.

Senator Snowe's eloquent statement at the beginning of this chapter provides a context for understanding the content of communications sent by Senators Mikulski, Cardin, Hutchison, and Cornyn to the citizens of their states: "I have always felt the special concern and the unique responsibility to single out those issues that are so important and critical to the future of women, and to make those changes, because [women's] voices can't be heard otherwise. . . ." Does the content of representational communications between senators and their constituents vary systematically with the gender of the senator, or is the story of four senators from Maryland and Texas unique? We intend to explore this question because the nature of communications flowing from representatives to citizens has implications for understanding the quality of representation in America's democracy. The U.S. Senate in the first decade of the 21st century provides a window to explore the relationship between representation and gender.[14]

In the wake of the 2012 federal elections, the number of women serving in the U.S. Senate has reached 20, a historic high. Well over 100 million citizens are represented by a woman in one of the most important representative institutions in the world.[15] In contrast, 25 years ago, after the 1986 midterm federal elections, only two female senators represented 6.7 million constituents, approximately 2% of the U.S. population. The face of representation changed for tens of millions of citizens in little over a quarter of a century. This is an unprecedented time in the history of U.S. representative institutions: almost half of the U.S. population looks to female senators to represent their hopes and concerns in the national government.

These dramatic changes provide an ideal moment to explore some of the more important implications and consequences of representative government. Many debates about the nature and effectiveness of representative governments focus on whether the demographic characteristics of representatives shape and color how politicians represent their constituents (see Pitkin 1967; Mansbridge 1999). We have a unique opportunity to explore whether a U.S. senator's gender influences the representational relationship between senators and citizens.

Scholars have investigated and continue to examine whether the "descriptive" characteristics of representatives influence the political outcomes of representative governments (e.g., see Kittilson 2008). To be sure, researchers have isolated differences in how men and women represent constituents. On balance, the evidence suggests that men and women legislators have different policy agendas; they vote differently on roll-call votes; they differ in their ideological orientation; and they behave differently in committee settings (e.g., Boles 2001; Burrell 1994; Diamond 1977; Dodson and Carroll 1991; Epstein, Niemi, and Powell 2005; Frederick 2010; Gerrity, Osborn, and Mendez 2007; Poole and Zeigler 1985; Reingold 2000; Schumaker and Burn 1988; Welch 1985). What is striking about this emerging literature, however, is the absence of research on how male and female representatives communicate with their constituents regarding fundamental aspects of representation.

Communications between representatives and the represented are vital not only for lawmakers to discover what constituents want and need from their government, but also for citizens to know what their legislators are doing on their behalf. The importance of the communication process flowing from members of the Senate and House to citizens is best captured by Fenno's (1978, 136) notion that legislators need to provide an "explanation of Washington activity." Fenno (1978, 136) observed that legislators must *"explain* what they have done while they have been away from home. By explaining we mean to include the *description,* the *interpretation,* and the *justification* of their behavior . . . members spend time at home explaining to others what they had done in Washington and why" (italics in the original).

The flow of information from elected officials to constituents is the forgotten side of representational communication. It has been dramatically understudied (for a few exceptions see Fenno 1978; Fenno 1996; Grimmer 2010).[16] We intend to examine how this stream of communication varies by the gender of the senator because the nature of these messages is essential for maintaining the stability and legitimacy of representative government (Dahl 1971, 1989; Pitkin 1967).

ELEMENTS OF REPRESENTATION

Where might we locate differences in senators' messages to constituents regarding the nature of representation? Three important aspects of representation center on: (1) the development of public policy, (2) the allocation of federal resources, and (3) symbolic activities and statements.[17] Elected officials must communicate to citizens on these topics in order to remain in their jobs. How legislators represent citizens' policy or issue concerns has attracted the most attention by scholars over a long period of time (e.g., Miller and Stokes 1963; Schwindt-Bayer and Mishler 2005). Eulau and Karps (1978, 63) write, "The premise underlying the specification of policy responsiveness is the presence of a meaningful connection between constituent policy preferences or demands and the representative's official behavior." It is very important for senators to communicate policy cohesiveness and policy responsiveness with their constituents, or at the very least to their "reelection constituency."

Allocation responsiveness captures the amount of federal dollars and projects that legislators are able to steer toward their districts or states. These federal projects involve advantages and benefits that accrue to a senator's state. Many of these projects can be seen as "public goods" (Eulau and Karps

1978). Federal projects are as divergent as expansive urban-renewal programs or environmental-protection programs, and are often visible and concrete projects, such as the building of post offices and dams.[18]

The delivery of federally funded projects benefits legislators in terms of capturing a higher proportion of both "core" (e.g., Cox and McCubbins 1986) and "swing" (e.g., Dixit and Londregan 1996; Stokes 2005) voters. In addition, federally funded projects appear to heighten turnout in the affected districts and states (Cox 2007). There are a number of reasons, then, to expect senators to "advertise" and "claim credit" for bringing projects back to the state.

Less obvious, but nevertheless important, are communications focused on symbolic representation. According to Pitkin (1967), symbolic representation is not concerned with what representatives actually do, but how they are perceived by those they represent. This aspect of representation is not about "concrete transactions"; rather, it is focused on building the trust and confidence that the represented give to the representative (Eulau and Karps 1977; Fenno 1978; Wahlke 1971). Senators routinely take part in symbolic activities (e.g., participating in a parade) and make symbolic statements (e.g., formally thanking veterans for "maintaining America's freedom"). In summary, senators must produce and disseminate messages to constituents regarding the policy, allocation, and symbolic activities they are engaged in on behalf of their constituents and their states.

These three types of representational messages form the backbone of communications regarding the governing of a nation. If the amount and content of these communications vary by the gender of the legislator, then the nature of representation also varies. For example, male and female senators may highlight divergent policy agendas; they could discuss the symbolism of politics in alternative ways; they could focus on the allocation of government goods and services in contrasting ways.

The variance in representational messages ultimately influences the actions and attitudes of the news media and constituents, the two other players in the communication relationship in contemporary democracies. These three sets of actors are inextricably linked because of the size and complexity of the U.S. democracy. The news media, since the earliest days of the founding of the United States, have played a number of important roles for busy and distracted citizens. Reporters and editors deliver information from legislators to constituents, interpret and comment on the swirl of complex and often contradictory communications flowing from Washington, D.C., and investigate legislators' messages in order to assist citizens in holding their elected officials accountable. How does the news media play these roles when covering U.S. senators? Are the journalists' tasks more difficult if male and female senators differ in their representational messages? Do news organizations reflect and accommodate these differences? Or, does the news media's coverage of senators ignore these differences?

Citizens, hurried and harried by the challenges and distractions of their personal lives, are the target of the messages instigated by senators. Citizens' beliefs about the actions of their legislators determine who will represent citizens, who will deal with the pressing issues that occupy and perplex democratic governments. Do messages shaped by the gender of the senator find their way to constituents either directly or indirectly via the news media? Does the potential variance in the messages alter citizens' assessments of male and female senators in meaningful ways?

In this book, we demonstrate that the gender of a U.S. senator affects not only the messages sent by each senator, but also the news media's coverage and citizens' awareness and assessment of each senator. The findings are striking. The senator's gender permeates all aspects of how representational messages are formulated, how these messages are delivered by the press, and ultimately how they are received by constituents. The findings remain consistent, even after accounting for a series of rival explanations. For example, we find citizens know more rudimentary and complex information about female, compared to male, senators, suggesting the nature of representation varies merely by the gender of the senator.

These remarkable conclusions rest on data gathered in 2006. The data were gathered in the midst of the first decade of the 21st century, not during the fledgling days of the women's movement in the 1960s and 1970s, when the press and citizens viewed female senators as novel, unique, and inexperienced in politics on the national stage. We conduct detailed content analyses of thousands of senators' messages and news stories to determine the content and tone of information flowing to citizens. The senators' messages and the news media's coverage of those messages focus on a variety of topics, including discussion of the senators' policy priorities, their ability to bring federal projects to their states, their engagement in symbolic politics, and the senators' discussions of their experiences and backgrounds.

This is the first study to examine systematically the representational messages of male and female senators. We find female and male senators emphasize different topics and priorities. female senators are more likely than men to prioritize issues related to health care, the environment, and education; they stress their political experience; they are more likely to take clear positions on issues; they emphasize their work and experience within the institution. Male senators, in contrast to female senators, focus more often on issues related to business, the economy, and defense; they talk about their backgrounds prior to holding office; they empathize with the plight of their constituents; and they remind citizens of federal dollars that the senators have delivered to their states.

The news media's coverage, too, reflects sharp differences related to the gender of the senator. Some of these differences in press treatment echo earlier studies examining gender differences in campaign news, but some of our findings depart in important ways from earlier work. Consistent with previous work (e.g., Kahn 1996; Heldman, Carroll, and Olson 2005), reporters and editors favor male senators over female senators in terms of the number of paragraphs written, the prominence of coverage, and the accuracy in which they represent the messages emanating from the senators' offices. However, unlike previous studies of news coverage, we find that female senators receive less critical coverage and are described more positively in terms of their personal traits.

The gender of the senator also influences citizens' understanding and assessments of U.S. senators. By examining attitudes of 18,000 citizens in 17 states, we find constituents know more about female than male senators. They have more rudimentary information (e.g., party of the senator) and they have more sophisticated information (e.g., roll-call votes on important pieces of legislation) about female senators, compared to their male counterparts. This advantage for female senators is a surprising and novel finding, especially given female senators' disadvantage in sheer amount of news attention. In addition, citizens assess female senators more positively than male senators in terms of their ability to deal with health-related issues. These findings suggest the quality of representation may be influenced to a significant degree by the gender of the U.S. senator.

In this book, we provide extensive evidence and discussion elaborating on these compelling findings. We begin our exploration by reviewing what we know about representatives' messages. That is, what are the different styles employed by representatives to communicate with constituents about their governing principles and priorities?

STYLES OF COMMUNICATIONS

Legislators deliver messages about their representational activities in a number of different ways. Two classic studies of members of Congress, Richard Fenno's (1978) *Home Style* and David Mayhew's (1974) *The Electoral Connection*, provide two frameworks for understanding the various styles that legislators employ to communicate representational messages with constituents. Fenno (1978) found that communicating with constituents is part of a legislator's "home style." All legislators fashion a particular style to communicate with constituents in their home districts or states. A politician's home style not only focuses on developing person-to-person relationships with citizens, but it also establishes an ongoing pattern of communications with constituents. Fenno found that each member's home style is composed of three components: (1) allocation of resources, (2) presentation of self, and (3) explanation of Washington activities. Although Fenno was most concerned with "face-to-face" communications, a representative's home style extends easily to different types of communication.

"Allocation of resources" details the amount of time and resources a member dedicates to the district. If the member visits often and develops a large and talented staff in several satellite offices throughout the district, communications between that member and those constituents presumably will be enhanced.

"Presentation of self" deals with how legislators provide information about themselves to their constituents. In an effort to gain trust, representatives and senators emphasize their qualifications when "presenting" themselves to their constituents, often disseminating information about their experiences prior to coming to Washington as well as their experiences in Congress (Fenno 1978; Fenno 1996). Members will often discuss their influence within their political party, their work on important committees, as well as their leadership assignments within their respective chamber. Messages about political experience indicate representatives' ability to "get things done" for their constituents in Congress.

Beyond qualifications, representatives and senators try to convey how well they identify with their constituents' lives. For instance, senators often talk about their childhoods, especially if they grew up in the district or state. They want people to know about their families: both the families in which they grew up and those they created. They provide stories about their careers outside of politics (e.g., small business owner, country veterinarian, alumni of the state college, family farmer), with special emphases on activities taking place in the district or state. Fenno (1978, 56–61) found that members of Congress use this type of information to tell constituents, "You can trust me because we are like one another" (Fenno 1978, 59).

The final aspect of home style is explaining "Washington activities." Representatives and senators need to discuss their votes on legislation, talk about bills they have introduced or cosponsored, and clarify their legislative priorities. Mayhew (1974), in his classic book, *The Electoral Connection,* describes three key communication strategies legislators employ to explain their Washington activities: (1) advertising, where members engage in activities so that they will be seen, such as holding press conferences, participating in press interviews, partaking in parades and ceremonies; (2) credit-claiming, where members discuss their particularistic policies, like projects for their state, as well as casework, to show how their efforts benefit constituents; and (3) position-taking, where members highlight roll-call votes as a way of staking out popular positions on issues.

MEDIUMS OF COMMUNICATIONS

Never before in history has it been so easy for senators to communicate with constituents. And, never before has it been so manageable for scholars to track these messages. The amount of information available about politics is enormous and increasing and can be found across a number of mediums, including network television, cable, satellite, e-mail, newspapers, magazines, and the Internet. Senators have developed extensive websites containing a great deal of information about their committee assignments, their schedules, their issue positions, their constituent services, and their backgrounds. They have created online "newsrooms" for citizens and the press, and they routinely post press releases on these websites. Within the last couple of years, elected officials have begun to provide information via social-media outlets, such as Facebook and Twitter, where they highlight their activities and emphasize their priorities.

While a plethora of information is available for citizens directly from senators; senators are more effective at disseminating their messages if the news media report these messages. The local news media is an essential conduit of information for U.S. senators as they present themselves to their constituents and explain their Washington activities. While senators try to in-

fluence the news media coverage (Lipinksi and Neddenriep 2004), journalists
are selective in what they report about senators' actions. Journalists, in covering a senator in the local paper, do not have the resources to report every
bill introduced, every vote taken, every speech made. Instead, journalists
and editors rely on specific criteria of newsworthiness when deciding what
to cover and what to publish in the newspaper (Graber 2010; Vinson 2003).
Stories that are more conflictual or stories that have the potential to influence a great number of readers are more likely to be covered by the local news
organizations (Kahn and Kenney 1999).

The relationship between journalists and senators is an adversarial one
(Cook 1989). Senators want coverage to highlight the positive contributions
to the constituents of their states. Reporters and editors, on the other hand,
want stories that will generate interest among readers. While these divergent
goals will sometimes converge on the same story, often the disparate goals
lead to unfavorable or scant coverage.

Most citizens learn about the beliefs and behaviors of their senators from
news reports in the local paper (e.g., Arnold 2004).[19] And while the circulation of local daily newspapers has been declining for the last quarter of a
century, online newspaper readership has been steadily increasing (Arango
2009).[20] Recent research suggests that online newspaper content mirrors the
content of print newspapers (see Hoffman 2006). Furthermore, print newspapers often serve as agenda-setters for other local media outlets, including
local television news programs, radio news programs, and online news
sources (Project for Excellence in Journalism 2006). Finally, citizens learn
more from local newspapers than from online news sources or from local
television news (Chaffee and Frank 1996; Druckman 2005; Scheufele and
Nisbet 2002; Tewksbury and Althaus 2000; Vinson 2003).

We examine whether local newspapers differ in how they cover male and
female senators. For example, are male and female senators given the same
amount of news attention in the local paper? Does the press focus on different themes for female senators compared with their male counterparts? Is
the tone of coverage different for male and female senators? By comparing
the coverage of senators in local newspapers with the messages presented by
these senators, we can see whether the news media replicate or distort the
representational messages delivered by male and female senators.

In summary, previous research provides a clear picture regarding the
broad content of messages disseminated by legislators (i.e., public policy, allocation, symbolic). In addition, scholars have discovered how these mes-

sages are organized and framed by legislators (i.e., presentation of self, explanation of Washington activity, advertising, position taking, credit claiming). We contend the exact focus and specific content of representational communications will vary by the gender of the representative. Specifically, we theorize that male and female senators will deliver quite different messages to citizens via their websites and press releases. Why? In the next section we present a theoretical explanation for the variance in messages sent by high-level politicians.

STRATEGIC STEREOTYPE THEORY

We present the strategic stereotype theory, an original theory, to explain why we expect representational communications to vary by the senator's gender. We weave together two established theories to explain the behaviors of male and female senators. First, the theory of rationality developed by Downs (1957) and utilized by others (e.g., Fenno 1978; Mayhew 1974; Jacobson and Kernell 1983) predicts legislators will develop messages aimed at creating positive feelings among constituents in the hopes of securing reelection. Second, gender-role theory explains people have shared expectations about appropriate qualities or behaviors of men and women, producing stereotypical beliefs about men and women (e.g., Eagly 1987; Wood and Eagly 2002).

We contend that gender stereotypes force politicians to emphasize stereotypical strengths in certain messages, while revising stereotypical weaknesses in other communications in order to maximize their chances of reelection. The interaction of senators' strategic behaviors and the persistence of gender stereotypes create the foundation for the strategic stereotype theory. This original theory helps us understand and predict the unique representational messages delivered by men and women in the U.S. Senate.

We start with the premise that people have expectations about gender roles, thereby producing beliefs about appropriate behavior for men and women. These gender roles, true of "social roles" more generally, are consensual beliefs found across cultures and time (Wood and Eagly 2002). According to Eagly (1987, 12), gender roles are "shared expectations (about appropriate qualities and behaviors) that apply to individuals on the basis of their socially identified gender." Gender-role expectations are comprised of two types of beliefs: beliefs about the characteristics that men and women *do* possess and beliefs about the characteristics that men and women *should* possess (Eagly and Karau 2002). Psychologists refer to shared beliefs about the attributes of men and women as "descriptive" stereotypes, while beliefs about the proper behavior for men and women are called "prescriptive" stereotypes (Cialdini and Trost 1998; Burgess and Borgida 1999).

The empirical support for gender-role expectations is strong and convincing. For example, not only are men expected to be more aggressive than women, but people also believe that men *should* be more aggressive than women (e.g., Broverman, Vogel, Broverman, Clarkson, and Rosenkrantz 1972; Deaux and Lewis 1983; Glick, Wilk, and Perreault 1995; Spence and Helmreich 1978; Ruble 1983). In addition, experimental research shows that the descriptive and prescriptive norms associated with gender roles are stronger and more entrenched than consensual roles related to race and age (e.g., Fiske, Haslam, and Fiske 1991; Stangor, Lynch, Duan, and Glass 1992).

The research on gender roles demonstrates that many of the beliefs about differences between men and women fall along two dimensions: the communal and agentic dimensions. The communal dimension can be described as a concern for the welfare of others, with women more strongly demonstrating this concern than men. Women, according to the evidence, are more likely to be viewed as caring, nurturing, affectionate, helpful, kind, sympathetic, sensitive, emotional, gentle, and soft-spoken. Men, in comparison, are seen as embodying the agentic dimension, displaying a more assertive and controlling demeanor. Men are seen as aggressive, ambitious, dominant, forceful, and acting as a leader, independent, self-reliant, and self-confident (for a summary see Eagly 1987). People not only describe men and women in these terms, but they believe that men and women should behave according to these prescriptions.

The communal and agentic norms are so pervasive that they produce dilemmas for women and men who pursue careers and jobs requiring that they act differently from the prescribed norms. For example, agentic characteristics correspond to the characteristics valued in potential leaders (Cann and Siegfried 1990; Dasgupta and Asgari 2004; Eagly and Karau 2002). Therefore, women leaders face a double-bind with regard to gender roles. Women are not perceived as strong leaders, especially compared to men, because they are not as likely to be seen as strong, assertive, and independent. Yet, when women highlight these agentic characteristics, they are violating prescriptive beliefs by failing to exhibit the communal behaviors preferred in women. By acting in a nonstereotypical way, women may be evaluated more negatively. Eagly and Karau (2002, 575) summarize the double-bind by saying, "Conforming to their gender role would produce a failure to meet the requirements of their leader role and conforming to their leader role would produce a failure to meet the requirements of their gender role."

Female politicians have acknowledged facing the double-bind created by people's adherence to gender stereotypes. In *Nine Women and Counting* (2000), a book written by the nine women serving in the U.S. Senate in the 106th Congress, the authors write, "Women in public life are never forgiven for their tears, but they are held in suspicion for displays of stoicism. Women are still forced to ride the ever-shifting teeterboard of proper feminine behavior. They must fight notions that they are not tough enough while also taking care that they don't appear to be too tough—that is, too much like a man" (Mikulski et al. 2000, 61–62.)

In summary, gender-role theory contends that people hold both descriptive and prescriptive norms regarding the appropriate behavior for men and women. These norms are deeply entrenched and have been found across cultures and time (e.g., Eagly, Wood, and Diekman 2000; Heilman and Okimoto 2007; Johnson, Murphy, Zewdie, and Reichard 2008; Kite, Deaux, and Haines 2008; Scott and Brown 2006; Williams, Satterwhite, and Best 1999). The strategic stereotype theory hypothesizes that senators consider these gender stereotypes when deciding how to communicate with the media and their constituents. In particular, senators will develop messages capitalizing on favorable stereotypes while simultaneously trying to revise potentially damaging stereotypes.

Although strategic stereotype theory accounts for the variance in the representational messages sent by female and male senators, the impact of this variability depends on the beliefs and behaviors of reporters, editors, and constituents. The size and impersonal nature of America's democracy of over 300 million citizens means that the impact of senators' representational messages depends, to a large extent, on whether their communications are mirrored in the news media. In addition, the influence of senators' messages, filtered or unfiltered by the news media, depends on whether they find receptive audiences among constituents. Based on a great deal of work from social psychology (e.g., Bodenhausen and Wyer 1985; Fiske and Neuberg 1990; Hastie 1981), we contend that senators' representational messages will be more influential when their messages reinforce existing gender stereotypes. When senators highlight their stereotypical strengths, the news media is likely to mirror these messages because these messages are consistent with journalists' own stereotypical views of men and women elites, ir-respective of whether these elites are politicians or other high performers (e.g., corporate executives). Furthermore, citizens are more likely to absorb stereotypically consistent messages, since these types of communications will be largely reinforced by the news media's coverage and fit nicely with citizens' own gender-role expectations.

However, senators' communications will be less influential when they try to deliver counterstereotypical messages as a way of alleviating poten-tially damaging stereotypes. Since these types of messages run counter to people's stereotypical views of male and female politicians, they may not be accurately covered by the news media and will not be as easily embraced by the public.

In addition, we believe that gender stereotypes will condition the com-munication process. Specifically, we expect constituents, as well as reporters and editors, to interpret and react to senators' messages through the lens of gender-role stereotypes. Gender-role stereotypes, then, need to be consid-ered alongside the typical criteria that citizens employ to interpret the po-litical world (e.g., party, ideology, issues). In the following section, we ex-plain how senators react strategically to pervasive gender stereotypes when developing and disseminating their representational messages.

SENATOR'S STRATEGIC MESSAGES

Senators' Communications About Legislation

U.S. senators must develop a communication strategy targeting the impor-tant issues of the day. We theorize that senators' policy messages will focus, to a large degree, on issues that highlight and emphasize a senator's stereo-typical strengths. People, a priori, expect male politicians to be better at is-sues where the primary goal is to defeat the competition (e.g., economy, business, defense), while people expect female politicians to be more effec-tive with communal issues, where the main goal is to help others, such as health care or caring for the environment (e.g., Huddy and Terkildsen 1993; Lammers, Gordijn, and Otten 2009). These attitudes follow directly from gender expectations; men are seen as competitive and assertive and women are perceived as communal and socially oriented. Therefore, female politi-cians are viewed as more capable at handling social issues, while male politicians are expected to be better equipped to handle economic, defense, and foreign-policy issues (e.g., Alexander and Andersen 1993; Falk and Kenski 2006; Kahn 1996; Lawless 2004; Matland 1994; McDermott 1998; Rosenwasser and Dean 1989; Sapiro 1982).

We expect both male and female senators to highlight their stereotypical strengths regarding issues for two reasons. First, we know that when men and women run for office they often emphasize different sets of issues, with male candidates focusing more on international affairs and budget policy and women emphasizing social-oriented issues like education and social welfare (Dabelko and Herrnson 1997; Herrnson, Lay, and Stokes 2003, Kahn 1996; but also see Bystrom, Banwart, Kaid, and Robertson 2004; Dolan 2005). We expect that candidates, once elected, will remain faithful to their issue priorities or risk facing negative electoral consequences (Pitkin 1967; Arnold 1992).

Furthermore, men and women emphasize different issues as candidates and as officeholders because they have distinct policy priorities. Research examining the issue agendas and legislative initiatives of male and female officeholders consistently demonstrate that women are more likely to work on issues of special concern to women (e.g., Bratton 1999; Swers 2002; Thomas 1991). Female legislators may emphasize distinct issues, compared to their male counterparts, because of their unique experiences.

For example, in debate on the family-leave bill, Senator Patty Murray stated, "When I was twenty-six years old and an executive secretary in Seattle, I became pregnant with my first child. At that time, even though I was working out of economic necessity, there were no options for working mothers. A family leave policy would have given me the message that in this country, your family is as important as your job" (Woods 2000, 183). Women's unique experiences lead them to emphasize issues of special relevance to women.

To summarize, we contend female senators will focus on different topics from their male colleagues because they have campaigned on and care about these issues. In particular, we hypothesize that senators will showcase their stereotypical strengths regarding issues. This strategic decision provides senators with an opportunity to shape citizens' issue priorities. Decades of agenda-setting research show that the public's agenda regarding the important issues of the day are malleable (e.g., Erbring, Goldenberg, and Miller 1980; Iyengar and Kinder 1987; McCombs 1993). Furthermore, by emphasizing certain issues, politicians may alter the criteria that constituents think about when assessing their representatives (e.g., Iyengar and Kinder 1987). Therefore, senators, by emphasizing their "preferred" issues in their communications, hope to set the public's agenda regarding the pressing issues of the day. By focusing on their policy strengths, senators hope to increase the salience of these issues and to "prime" the public to consider these policy dimensions when thinking about their sitting senators.

Senators' Communications about Personal Traits

Legislators want citizens to know who they are, where they came from, and what they are like. And, citizens want to know about the character of their representatives. According to Fenno, House members and senators (1978; 1996) want citizens to consider them to be "good" people. In fact, politicians believe that this characterization is as important as policy responsiveness. Fenno (1978, 240–41) concludes that citizens "want 'a good man' or 'a good woman,' someone whose assurances they can trust, as much as they want good policy." While being viewed as a "good person" or trustworthy is important, representatives also want their constituents to view them as strong leaders, competent, effective, and empathetic.

Senators deliver messages aimed at encouraging people to develop positive trait impressions because trait evaluations are powerful and strongly related to vote choice. A plethora of empirical studies demonstrate that trait evaluations can have a strong effect on people's impressions of politicians (e.g. Fenno 1978; Fridkin and Kenney 2011; Funk 1996; Funk 1999; Hayes 2005; Herrnson 1995; Kahn and Kenney 1999; Kinder 1986; Markus 1982; Pierce 1983). These trait assessments are easy for citizens to make since they make personality evaluations routinely in their everyday lives (Fridkin and Kenney 2011).

Legislators strive to enhance people's views of their personality characteristics in their representational messages. For example, senators may discuss their leadership qualifications on their websites, or they may highlight their humble backgrounds in a press conference, or they may emphasize their empathy for the citizens of their states. In deciding the types of traits to highlight in their representational messages, men and women face different obstacles. Research in social psychology demonstrates that people hold leadership prototypes, and these prototypes organize how information is processed and how leaders are evaluated (e.g., Scott and Brown 2006; Lord and Maher 1991). If the traits of leaders resonate with the prototypes, then people perceive the leaders more favorably (Gaffney and Blaylock 2010). These leadership prototypes are pervasive and persistent across time (e.g., Lord and Maher 1991; Lord, Brown, and Harvey 2001)

As discussed earlier, there is considerable evidence that the traits associated with the leadership prototype are agentic traits, like intelligence, dominance, and decisiveness (e.g. Lord, De Vader, and Alliger 1986). And, research in political science demonstrates that traits associated with the prototypical political leader are also agentic in nature, such as experience, competence, and strength (e.g., Huddy and Terkildsen 1993; Markus 1982; Kinder, Peters, Abelson, and Fiske 1980; Kinder 1986).

Given the salience of agentic traits for the evaluations of leaders, U.S. senators need to assure their constituents that they embody these characteristics. Since there is a clear overlap between men's stereotypical strengths and the prototypical characteristics of leaders, female senators need to revise constituents' views regarding their possession of agentic traits. Female senators, more than their male colleagues, need to highlight their experience, strength, and competence in their representational messages.[21]

Of course, given the prescriptive nature of gender stereotypes, constituents may develop negative impressions of a female senator acting in a non-feminine way. However, focusing on agentic traits may be worth the risk for these senators given the stable nature of the leadership prototype. Similarly, the six-year term of office may provide senators with some flexibility as they try to modify constituents' views of their personal characteristics.

Male senators, on the other hand, do not need to highlight their agentic traits. People's adherence to gender stereotypes leads them to see men as more decisive, stronger, and knowledgeable. Instead, male senators may feel more of a need to shore up their communal qualities in their communications. Since gender-role stereotypes lead people to view male senators as less empathetic, less helpful, and less caring than their female counterparts, male senators may spend time trying to improve their constituents' views of their communal credentials. Demonstrating empathy is an important quality linked with electoral success (Fenno 1978; Fenno 1998).

Personal Traits and Symbolic Responsiveness

Besides specifically emphasizing traits like leadership or compassion in their representational messages, senators may engage in different representational acts as a way of illustrating their embodiment of certain personal traits. For example, representatives take part in a range of "symbolic" activities in order to generate trust among citizens. Fenno (1978; 1986) explains that legislators believe that acts of symbolism help foster feelings of empathy, trust, and responsiveness.

Symbolic acts of representation are intended to be nonpartisan, noncontroversial, and aimed at evoking positive emotions. Symbolic activities include marching in a parade on the Fourth of July, taking part in Memorial Day services, or visiting constituents in the aftermath of natural disasters. Symbolic statements include messages recognizing the death of important constituents, sending citizens personal letters of thanks or recognition of an accomplishment (e.g., congratulating an Olympic athlete), or putting forth a press release honoring fallen soldiers in distant wars.

Male and female senators may differ in their reliance on symbolic acts of representation. We contend that male senators need to improve constituents' views of their empathy since they are viewed as less communal than female senators. Women, in contrast, because of existing stereotypes, have an advantage on this personality dimension. Male senators, therefore, may spend more time highlighting their symbolic activities as a way of increasing rapport with their constituents and revising citizens' stereotypical views of their empathetic qualities.

Personal Traits and Allocation Responsiveness

U.S. senators, in cooperation with members of the House of Representatives, allocate billions of dollars each year for what is known as "distributive" projects. These are projects where the benefits are targeted at or distributed to specific localities and states, but the costs are spread across all states and districts and are paid for by general revenues (Collie 1988; Weingast 1994).[22] Classic examples of these types of projects are roads, bridges, urban renewal, rivers and harbors programs, dams, post offices, defense procurements, public land and resource policies, and agricultural subsidies, to name just a few (e.g., Collie 1988; Ferejohn 1974; Lowi 1964). These are the kinds of projects citizens often witness and reap the benefits from in direct and personal ways.

Senators' emphasis on allocation responsiveness may encourage constituents to alter their trait assessments of their legislators. In particular, when senators send messages showing how they are taking care of the state by bringing jobs and projects "home," citizens may come to view the senators as more concerned and more connected to the state. Male senators may be more motivated to focus on allocation activities in their representational messages as a way of revising negative views of the male senators' "connectedness." Male senators may also feel more compelled to demonstrate that they "care" for their state, since people are less likely to view male legislators as sympathetic and compassionate, compared with their female colleagues. Therefore, we expect that male senators will spend more time advertising their allocation responsiveness as a way of altering people's stereotypical views of their empathetic qualities.[23]

However, credit claiming is an electorally advantageous strategy for incumbent senators. And, while male senators may feel a greater need to show how they can take "care" of their states, female senators may be more likely to claim credit for bringing home money for certain kinds of projects (i.e., projects that reinforce women's stereotypical strengths). More specifically, women may be more likely to claim credit for projects that focus on their perceived policy strengths (e.g., the building of a day-care center), while men may be more likely to claim credit for projects complementing their stereotypical issue strengths (e.g., the expansion of a military base).

In summary, strategic stereotype theory predicts that senators will highlight their stereotypical strengths regarding policy matters. Gender stereotypes about men's and women's perceived areas of issue expertise often correspond to authentic differences in the policy priorities of male and female senators. Furthermore, since the public's policy priorities are malleable, senators may be effective in persuading constituents to care about issues that highlight the senators' perceived strengths. However, the salience of personal traits is more intransient, leading senators to try to revise potentially damaging stereotypes about their personalities. Female senators will stress their agentic strengths, like their leadership qualities and decisiveness, while male senators will stress their empathy and caring qualities.

NEWS MEDIA'S COMMUNICATIONS ABOUT SENATORS

The news media's coverage of senators will be influenced by a number of factors, including the senators' own messages, the constraints facing news organizations (Graber 2010), and the gender stereotypes held by news personnel. Journalists, like all citizens, hold gender stereotypes about men and women. In particular, news personnel are likely to associate agentic traits (e.g., leadership, competence) with male senators and communal traits (e.g., compassionate, empathetic) with female senators. Therefore, news personnel may view male senators as stronger leaders and more informed. If this is the case, then female senators may receive less news attention since gender stereotypes encourage reporters and editors to view female senators less positively along a variety of leadership dimensions.

Our expectation is supported by prior studies investigating gender differences in press treatment. In the campaign setting, Kahn (1996) found that women candidates for statewide office receive less attention than their male counterparts, controlling for incumbency and the competitiveness of the race.[24] In a more recent study exploring press treatment of men and women in Congress, Niven (2005) examined newspaper coverage of all women serving in the U.S. Senate and in the U.S. House between 2001 and 2003. Niven found that female politicians received significantly less coverage than their male counterparts in statewide and national newspapers. In a related study, Niven and Zilber (2001b) interviewed press secretaries of male and female members of Congress in 1998 to see how these staffers viewed news coverage of their bosses. Press secretaries for female members overwhelmingly complained about a lack of press coverage for their members, compared to the press secretaries working for male members.

Women are also less likely than men to be used as sources in the news (Armstrong 2004; Rogers, Thorson, and Antecol 2000; Zoch and Turk 1998) thereby reducing the amount of attention they receive in the press. The reluctance to use women as sources may reflect the stereotypical belief that men are more knowledgeable and informed about politics and public policy and consequently make more authoritative sources. For example, a study conducted by the Project for Excellence in Journalism in 2005 found significant gender differences in the use of women as expert sources in newspapers, television, and online. Researchers examined sixteen newspapers, four nightly newscast programs, three network morning news programs, nine different cable news programs, and nine websites. Across these various media outlets, three-quarters (76%) of the stories contained at least one male source, while only a third (33%) contained a female source.

In addition, we expect gender-role expectations to influence the tone of coverage devoted to male and female senators in their state newspapers. Gender differences in the tone of coverage may reflect the greater congruity between stereotypical male traits (e.g., agentic traits) and the leadership prototype. Female senators, in contrast to their male colleagues, are violating prescriptive stereotypes by simply being U.S. senators. Therefore, female senators may be treated more harshly by the press. Prior research looking at female candidates find that women often receive more critical coverage than their male counterparts (e.g., Aday and Devitt 2000; Carroll 2009; Falk 2010; Heldman, Carroll, and Olson 2005; Lawrence and Rose 2009).

While gender-role expectations may influence how male and female senators are covered in the news, it is also important to consider how the senators' messages influence patterns of press attention. In certain instances, the messages of male and female senators reinforce common gender stereotypes. When gender stereotypes are reinforced by the behavior of male and female senators, we expect greater correspondence between the senators' preferred messages and coverage of the senators in the press.

The strategic stereotype theory predicts that senators are likely to highlight their stereotypical policy strengths in their representational messages. And, we expect coverage in the news will largely mirror the senators' preferred themes. Scholars looking at campaign coverage of senatorial and presidential candidates find support for our contention: the news media often highlight "communal" policy for female candidates and "agentic" policy for male candidates (e.g., Heldman, Carroll, and Olson 2005; Larson 2001; Kahn 1996).[25]

While male and female senators' messages about policy are expected to reinforce gender stereotypes, the strategic stereotype theory predicts male and female senators will revise stereotypes regarding their personal traits. In particular, women will stress their leadership credentials, their decisiveness, and their experience in their representational messages. Men, in contrast, will highlight their empathy and connectedness, spending more time advertising their allocation and symbolic responsiveness in their communications with constituents. Since senators' messages about traits contradict prevailing gender stereotypes, it is unlikely that news coverage will simply mirror the messages disseminated by these senators. Instead, the news media's coverage may ignore the senators' own messages and instead reinforce common gender stereotypes. That is, news coverage may highlight agentic traits for male senators, while focusing on communal traits of female senators.[26] Or, coverage in local newspapers may reflect a mix, sometimes reflecting the senators' preferred messages and sometimes reinforcing gender stereotypes.

To summarize, gender-role expectations may lead news personnel to cover male and female senators differently, with women receiving less coverage and less positive coverage. Furthermore, when male and female senators emphasize themes that resonate with common gender stereotypes, we expect news media coverage to reflect these messages. However, when male and female senators try to revise potentially damaging stereotypes with their representational messages, news media coverage may not portray these messages as accurately.

CONSTITUENTS' IMPRESSIONS OF SENATORS

Citizens' beliefs and attitudes about male and female senators will be influenced by a confluence of several factors including: (1) the messages delivered by their senators, via news conferences, newsletters, web pages, and townhall meetings; (2) the news coverage of their senators on local television news programs and in their local newspapers; (3) the citizens' own adherence to gender-role stereotypes; and (4) citizens' party and ideological predispositions.

Under certain circumstances, the messages disseminated by the news media and the senators will be consistent with citizens' stereotypical views. We expect this correspondence in the area of policy matters. In particular, we expect male and female senators will focus on issues corresponding to their stereotypical strengths. These differences in issue emphases are expected to be reinforced by the news media's attention. And, we expect constituents to view male senators as better able to deal with "competitive" issues, while female senators will be considered better at dealing with "compassion" issues.

While messages about policy disseminated by the senators and the news media correspond to citizens' own stereotypical views, we expect less congruence when it comes to messages about the senators' personal characteristics. The strategic stereotype theory leads us to expect that male and female senators will try to revise stereotypical views of their personality in their representational messages. However, these messages may not be reinforced by the news media's messages. And, the senators' messages about traits may violate constituents' own conceptions regarding the typical and proper behavior of men and women. Therefore, male and female senators may not be especially effective at changing people's perceptions of their personality characteristics.

In summary, we theorize that people will retain their stereotypical views of women and men senators when these stereotypes are reinforced by the senators and the news media. When senators' messages about their personality are inconsistent with the news media's messages and conflict with common gender stereotypes, we are less confident about how constituents will respond to the senators' communications. Constituents may continue to view male senators as embodying agentic traits and female senators as exemplifying communal characteristics. On the other hand, constituents may respond to the senators' messages and begin to revise their stereotypical views of the traits associated with male and female senators.

A LOOK AHEAD

The next chapter introduces the content analyses and surveys that serve as our main source of evidence for our empirical claims. We provide extensive details of the content analyses of senators' controlled communications, including campaign and official websites, press releases, and political advertisements. We also discuss our examination of "uncontrolled" media, an extensive content analysis of news coverage of U.S. senators. We explain why we examined newspapers, how we sampled news articles, what aspects of content we analyzed, and how we drew our sample of newspaper and news articles. We introduce the surveys employed to query citizens about what they know about senators and how they evaluate these politicians. In addition to describing and explaining the survey instrument, we discuss our samples of nearly 20,000 respondents, most interviewed outside of the campaign period, but many interviewed during the 2006 campaign.

Chapters 3 and 4 examine the messages emanating from U.S. senators. These chapters provide evidence of senators' controlled communications, illustrating what messages senators choose to emphasize regarding their representational style. Chapter 3 examines information presented on senators' official websites while chapter 4 examines the content of senators' press releases. The influence of the gender of senators on the content of communications is evident immediately. On their websites, male and female senators stress different policy priorities, even when they are in the same party, representing the same state. They talk about distinct personal traits, they reflect on different experiences prior to public office, and they stress different successes in the U.S. Senate.

Press releases, too, vary with the senator's gender. Male senators spread their messages more equally across policy and allocation successes. They stress issues that resonate with their stereotypical strengths. Male senators are also more likely to boast about what they have done for their state's constituents. Female senators use their press releases to discuss their policy agenda. They also work hard to revise views of their stereotypical trait weaknesses. For example, female senators emphasize their leadership and experience in the Senate and readily reveal where they stand on issues as a way to remind citizens they are decisive.

With senators' messages documented, described, and analyzed, chapter 5 turns to an examination of the news coverage of senators in local newspapers. As we expected, we find that male senators, when compared with female senators, receive more coverage, more prominent coverage, and they are more likely to be quoted in the press. We also find that the news media's coverage largely reinforces gender stereotypes along issue and trait dimensions, largely ignoring the senators' attempts to revise stereotypical views of their personality characteristics.

In chapter 6, we spend considerable time determining what citizens know and how they evaluate their senators in light of these messages. Across a number of different measures, ranging from quite simple to much more complex, constituents consistently know more about female senators than their male counterparts. In addition, we uncover a persistent and sizeable gender gap in citizens' knowledge about their senators, with female respondents being less informed about their senators when compared with male respondents. However, we also demonstrate that this gender gap in knowledge levels is diminished significantly when people are assessing female senators.

In chapter 7, we turn our attention to senators as they run for reelection. We find male and female senators continue to emphasize divergent themes when campaigning for reelection, and that the news media cover men and women differently in their bids for reelection. However, compared with political elites, citizens are less likely to use gender as a cue when evaluating male and female senators in the midst of the campaign. For example, when we examine overall evaluations of incumbent senators on the eve of their reelection, we find that the senator's gender fails to powerfully influence citizens' impressions of that senator.

Finally, in chapter 8, we review our findings on the relationship between gender and representational messages and place these findings in a broader context. We discuss how the results of our study contribute to and inform several debates in American politics, including how gender roles influence our understanding of political behavior, how the news media perpetuates stereotypes about women, and insights regarding the importance of descriptive representation. Finally, by demonstrating that male and female senators communicate differently with their constituents, we confirm the unique role that women play in a representative democracy.

CHAPTER 2

Measuring the Content and Impact
of Representational Messages

THERE ARE THREE fundamental questions motivating this book: (1) Do male and female senators articulate different types of messages when governing and campaigning? (2) Do reporters and editors cover male and female senators differently? (3) Do citizens' understanding and assessments of senators vary with the senator's gender? To answer these questions, we need data capturing the communications disseminated by senators, we need data measuring the messages produced by news media about these senators, and we need data revealing what citizens know and think about these elected officials. We have assembled a large and impressive data set for U.S. senators in 2006 providing extensive information to answer these important questions.

We look at two different but complementary sources to capture the content of senators' representational messages: (1) the senators' official websites, and (2) the senators' press releases. Both of these data sources measure messages that are directly "controlled" by the senators, allowing us to make judgments about the type of information senators want to communicate to citizens. During the senators' reelection campaign, we turn to two additional sources of data: the senators' campaign websites and their televised political advertisements. To measure news media coverage of the senators' messages, we examine the largest circulating newspaper in each senator's state during governing and campaigning periods. Finally, to examine citizens' knowledge and evaluations of their senators, we rely on a large and representative survey of constituents, the Cooperative Congressional Election Study (CCES). During the senators' reelection campaign, we turn to a specific module of 1,045 respondents designed to explicitly evaluate gender differences in evaluations of senate incumbents approaching reelection.

These various data sets allow us to determine what senators choose to emphasize when they communicate with their constituents. We can explore whether the content and style of their representational message varies with the senator's gender. Furthermore, by comparing news coverage with the senators' own messages, we can see whether male and female senators differ in their ability to draw attention to their preferred messages. Finally, we can examine the connection between the content of the senators' communications and the attitudes citizens hold toward their senators.

WHY THE SENATE?

We have decided to study the U.S. Senate for a number of reasons. The constitutional structure of the U.S. Senate makes it an ideal laboratory for studying representation. First, the staggered electoral cycle means that one-third of senators in the chamber in any given year will face reelection, while one-third of the senators will be two years away from their reelection campaign, and one-third will be four years away from the demands of reelection. Therefore, when looking at a single year, we can compare how the senators' representational messages change with their proximity to reelection.

Second, the dual member districts of the U.S. Senate, two senators serving the same state, provide useful analytical leverage for a number of interesting comparisons. We can compare senators with the same constituency to see how they differ in their communication patterns and in the news media's representation of these messages. For instance, we can explore whether male and female senators serving the same constituency differ in their representational messages. While we expect male and female senators to distribute different messages, will this hold true for senators sharing the exact same constituency? And if male and female senators representing the same constituency deliver divergent messages, will the press echo these distinctions in their news coverage?

Third, 20 women are currently serving in the U.S. Senate. Their constituents represent nearly half of the U.S. population. In contrast, while there are more women in the U.S. House of Representatives, these congresswomen represent only about 15% of the U.S. population. In addition, the U.S. Senate is a better choice than the U.S. House for examining the mediated nature of communication since news coverage of senators is much more extensive than coverage of U.S. House members (Arnold 2004; Cook 1990; Krasno 1997; Westlye 1991).

Fourth, there is a long history of women serving in the U.S. Senate. The first woman to serve in the U.S. Senate was Rebecca Latimer Felton (D-GA) in 1922. She was appointed to fill the unexpired term of a senator who had died in office.[1] Hattie Caraway (D-AR), who was initially appointed in 1931 to fill the vacancy caused by the death of her husband, was the first women to be elected to a full six-year Senate term.[2] Margaret Chase Smith (R-ME) was the first woman elected to the Senate without having first been appointed; she served from 1949 to 1979. Senator Barbara Mikulski (D-MD) holds the record for length of service. She entered the U.S. Senate in January 1987 (Manning, Shogan, and Smelcer 2011). Consequently, there has been plenty of time for female senators to gain their own voice and distribute their own unique messages, if indeed their communications are distinct from their male colleagues.

The unique constitutional structure of the U.S. Senate, along with the significant number of women in the institution, allow us to explore possible gender differences in the substance and impact of men and women's representational messages. In our study, we sampled 32 U.S. senators from the 109th Congress (2005–2006) in order to examine how male and female senators communicate with their constituents. We included *all* of the sitting female senators in 2006 ($n = 14$) in our sample.[3] For female senators serving in a state with a male senator, we always included the male senator in our sample (e.g., Debbie Stabenow and Carl Levin of Michigan). Finally, we selected additional male senators who matched the female senators in terms of ADA scores, seniority, and proximity to reelection.

The senators in our sample represent both large (e.g., California, New York) and small states (e.g., Alaska), as well as different regions of the country. Included in our sample of senators are 18 Democrats and 14 Republicans. The senators vary in their seniority, with 9 senators in the midst of their first term, 4 senators serving in the Senate for over 20 years, and the bulk of the legislators arriving in the Senate in the 1990s. Furthermore, these senators vary in their proximity to their next election, with 9 senators facing reelection in 2006, 11 senators 2 years away from reelection, and 12 senators 4 years away from their next reelection bid. We provide a list of the senators included in the sample, along with the senator's party affiliation, seniority, and ADA score in appendix A.

MEASURING SENATORS' MESSAGES

Senators' Websites

Each senator has an official website located at www.senate.gov. We looked at
websites in February 2006 and in September 2006. A senator's official website was examined at least once for each of the 32 senators. For 19 of the 32
(59%) senators, we examined their official websites twice, once in February
and once in September. Overall, 27 of the 32 websites (84%) were examined
in February and 24 of the 32 websites (75%) were examined in September.

Senators use their websites to advertise their accomplishments, to bring
attention to their priorities, and to help provide services for their constituents. For instance, Senator Barbara Boxer provided a link on her website with
information to help students prepare for college, as well as a link telling Cal-
ifornians where they could obtain a flu shot. Senator Boxer also announced
on her main page that she was introducing a bill in the Senate to improve the
safety of public schools. Senator Carl Levin of Michigan also highlighted
links on his main page, with one of the links guiding students and teachers
to useful resources. Senator Levin's main page also illustrated his policy priorities, including an announcement released by the Senate Intelligence
Committee stating that the pre-Iraq War intelligence put forth by the Bush-
Cheney administration was full of "misinformation." The main page of Senator Ken Salazar's (D-CO) web page contained constituent-friendly links,
such as a notice that Medicare Part D enrollment would begin soon. Senator
Salazar's main page also illustrated his issue concerns and his work deliver-
ing federal dollars to his home state of Colorado. For example, in a section
titled "*Hot Topic*" (in red), Senator Salazar highlighted his efforts to improve
Colorado. The headline in the section read "Senator Unveils Fountain Creek
Vision."

In coding the senators' official websites, we looked at the main page and
the biography page of each website. On the main page, we examined the images, such as photographs of the senators and images of the American flag.
We also note the senator's blog, links to press releases, links to video archives
and photo albums, as well as legislative and committee links. On the biography page, we analyzed descriptions of the senator's background, including
facts about the senator's family and discussion of the senator's ties to the
state. We also examined the presentations of political qualifications (e.g.,
prior political office, committee assignments, and legislative accomplish-

ments). When examining the biography page, we coded the discussion of issues, including mentions of the senator's "top accomplishment." Finally, we coded the discussion of personality traits on the biography page, with more than 30 different traits examined.[4]

In conducting our content analysis, we followed the procedures described by Neuendorf (2002). A team of six research assistants (i.e., political science graduate and undergraduate students) coded the web pages. Coders participated in a series of training sessions where they were given the code sheets, as well as a codebook, containing detailed instructions for coding each variable on the code sheet. These guidelines helped reduce individual differences among coders. During the content-analysis training sessions, the coders completed pilot coding of one entire web page. Differences among coders were discussed and necessary adjustments were made to the code sheet and codebook. Coders were kept blind to the purpose of the study as a way to reduce potential bias. Once coding began, team meetings were held every week to review progress and problems that may have arisen during coding. In addition, random reliability checks of coding were periodically tested. One of the authors conducted the reliability checks, comparing the author's coding of the web page with the coding by the research assistants. In addition, a second author coded 10 full websites and these were matched to coders to assess reliability. Cohen's kappa was used to measure intercoder reliability, with a resulting score of .82 ($p < .001$), indicating a high level of agreement among coders.[5] A copy of our content analysis code sheet for the websites can be found in appendix B.

Senators' Press Releases

For each senator in our study, we collected all press releases from the senator's official website for January–April 2006 and August–November 2006. Senators vary dramatically in the number of press releases posted on their websites. For instance, for the month of February, the average number of press releases posted on senators' websites was 17, with 3 senators posting as few as 3 press releases (i.e., Bill Nelson of Florida, Paul Sarbanes of Maryland, and Ron Wyden or Oregon), while Susan Collins of Maine posted the most press releases in February, at 53. Given the large number of press releases posted on senate websites, we sampled every other day.[6] We coded nearly 2,000 press releases (i.e., 1,920), with an average of 50 press releases per senator for the entire period (January–April and August–November 2006).

Press releases focused on a variety of topics. For example, Senator Dick Durbin's (D-IL) press release on April 18, 2006, touted the "Reverse the Raid on Student Aid Act of 2006 (RRSA Act), which would make a college education more accessible and affordable. The bill cuts interest rates on college loans in half for student borrowers with the most financial need and for parent borrowers, increases Pell Grant awards, and gives students the opportunity to choose the best deals with consolidating loans. Durbin introduced the bill on Friday, April 7, 2006, just before the spring recess began."[7]

Senator Mel Martinez (R-FL) issued a very different type of press release on January 27, 2006. The press release explained that Senator Martinez "today presented Senator Santorum (R-PA) with the proceeds promised in a friendly wager between the two senators on the outcome of the 2006 Orange Bowl in which Penn State beat FSU 26–23. Martinez wagered smoked sausage from Bradley's Country Store in Tallahassee and delivered 23 pounds of it to Santorum, representing the 23 points the Seminoles scored against the Nittany Lions."

In coding the press releases, we attempted to measure three different types of responsiveness: legislative responsiveness (e.g., discussion of policy, bill sponsorships), allocation responsiveness (e.g., discussion of federal projects in states), and symbolic responsiveness (e.g., discussion of "nontangible" actions, such as participating in a parade or touting the state's NFL team).[8] Overall, the majority of the press releases discussed policy (58%), while almost one quarter of the press releases announced a new or ongoing federal project (24%). And approximately one-tenth of all the press releases discussed symbolic actions and statements (11%). Finally, 6% of the press releases focused on something other than policy, projects, or symbolism; for example, a press release announcing a visit by a national or state leader.

A team of eight research assistants (i.e., political science graduate and undergraduate students) coded the press releases. Coders were provided with the code sheet (see appendix C) and a codebook containing detailed instructions for coding each variable. The comprehensive guidelines in the codebook helped to reduce individual differences among coders. During the content-analysis training sessions, the coders completed a pilot coding of ten press releases. Differences among coders were discussed, if necessary, adjustments were made to the code sheet and codebook. Given the comprehensiveness of the training procedures, maturation effects by coders during the content-analysis process were reduced. In addition, coders were again kept blind to the purpose of the study as a way to reduce possible bias. As with the coding of the official websites, team meetings were held every week to review progress and problems that may have arisen during coding. Eighty press releases (ten per coder) were subject to reliability analysis. One of the authors conducted the reliability checks and Cohen's kappa was used to assess intercoder reliability, with a resulting reliability score of .93 ($p < .001$).

MEASURING COVERAGE OF SENATORS IN THE NEWS

To measure how the news media portray senators' representational messages, we selected the largest circulating newspaper in each state for analysis.[9] We chose newspapers for several reasons. First, newspapers allocate more resources and more space to their coverage of statewide campaigns, compared with television, thereby producing more comprehensive coverage (Kahn and Kenney 1999). Westlye (1991, 45) finds that, compared with local broadcast news, "newspapers present an amount of information that more closely approximates what campaigns are issuing." In addition, while people rely heavily on television news to keep informed about national politics, they depend on local newspapers for coverage of senatorial and gubernatorial campaigns (Kahn and Kenney 2004). Furthermore, a recent study comparing the impact of different information outlets on political knowledge demonstrates that people learn more from local daily newspapers, compared to local and national network news programs, online newspaper websites, and online political blogs (Oxley 2012).

While studies of news content on websites is still in its infancy, recent work suggests that the content of Internet news sites mirrors the coverage in traditional news sources (Hoffman 2006; Maier 2010). Furthermore, a recent study conducted by the Project for Excellence in Journalism (2010) compared news content in print, television, radio, and the Internet and demonstrated that most original content emanated from newspapers, compared to other mediums. In other words, newspapers were shown to set the narrative for most of the other media outlets.

We examined newspaper coverage from January 1 to April 30, 2006, and from August 1 to November 8, 2006. We relied on Access World News to search for all news items in the largest circulating newspaper that contained any reference to the U.S. senator. The number of articles examined ranged from 13 articles published about Paul Sarbanes in the *Baltimore Sun* to 244 articles published about Ken Salazar in the *Denver Post*. Overall, 3,822 articles were coded for the 32 senators.

Articles about the senators varied in length, subject matter, and tone. As an illustration, an article published in the New Orleans *Times-Picayune* on August 3, 2006, titled, "La. Delegation Against Pullout," discussed the call by 12 Democratic congressional leaders for a phased withdrawal of U.S. troops from Iraq. In the sixth paragraph of the article, the author mentioned Senator David Vitter's (R-LA) position on the proposal by explaining that Senator Vitter "accused Democratic leaders who signed the letter of advocating a 'cut and run' policy for Iraq." The article also quotes Senator Vitter, "I pray we'll be able to bring troops home soon . . . We all want that. But what the Democrats are calling for are arbitrary set deadlines for withdrawal no matter what the situation is on the ground" (Alpert 2006).

An article about Senator Ted Stevens of Alaska, published in the *Anchorage Daily News* on January 5, 2006, dealt with a much different subject. The headline of this article, appeared on the front page of the newspaper and read, "Alaska Lawmakers got Cash from Abramoff Clients; Stevens has Donated the Contributions he Received to Charity." In the lead paragraph, the reporter, Liz Ruskin, writes, "Senator Ted Stevens has joined an expanding list of lawmakers who are forfeiting campaign contributions from lobbyist Jack Abramoff and his clients." The story explains that Senator Stevens received more than $10,000 from Abramoff and his clients, but Senator Stevens's campaign would donate about $17,000 to charities to offset the contributions from Abramoff's clients (Ruskin 2006).

Finally, another front-page article, published on February 1, 2006, in the Raleigh, North Carolina, *News and Observer* focused on Senator Richard Burr. The article discussed Senator Burr's biography on *Wikipedia*. In the lead paragraph, the reporter, Jim Nesbitt, explains, "For the record, U.S. Sen. Richard Burr says he was never nicknamed 'The Flying Cheetah' by his high school classmates in Winston-Salem." The article continues by quoting Senator Burr's spokesman, "He has no idea where that nickname came from in the bio. He hadn't even heard of Wikipedia until the other day" (Nesbitt 2006).

Given the large variation in how senators are covered in the news, we took special care in developing a valid but reliable content analysis of news coverage. In designing our content analysis of newspaper coverage, we wanted to capture how the media portrayed the senator in the news. We also wanted to measure how closely the news coverage mirrored the senator's messages. We matched the content analysis of the newspapers with the content analysis of the senator's web pages and press releases whenever possible. We coded the amount and substance of trait discussion in the news. We also examined the content of the policy discussion in the press, including coverage of the senator's position on issues, whether the senator offered a plan or program to deal with a particular issue, and whether the senator was given credit for a policy success or blamed for a policy failure.

In addition, we examined media discussion of the senator's leadership position in the U.S. Senate, as well as discussion of the senator sponsoring or cosponsoring legislation. The content analysis also measured coverage of the senator's ability to bring federal projects to the state, as well as coverage of the senator's symbolic actions, such as participating in a parade or appearance at a ribbon-cutting ceremony. We also assessed the tone of the coverage by recording the number of criticisms in the press. We also measured the sheer amount of coverage given to the candidates and the prominence of coverage.

The coding of the articles was a labor-intensive enterprise. Coders were trained to locate articles from the Access World News website, while another set of coders were taught how to content analyze the articles. In all, 20 coders, graduate and undergraduate students in political science, were trained and participated in the news media portion of the project. As with the content analyses of press releases and websites, we followed the procedures described by Neuendorf (2002).[10] See appendix D for a copy of the newspaper code sheet.

MEASURING CONSTITUENTS' VIEWS OF THEIR SENATORS

To explore citizens' assessments of their U.S. senators, we rely on the 2006 Cooperative Congressional Election Survey (CCES). The CCES was conducted by Polimetrix, Inc., during the 2006 election. Respondents completed the survey on the Internet, answering a common content section that all respondents received, as well as a specific section of group content constructed by individual research teams. The 2006 CCES contained a large sample of 36,500 respondents. In obtaining the sample, Polimetrix employs a matched sampling method, matching key characteristics of a true representative sample of the U.S. population. Analyses suggest that this method compares favorably with traditional survey sampling methods (Hill, Lo,

Vavreck, and Zaller 2007).[11] We rely on the common content to assess understanding of U.S. senators.

In our analysis, we restrict our attention to the 32 senators examined in our study, resulting in a survey sample of about 18,000 respondents in 17 states. We look at people's basic understanding about the senators, including their ability to correctly recognize the name, party identification, and ideology of the senators. In the 2006 Cooperative Congressional Election Survey, respondents were also asked directly about salient roll-call votes. Several key roll-call votes, as identified by *Congressional Quarterly* and the *Washington Post,* were included. These votes captured a range of domestic- and foreign-policy questions and were highly salient (see Ansolabehere and Jones 2010, for a more extensive discussion of CCES methodology). In the CCES, respondents are asked to identify their own preferences on these roll-call measures, as well as identify the votes of their senators for each of the roll-call votes. In this book, we examine five roll-call votes examined in the preelection wave of the CCES: (1) federal funding for stem-cell research, (2) extending capital gains tax cuts, (3) immigration reform, (4) increasing the minimum wage, and (5) withdrawing forces from Iraq. In appendix E, we include the exact question wording for the survey questions used in our study.

ASSESSING THE CONTENT AND IMPACT OF
MESSAGES DURING CAMPAIGNS

At the end of six years in office, senators must explain and justify to citizens why they should be given six more years to govern. Citizens, weighing these messages, must decide whether their sitting senator should be retained or retired. We are interested in whether representational messages disseminated by senators during their "governing" phase are consistent with messages put forth during the "reelection" phase. Most important for this analysis, are gender differences in senators' governing messages replicated during the campaign period? And do the news media cover male and female senators in similar ways when reporting on reelection bids? Finally, how do citizens react to male and female senators as they head for the ballot box?

To examine the content and impact of campaign messages, it is necessary to supplement our original sample of senators with additional senators facing reelection in 2006. In our sample of 32 senators, only 8 senators were up for reelection. Therefore, we expanded our sample by selecting 13 additional senators who were up for reelection. In drawing our sample, we stratified by the competitiveness of the race. Thus, we compiled a sample of 21 senators competing for reelection, including the population of 6 female senators who were up for reelection in 2006 (See appendix F for a complete list).

The reelection campaigns in our sample varied dramatically in terms of the closeness of the election, the amount of campaign spending by the contestants, and the amount of news attention given to the candidates. For example, in Ohio, preelection polls showed Senator Mike DeWine running 7 points behind his challenger, U.S. House member Sherrod Brown. In contrast, Senator Orin Hatch was 37 points ahead of his challenger, businessman Pete Ashdown. With regard to campaign spending, Senator Dianne Feinstein spent only 31 cents per potential voter in her reelection campaign in California, while Senator Conrad Burns spent more than $10 per potential voter in his contest against Jon Tester in Montana. The amount of news attention varied dramatically across these contests as well. Among the largest circulating newspapers in the each of the 21 states, the Virginia contest between Senator George Allen and former Navy secretary James Webb generated the most attention, with the *Richmond Times-Dispatch* publishing 187 news articles between October 1 and Election Day 2006. The least covered contest was in Wyoming, where the *Cheyenne Tribune-Eagle* published a mere 19 articles about the race between Senator Craig Thomas and engineer Dale Groutage.

To measure the senators' messages during the campaign, we rely on two complementary data sets: (1) the senators' campaign websites, and (2) the senators' political advertisements. The data on campaign websites was collected by Druckman, Kifer, and Parkin (2009).[12] Druckman et al. obtained their sample of websites by following links from the *National Journal*'s website (www.nationaljournal.com) and using search engines such as Google. Each of the campaign websites for the 21 senators in our sample is included in the Druckman et al. data set.

Campaign websites offer some of the same advantages as the senator's official websites. The campaign websites represent the controlled message of the senators. Second, campaign websites are available for all senators running for reelection. In contrast, political advertisements are only available for the more competitive campaigns (Kahn and Kenney 1999; Goldstein and Rivlin 2005).

However, campaign websites do not represent all types of campaign messages. For example, senators are less likely to explicitly mention traits on

their campaign websites compared to their political advertisements. Therefore, candidate traits need to be inferred using proxy measures. For example,
to measure "empathy," Druckman et al. code whether the candidate presents
details about his or her family on the campaign website.[13]

In addition to relying on the campaign website data, we conducted a
content analysis of televised campaign advertisements. We collected political advertisements from the *National Journal*'s website. The *National Journal*'s
website included downloadable links to almost all senate advertisements
publicly available (Grose and Globetti 2007). We searched the candidates'
own websites and additional websites to increase the completeness of candidates' advertisement samples. We examined 131 advertisements for the 21
incumbents. Advertisements could not be located for five senators: Hillary
Clinton, Diane Feinstein, Bill Nelson, Olympia Snowe, and Craig Thomas.
These incumbents were competing in races labeled as "solid" Republican
(Olympia Snowe, Craig Thomas) or "solid" Democrat (Hillary Clinton, Dianne Feinstein, Bill Nelson) by the *Cook Political Report* (2006). This categorization indicates these races were not considered competitive and senators
easily won reelection.[14]

In coding the political advertisements, we assessed a variety of factors
associated with the content of each advertisement, including the substance
of the policy discussion, as well as the type and amount of discussion regarding personality characteristics. Six research assistants coded these advertisements and a sample of advertisements was subject to reliability analysis.[15]
See appendix G for a copy of the political advertisement code sheet.

In addition to looking at the controlled messages of the senators in the
midst of their reelection campaign, we also examined news coverage of the
senators' reelection campaigns in their state's largest newspaper. In particular, we collected newspaper data from each state's largest circulating newspaper from October 1 through Election Day 2006. We coded 2,077 news articles
for the 21 senate incumbents. To access the newspaper data, we relied on Access World News. In coding the news content, we looked at the amount and
prominence of news coverage, the substance of coverage about the senator,
including issue and trait discussion, as well as the tone of news coverage.[16]
See appendix H for a copy of the campaign news code sheet.

Finally, to assess citizens' reactions to senators running for reelection, we
utilized the 2006 Cooperative Congressional Election Study (CCES). Instead
of relying on the common content of the CCES discussed earlier, we created
a unique "module" where we controlled the survey content. For our "mod-

ule," Polimetrix sampled approximately 75 respondents for each of the 21 states included in our campaign sample for a total of 1,045 respondents. Our portion of the 2006 CCES questionnaire explored, among other topics, how citizens evaluated male and female senators along a series of trait and issue dimensions. See appendix I for the exact question wording for the survey questions in our campaign "module."

We analyzed citizens' evaluations of senators for four personal traits: honesty, caring, experience, and leadership. Previous research finds these trait dimensions influence overall evaluations of candidates in presidential elections (e.g., Bartels 2002; Funk 1996; Kinder 1986; Markus 1982; McGraw 2003; Pierce 1993). In addition, gender stereotypes lead people to view men as more experienced and strong leaders; whereas, women are viewed as more caring and more honest than men (e.g., Alexander and Andersen 1993; Huddy and Terkildsen 1993; Rosenwasser and Seale 1988). We relied on the measure of personality traits developed and employed by the American National Election Study (ANES) when examining impressions of presidential candidates.

We also measured respondents' assessments of the Senate incumbent's ability to deal with two issues: the economy and health care. We included these two issues because prior studies suggest gender stereotypes lead people to view female candidates as more competent at dealing with health-care issues, while male candidates are seen as better able to deal with economic issues (e.g., Huddy and Capelos 2002; Kahn 1996; Sapiro 1981/82). Also, health care and the economy were prominent issues in the 2006 campaign (Fridkin and Kenney 2007). We relied on the issue competence measure developed and employed by political scientists studying gender stereotypes (e.g., Sapiro 1981/82). Finally, we included a series of measures assessing forces known to influence people's evaluations of senatorial candidates. These variables include party identification (e.g., Abramowitz and Segal 1990; Kahn and Kenney 1997), ideology (e.g., Wright and Berkman 1986), and national political conditions (e.g., Hetherington 1996; Jacobson and Kernell 1983).[17]

CONCLUSION

We are fortunate to embark on this project in an era when there is ready access to senators' representational messages and to the news media's coverage of U.S. senators. We have gathered and analyzed hundreds of senators' messages from their websites and press releases. Likewise, we have sampled and examined thousands of news stories about these same senators. These messages are aimed at citizens who read, listen, and react to the content of the messages when they assess the nature and quality of their representatives' performances. Fortunately, too, we have a sample of nearly 20,000 constituents to measure and gauge their evaluations in real time. Although the data are gathered in 2006, the unique constitutional design of the U.S. Senate provides us with crucial variance in the senators' proximity to their next election. Thus, we can examine messages at various times during the governing and electoral cycles.

However, given we are looking at only one year, we need to be cautious about our conclusions. Patterns of representational communication, originating from senators and disseminated to the news media and to constituents, may change over time. For instance, the unpopularity of the Iraq War and the dissatisfaction with the incumbent president (Gartner and Segura 2008) may have influenced the content and flow of senators' messages, as well as the impact these messages had on constituents.

Nevertheless, with the large and diverse data sets employed here, we can examine a number of important questions regarding how the gender of U.S. senators shapes, colors, and permeates the attitudes and actions of senators, reporters, editors, and citizens. Until now, the small number of women serving in the U.S. Senate has limited scholars' ability to explore these types of questions. But, almost overnight, in the first decade of the 21st century, women represent tens of millions of constituents in the U.S. Senate, and their priorities and concerns are on display on their websites and in their press releases. We turn first to an exploration into differences in how male and female senators choose to portray their representational messages on their official websites.

CHAPTER 3

The Websites of Senators and Presentation of Self

CONSTITUENTS INTERESTED IN learning more about their senator can click on their senator's official website.[1] Today, all U.S. senators have their own websites (Gulati 2004). The website of Senator John Cornyn of Texas currently features a picture of the senator with the slogan "United States Senator *for* Texas" at the top of the screen. In the center of the home page is a large picture of Senator Cornyn standing at a podium with the words, "Cornyn: Voter ID Decision Purely Political" appearing below the picture. Visitors interested in reading more about the Justice Department's decision to oppose Texas' voter identification law can click and read more about Senator Cornyn's view on this decision. Senator Cornyn's home page also features links to "Hot Topics," which include "Senate GOP Jobs Plan" and Recent News, including news titled "The President Lobbying Against Jobs" and "Cornyn Responds to Reports of White House Lobbying Against Keystone." Additional links guide visitors to information about services, issues, and more information about Senator Cornyn.

Senator Cornyn's colleague, Senator Kay Bailey Hutchison, has an official website with many of the same features. At the center of Senator Hutchison's home page is a scroll with links to pictures and videos featuring Senator Hutchison in different venues, including on the floor of the U.S. Senate, in a press conference, and in a committee meeting. In the lower left of the main page is a large box with the question, "How Can I Help You?" The box takes up about one-quarter of the space on the main page and includes links to ten services, including help with federal agencies, tour requests, flag requests, congratulatory letters, coffee with the senator, internships, and the senator page program. To the right of the box, a list of four news items is displayed;

the two most recent headlines read "Mikulski, Collins, Hutchison Announce Senate Passage of Resolution Designating 2012 'Year of the Girl' to Celebrate 100th Anniversary of the Girl Scouts" and "Senator Hutchison and Senator Toomey Conduct Press Conference Call Urging Senate Consideration of Jobs Act." Visitors have the option of clicking on the headlines to read the entire press release. Like Senator Cornyn's website, Senator Hutchison's main page has a number of additional links. For example, visitors can read more "about Kay" or about "Key Issues," or they can view more videos or read the senator's weekly column.

Historically, U.S. senators have used a variety of means to disseminate information, including personal letters, newsletters, speeches, small group meetings, press releases, and television interviews. The senator's official web page is a relatively new medium (Lipinski and Neddenriep 2004). These official websites were first introduced during the 104th Congress in the mid-1990s (Johnson 2004). Congressional websites can be used to communicate directly with constituents as the websites are free and easily accessible for people with computers or mobile devices. In addition, the websites offer senators another mechanism for influencing news coverage. Lipinski and Neddenriep (2004) found congressional websites are often designed to be "media friendly," making it easier for journalists to rely on the websites when covering members of Congress.

Most senators organize their websites in a similar fashion, like Senator Cornyn and Senator Hutchison, including links to the senator's biography, information about the senator's state, and news about the senator published in local newspapers or broadcast on local television stations. Senators' websites also provide links to the senator's policy priorities and legislative accomplishments, as well as offering a place for senators to catalogue their press releases. Senators also provide specific links for students seeking information about the U.S. Senate, as well as help for constituents trying to locate assistance (e.g., ordering flags, tours of Washington, grants, nominating constituents to attend the military academies).

There is a generic or standard contour for the main web page of all senators, regardless of the senator's gender. Indeed, the data in figure 3.1 reveals that male and female senators present the same images and links on their main pages.[2] For instance, 85% of the female senators and 80% of the male senators include a photograph of themselves on their main page, while 42% of women and 44% of men include an image of the flag on

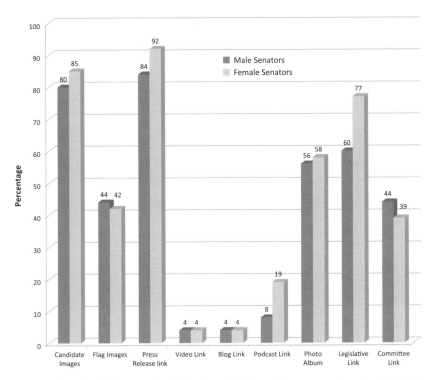

Fig. 3.1. Gender Differences in Main Page Links and Images on Senators' Official Websites

their main page. Similarly, men and women display similar links, with a small fraction of men and women employing links to blogs and videos on their websites.[3]

Since the use of social-networking sites (e.g., Facebook, Twitter) has exploded in recent years, we looked at the population of U.S. Senate races in 2010 and examined the popularity of these types of sites on the senators' web pages. We find that 64% of the senators had a link to YouTube on their websites, 40% had a Facebook link, and 32% had a Twitter link. However, male and female senators were equally likely to display these social networking sites on their web pages.

Although websites are a relatively new phenomenon, scholars have begun to investigate how politicians present themselves on these forums. However, the vast majority of these studies examine campaign websites (e.g.,

Druckman, Kifer, and Parkin 2007; Druckman, Kifer, and Parkin 2009; Puopolo 2000; Xenos and Foot 2005) rather than senators' official websites. Several researchers have investigated gender differences in the campaign websites of congressional candidates. Thus far, the results are inconsistent. Some researchers have found that female candidates for Congress are more likely than their male colleagues to focus on compassion issues, like health care, education, and the environment in their messages on their websites (e.g., Gershon 2008). In contrast, other scholars found only modest differences in the issue emphasis of male and female candidates (e.g., Bystrom, Banwart, Kaid, and Robertson 2004; Dolan 2005). In addition, Gulati (2004) examined images on congressional campaign websites and found that women were more likely than men to use images that convey their "outsider status"; for example, women present fewer pictures of Washington, D.C. and more pictures of local venues compared to their male colleagues. Bystrom et al. (2004) looked at mixed-gender races for senatorial and gubernatorial elections and discovered some gender differences in trait emphases on the candidates' websites. For example, men were more likely than women to emphasize their leadership and knowledge.

A few researchers have looked at how legislators describe themselves on official websites (e.g., Adler, Gent, and Overmeyer 1998; Niven and Zilber 2001a). Niven and Zilber examined 388 House websites during the summer of 1998. They found that women were more likely than their male colleagues to talk about women's issues (e.g., family leave, child care, sexual-harassment policy) and compassion issues (e.g., poverty, education). They also found congressmen and congresswomen described their legislative experience somewhat differently. Specifically, the authors found that women were more likely than men to discuss their qualifications. And women were more likely to describe themselves as "fighting for" others on their website, while men were more likely to use terms like "leading" or "leader."

While the research on websites is still in its infancy, studies suggest that male and female legislators may cultivate different images on their Internet sites. We intend to advance this literature by exploring and explaining the communications associated with representation and governing. It is our intention to move beyond campaign messages. Given the theoretical contours we developed in chapter 1, we have clear expectations regarding how male and female senators communicate on their websites and we subject these expectations to empirical testing in this chapter.

STRATEGIC STEREOTYPES AND PRESENTATIONS
ON THE SENATORS' OFFICIAL WEBSITES

Official websites can be considered a mechanism where senators present themselves to their constituents. These websites offer senators a way to introduce themselves to their constituents, to explain their priorities and their goals, to discuss their backgrounds, and to present their biographies. Given gender-role expectations, we expect male and female senators to act strategically when presenting themselves on their websites.

We expect senators will emphasize policy matters that correspond to their stereotypical strengths. More specifically, we expect male senators to focus more extensively on competitive issues, like the economy and defense policy, while female senators will spend more time highlighting their concern for communal issues, like health care, the environment, and social-welfare programs. By focusing on their stereotypical policy strengths, senators hope to increase the salience of these issues among their constituents. Furthermore, if senators can "prime" issues corresponding to their stereotypical strengths, then constituents will develop more favorable views of their senators (e.g., Scheufele and Tewksbury 2007).

While citizens' views about the important issues of the day are quite malleable (see McCombs 2005 for a review of the agenda-setting literature), the public's leadership prototype is less flexible (e.g., Koenig, Eagly, Mitchell, and Risikari 2011). Therefore, male and female senators will try to revise stereotypical views regarding their personality. Female senators need to demonstrate their possession of agentic traits. Therefore, female senators will be more likely than male senators to emphasize their experience, their competence, and their leadership skills on their official websites. Male senators, in contrast, are expected to spend more time convincing constituents they are compassionate, empathetic, and care about the citizens of their state. We explore these hypotheses by examining different areas of content located on the biography page. The biography page is an important link appearing on every senator's main page.[4]

Biographical Information

On the biography page, senators present a plethora of information about themselves, including a discussion of their family background, their history in the state, their legislative accomplishments, their personal achievements, and their policy goals. As an illustration, the following is the first sentence from Senator Lincoln Chafee's (R-RI) biography page: "Since 1999, Senator Lincoln Chafee has represented Rhode Island with dignity, integrity, and compassion and has been an unwavering advocate for Rhode Island's interests in the U.S. Senate." Senator Mary Landrieu's biography page begins with "Mary L. Landrieu has been referred to as 'one of the Senate's foremost leaders on education' by her colleagues in the Senate."[5]

We begin by looking at how senators present their life story, including discussions of their family backgrounds. We expect men to be more likely than women to discuss and highlight their family in their biographical messages; men want to stress their familial connections as a way of demonstrating their communal characteristics. For female senators, emphasizing family may be a liability since the "feminine" prototype and the "leadership" prototype are at odds. Female senators may be expected to put family first, especially if they draw attention to their role as mother and wife in their political communications. For instance, Senator Patty Murray explains, "Over the years, many people criticized me because I wasn't home with the kids. And they criticized me because my husband 'had to' move to Washington when I got elected. What kind of mother was I? What kind of wife was I?" (Mikulski et al. 2000, 100–101). Similarly, when Blanche Lincoln ran for the U.S. Senate, she had young twins. She was lambasted by conservative columnist, Mona Charen, who said, "Running for the U.S. Senate is incompatible with being a good mother to very young children" (Mikulski et al. 2000, 96).

Given these gender-role expectations, we expect female senators to spend less time discussing their family on their biography page compared to their male counterparts. This is exactly what we find. According to our analysis of the senators' official websites, virtually all of the men (96%) mention their family, while only 77% of the women spend time emphasizing their family backgrounds on their biography pages.

We also expect men to be more likely than women to emphasize their ties to the state as a way of demonstrating their connection to their constituents. These connections are a way for male senators to buttress their empathetic profiles. For example, Senator Ken Salazar's biography page begins, "A fifth generation Coloradan, Ken and his family have been farmers and ranchers in the San Luis Valley since before Colorado became a state." Similarly, Senator Paul Sarbanes's biography on his web page begins, "Paul Sarbanes was born in Salisbury, on Maryland's Eastern Shore on February 3,

1933. He was the son of Greek immigrants. . . . who owned the Mayflower Restaurant on Salisbury's Main Street." The emphasis on family roots and connections with the state allow male senators to shore up evaluations of their communal qualities. According to our analysis, men mentioned their ties to the state 96% of the time, while women made these references 81% of the time on their biography pages.

We explore whether these gender differences in reference to family and ties to the state persist when we take into account additional forces, such as the seniority of the senator, the senator's party, and whether the senator is up for reelection. It may be the case, for example, that Republicans are more likely to mention their families in their communications or that senators facing reelection are more likely to emphasize their ties to their state. Therefore, it is necessary to control for these characteristics of senators to see whether gender continues to influence how senators present information on their web pages. In table 3.1, we look at the impact of the gender of the senator in multivariate models. In particular, we present two logistic regres-

TABLE 3.1. Logistic Regression Predicting Mentioning Family and Ties to the State on Biography Page[a]

	Family	Ties to the State
Female Senator	−2.27*	−3.52*
	(1.27)	(1.82)
Years of Seniority in Senate	−.07	.78*
	(.06)	(.47)
Democratic Senator	−.46	1.10
	(.94)	(2.51)
Election Year	.52	−3.49
	(.98)	(2.93)
Constant	4.07**	0.94
	(1.55)	(1.58)
Correctly Predicted	86%	92%
Number of Cases	51; 32[b]	51; 32

Note: The dependent variable is (1) whether family is mentioned on the biography page of the senator's official website; (2) whether ties to the state are mentioned on the biography page of the senator's official website. Female Senator is coded 1 for female senators, 0 for male senators. Years of Seniority in Senate is coded as years in office. Democratic Senator is coded 1 for Democratic senators and 0 for Republican senators. Election Year is coded 1 for senators up for reelection in 2006, 0 for other senators.

[a]Standard errors are in parentheses.

[b]The numbers represent the number of websites, followed by the number of senators.

***$p < .01$; **$p < .05$; *$p < 10$

sions predicting the likelihood that senators will mention their families and their ties to the state in the biographical section of their website. The negative and statistically significant coefficients for gender in both equations indicate women are less likely than men to mention their families, and they are less likely to mention ties to their states when presenting their histories on their official web pages. These findings persist after controlling for three rival explanations (i.e., seniority of the senator, party of the senator, and whether the senator is facing an election).

Political Qualifications

We also expect common gender stereotypes to influence how men and women discuss their political qualifications on their web pages. Given the importance of "competence" and "experience" in the leadership prototype (Lord and Maher 1991), we expect women to highlight their political qualifications more than men in order to revise stereotypes suggesting that women are less experienced and less qualified than men in the world of politics.

Senator Olympia Snowe's political qualifications are described on her biography page. The discussion begins by recounting Senator Snowe's experience in the Maine legislature: "She served in both Houses of the Maine Legislature, first elected to the Maine House—representing her home town of Auburn—in 1973." The biography goes on to explain how Senator Snowe's House experience launched her to the U.S. Senate: "Before her election to the Senate, Olympia Snowe represented Maine's Second Congressional District in the U.S. House of Representatives for sixteen years." In addition, the biography focuses on what Senator Snowe has done for Maine: "She has also led efforts important to Maine, including successfully working to overturn the Department of Defense's recommendations in 2005 to close two of Maine's military installations, a successful push for federal disaster funds in response to a devastating 1998 ice storm and the recent flooding in Southern Maine, increased funding for the Togus veterans hospital, reauthorization of the Northeast Dairy Compact so critical to the survival of Maine's small family dairy farms, and opposition to a proposed federal rule that would have devastated the state's lobster fishery."

Similarly, Senator Debbie Stabenow's political experience is emphasized in her biography: "Inspired to first run for office by the closing of a local nursing home, she was elected to the Ingham County Board of Commissioners in 1974 and was the youngest person and first woman to chair the Board

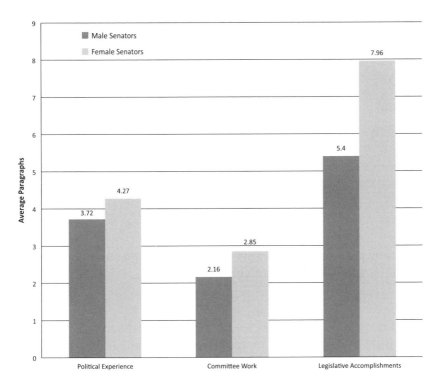

Fig. 3.2. Gender Differences in Discussion of Political Experience on Biography Page

(1977–78). She was elected to the Michigan House of Representatives where she served for twelve years (1979–90) and rose in leadership, becoming the first woman to preside over the House. She served in the State Senate for four years (1991–94). Elected to Congress in 1996 representing Michigan's Eighth Congressional District, she won election to the U.S. Senate four years later."

In figure 3.2, we look at whether female senators are more likely than their male counterparts to focus on their political qualifications and accomplishments on their biography pages. We examine three measures of political experience: mention of political office, committee work in the Senate, and legislative accomplishments. We find female senators are more likely than men to emphasize their political experience when discussing their biography. While these differences are consistent across each of the three measures, the most significant gender difference occurs when senators talk about their legislative accomplishments. Female senators, on average, mention their legislative accomplishments almost eight times on their biography page, while male senators average about five mentions on their biography page.[6]

These findings suggest that male and female senators do choose different topics to emphasize in their biographical messages, with women spending more time on their political qualifications and men focusing on their family and their connections to the state. Besides discussing their backgrounds, male and female senators often make explicit references to their personality characteristics on their biography pages. We turn next to an examination of gender differences in trait discussion on the senators' biography page.

Personal Traits

We expect male and female senators to try to revise stereotypes about their perceived trait weaknesses, leading women to emphasize their agentic traits, while men focus on their communal traits. Kay Bailey Hutchison noted the problem of constantly having to battle perceptions that she was not as tough as her male colleagues: "There was always the feeling, particularly among men, that because I was a woman, maybe I wouldn't be tough enough. 'She's going to go soft,' they'd grumble" (Mikulski et al. 2000, 51).

Senator Mary Landrieu, in an interview with Helen Thomas, noted the leadership conundrum facing women, "I think women still have to—when they show themselves to be leaders—have to conform to a male model of leadership . . . Sometimes if a woman doesn't come across as very fierce or very strong, she is perceived to be weak—when the fact is she could be a very good leader, she just has a different style" (Mara 2005, 89).

Overall, almost all senators (94%) mention traits on their biography page, with senators averaging about 7.6 mentions per page. When we look at the substance of the trait discussion, we find that traits corresponding to men's stereotypical strengths are more common than traits complementing women's stereotypical strengths. The data in table 3.2 illustrate that the most common trait mentioned on a senator's biography page is the senator's elective experience (agentic trait), followed by the senator as a "strong leader" (also an agentic trait). On average, agentic traits are much more likely to be mentioned on a senator's biography page than communal traits. In particular, agentic traits are mentioned on average 3.67 times on senators' biography pages, while communal traits are discussed on average 2.02 times per page.[7] Senators are signaling the central importance of agentic traits when communicating with constituents in their controlled messages on the Internet.

Although agentic traits are listed more often than communal traits on senators' biography pages, are female senators significantly more likely to focus on these traits compared to their male colleagues. In table 3.3, we rely on binomial regression to answer this question.[8] The significant and positive regression estimates for the gender of the senator suggest women are significantly more likely than men to mention agentic traits like leadership and experience on their biography pages.[9] But female senators, contrary to our expectations, are also more likely than their male counterparts to highlight their possession of communal traits, like empathy and advocacy. For example, Senator Susan Collins says she is a "tireless advocate for education," while Senators Barbara Boxer and Hillary Clinton both say they are advocates "for children and families."

Overall, we find that women focus on personal characteristics more than men on their biography pages. Women seem to be pursuing a dual strategy

TABLE 3.2. Emphasis on Personal Traits on Senators' Biography Pages: Average Number of Mentions for Top Traits

	Overall	Men	Women
Agentic Traits			
Accomplished	.39	.64	.15
Aggressive	.37	.28	.46
Ambitious	.02	.04	.00
Competence	.47	.28	.65
Consistent	.06	.08	.04
Elective Experience	.94	.80	1.08
Hardworking	.39	.36	.42
Independent	.25	.12	.38
Strong Leader[a]	.76	.40	1.12
Communal Traits			
Advocate[b]	.61	.28	.92
Caring	.69	.48	.88
Honest	.02	.04	.00
Moral	.20	.04	.35

[a]This difference is statistically significant at $p < .10$, based on the F-statistic (two-tailed test).

[b]This difference is statistically significant at $p < .05$, based on the F-statistic (two-tailed test).

of highlighting their stereotypical strengths (e.g., advocacy, empathy), as well as trying to revise their stereotypical weaknesses by emphasizing their competence and experience. The gender difference in emphasis on personal traits persists even in the face of controls for partisanship, election year, and seniority.

Turning to the control variables in table 3.3, Democrats and Republicans do not differ in their emphasis on personality dimensions on their biography pages. However, senators appear to be less likely to focus on communal traits when they are nearing their reelection bid, while senators with more seniority appear to prefer to emphasize agentic traits like leadership and competence on their websites. The preference for agentic traits among senior senators and the avoidance of communal traits for senators facing reelection suggest senators consider agentic traits to be more important.

Amount of Policy Discussion

Male and female senators may deliver different messages when talking about their commitments to policy matters on their biography pages. Just as discussion of family and connections to the state may bolster views regarding a senator's communal qualities, senators' emphasis on their policy expertise

TABLE 3.3. Negative Binomial Regression Estimates Predicting Number of Trait Paragraphs on Senator's Biography Page[a]

	All Traits	Agentic Traits	Communal Traits
Female Senator	.38 (.20)*	.44 (.26)*	.95 (.40)**
Democratic Senator	.26 (.19)	−.40 (.25)	.59 (41)
Election Year	−.39 (.23)	−.25 (.30)	−.95(.48)**
Seniority	.03 (.01)***	.02 (.01)*	.02 (.02)
Constant	1.42 (.20)***	.62 (.28)**	−.29 (.39)
Likelihood Ratio χ^2	13.77***	8.16*	10.27**
Degrees of Freedom	4	4	4
Number of Observations	51; 32[b]	51; 32	51; 32

Note: The dependent variable is (1) the number of traits, (2) the number of agentic trait mentions, (3) the number of communal trait mentions. Agentic traits include experience, strong leader, competent, accomplished, hardworking, aggressive, independent, consistent, and ambitious. Communal traits include caring, advocate, moral, compassionate, and honest. Female Senator is coded 1 for female senators, 0 for male senators. Seniority is coded as years in office. Democratic Senator is coded 1 for Democratic senators and 0 for Republican senators. Election Year is coded 1 for senators up for reelection in 2006, 0 for other senators.
[a]Standard errors are in parentheses, followed by levels of significance.
[b]The numbers represent the number of websites, followed by the number of senators.
***$p < .01$; **$p < .05$; *$p < .10$

and legislative accomplishments can lead constituents to view senators as more knowledgeable and effective. We expect women to be more likely than men to discuss issues on their biography page as a way of illustrating and augmenting constituents' views of their competence and political skills.

To examine the validity of our expectations, we begin by looking at men and women's "top accomplishment," as detailed on their biography pages. Almost half (43%) of the senators describe a top accomplishment and the vast majority of these accomplishments are issue based (83%). We also find, as expected, that female senators are more likely than their male colleagues to describe a policy success as a top accomplishment: 54% of the women and 20% of the men describe a policy as a top accomplishment on their biography page.[10] As the findings in table 3.4 show, women's greater likelihood of mentioning policy achievements more frequently than men is statistically significant, even when we control for the senator's party, seniority, and proximity to election.[11] In fact, the gender of the senator is among the most important variable in the model. We also find Democrats are more likely than

TABLE 3.4. Logistic Regression Predicting Mentioning Issues as Top Accomplishment[a]

Female Senator	2.42**
	(.82)
Years of Seniority in Senate	.007
	(.042)
Democratic Senator	1.44*
	(.77)
Election Year	−2.42**
	(.97)
Constant	−2.20**
	(.85)
Correctly Predicted	76.5%
Number of Cases	51; 32[b]

Note: The dependent variable is whether the senator mentions issues as a top accomplishment on the biography page of the senator's official website. Female Senator is coded 1 for female senators, 0 for male senators. Years of Seniority in Senate is coded as years in office. Democratic Senator is coded 1 for Democratic senators and 0 for Republican senators. Election Year is coded 1 for senators up for reelection in 2006, 0 for other senators.

[a]Standard errors are in parentheses, followed by levels of significance.

[b]The numbers represent the number of websites, followed by the number of senators.

***$p < .01$; **$p < .05$; *$p < .10$

Republicans to tout policy as a top accomplishment, and senators who are not facing reelection talk about policy accomplishments more readily, perhaps because they are less fearful of alienating potential supporters with their policy stance.

Substance of Policy Discussion

While we expect male and female senators to try and revise expectations about their communal and agentic characteristics, we argue that senators will play to their stereotypical strengths when it comes to policy dimensions. People, a priori, expect male politicians to be better at issues where the primary goal is to defeat the competition (e.g., economy, business, defense), while people expect female politicians to be more effective with communal issues, where the main goal is to help others (e.g., Huddy and Terkildsen 1993; Lammers, Gordijn, and Otten 2009). Therefore, female politicians are viewed as more capable at handling social issues, while male politicians are expected to be better equipped to handle economic, defense, and foreign-policy issues (e.g., Alexander and Andersen 1993; Falk and Kenski 2006; Kahn 1996; Lawless 2004; Matland 1994; McDermott 1998; Rosenwasser and Dean 1989; Sapiro 1982).

Men and women may emphasize their stereotypical strengths regarding issues because they believe such a strategy will be effective. Or, it may be the case that male and female senators have authentic differences in policy priorities, corresponding to their stereotypical strengths. Women in the U.S. Senate often point to their unique experiences as driving their interest in policy. For example, Senator Patty Murray explained, "I'm running *because* I have young kids. We need policymakers who understand what women are going through so these policies work for women" (Mikulski et al. 2000, 45, italics in the original). Similarly, Senator Kay Bailey Hutchison suggested, "We bring our life experiences to the table. Nobody fought for homemakers to have retirement accounts until we did in the Senate in 1993, for God's sake . . . When a woman has worked inside the home, what is she to do when her husband dies or leaves her after a thirty-year marriage? It wasn't that men were against these changes. They just hadn't considered the issue before because they hadn't experienced the problem in their own lives" (Mikulski et al. 2000, 53).

Do male and female senators emphasize issues corresponding to their stereotypical strengths? To examine this question, we look at the number of

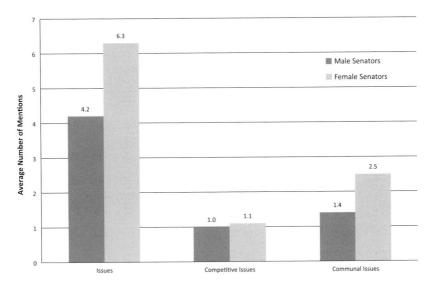

Fig. 3.3. Mean Number of Issue Mentions on Biography Page. (*Note: Competitive Issues* include defense, foreign policy, business, inflation, economy, budget, energy, farm, and taxes. *Communal Issues* include health care, elderly, welfare, child care, education, and the environment.)

issue mentions on the senator's biography page: we look at all issues and then divide issues into competitive and communal issues based on the gender stereotype literature. Communal issues (i.e., issues corresponding to women's stereotypical strengths) include health care, the elderly, welfare, child care, education, and the environment, while competitive issues (i.e., issues corresponding to men's stereotypical strengths) encompass defense, foreign policy, business, the economy, inflation, the budget, energy, farms, and taxes (e.g., Atkeson and Krebs 2008; Huddy and Terkildsen 1993; Jalalzai 2006; Kahn 1996).[12]

The data in figure 3.3 indicate that women mention issues significantly more than their male counterparts and they are more likely than men to focus on communal issues. Female senators discuss communal issues an average of 2.5 times on their biography page, while men mention these same issues only about 1.4 times. With regard to competitive issues, men and women both mention these types of issues approximately once on their biography pages.

Female senators' greater likelihood of discussing issues, as well as com-

munal issues in particular, persists when we control for the senator's seniority, party, and proximity to election (see table 3.5). Our results also show
Democrats are more likely than Republicans to mention issues and competitive and communal issues on their biography pages. Also, as senators' seniority increases, they are less likely to talk about issues generally and communal
issues, particularly.[13]

Finally, we conduct a natural experiment by looking at a subset of male
and female senators who share the same party and represent the same state.
There are seven pairs of senators serving the same state, and sharing the
same party, differing only in their gender: (1) Lisa Murkoski (R-AK) and Ted
Stevens (R-AK), (2) Blanche Lincoln (D-AR) and Mark Pryor (D-AR), (3) Barbara Mikulski (D-MD) and Paul Sarbanes (D-MD), (4) Debbie Stabenow (D-
MI) and Carl Levin (D-MI), (5) Elizabeth Dole (R-NC) and Richard Burr (R-
NC), (6) Hillary Clinton (D-NY) and Charles Schumer (D-NY), (7) Kay Bailey
Hutchison (R-TX) and John Cornyn (R-TX). Since these senators represent
the same constituency and are members of the same party, it is reasonable to
assume that they would be concerned with similar types of issues. However,
if a senator's gender is a powerful force influencing communications with

TABLE 3.5. Negative Binomial Regression Predicting Mentioning Issues[a]

	All Issues	Communal Issues	Competitive Issues
Female Senator	.47 (.23)**	.67 (.26)**	.10 (.31)
Years of Seniority in Senate	−.03 (.01)**	−.06(.02)***	−.03 (.02)
Democratic Senator	1.11 (.24)***	.89 (.27)***	.88 (.33)***
Election Year	−.46 (.28)*	−.38 (.28)	−.25 (.35)
Constant	1.07 (.24)***	.30 (.27)	−.29 (.33)
Likelihood Ratio χ^2	21.85***	20.89***	8.40*
Degrees of Freedom	4	4	4
Number of Cases	51; 32[b]	51; 32	51; 32

Note: The dependent variable is (1) the number of issues mentioned on the biography page of
the senator's official website; (2) the number of "communal" issues mentioned on the biography
page of the senator's official website; (3) the number of "competitive" issues mentioned on the
biography page of the senator's official website. Competitive issues are defense, foreign policy,
business, inflation, economy, budget, energy, farm, and taxes. Communal issues are health care,
elderly, welfare, child care, education, and the environment. Female Senator is coded 1 for female
senators, 0 for male senators. Years of Seniority in Senate is coded as years in office. Democratic
Senator is coded 1 for Democratic senators and 0 for Republican senators. Election Year is coded 1
for senators up for reelection in 2006, 0 for other senators.
[a]Standard errors are in parentheses, followed by levels of significance.
[b]The numbers represent the number of websites, followed by the number of senators.
***$p < .01$; **$p < .05$; *$p < .10$

constituents, as our earlier analyses suggest, then these senators may emphasize different issues that correspond with their stereotypical strengths.

We examine the proportion of issues mentioning competitive and communal issues on their biography pages. The two senators from Texas do not discuss these issues on their biography pages. Of the six remaining pairs of senators, we find male and female senators focus on different issues. In five of the six cases, the female senator spent more time on her biography discussing communal issues, while the male senator was more likely to talk about competitive issues. For example, in Alaska, 83% of Lisa Murkowski's issue mentions focused on communal issues, while Ted Stevens only discussed competitive issues.[14]

Similarly, in Maryland, Barbara Mikulski talked exclusively about communal issues on her biography page, while Paul Sarbanes spoke only about competitive issues. A portion of Senator Mikulski's biography page has the following description, illustrating her emphasis on communal issues.

As a United States Senator, Mikulski puts her values into action to make a difference in people's lives.

Fighting for access to quality education: Mikulski is working for every student to have access to higher education so they can follow the American dream. She has been fighting to double Pell grants, to institute a tuition tax credit and for public schools families can depend on.

Standing up for America's seniors: Mikulski is a strong supporter of the Older Americans Act and is fighting for pensions people can count on. She wrote the Spousal Anti-Impoverishment Act to keep seniors from going bankrupt while paying for a spouse's nursing home care. She fights to reform Medicare.

Working on the side of cures and research: Mikulski is fighting to increase Alzheimer's and stem cell research. She has also worked to increase the budget for the National Institutes of Health and continues to be a leader in increasing funding for uterine fibroid research.

Continuing to lead on women's health: Mikulski fought to have women included in clinical trials and medical research at the National Institutes of Health. She wrote the law requiring federal standards for mammograms and fought for uninsured women to get screenings and treatment for breast and cervical cancer.[15]

In contrast, Senator Sarbanes, also a Democrat serving the people of Maryland, talks entirely about competitive issues on his biography page, as the following excerpt illustrates.

> In response to the failure of Enron Corporation in 2001, which, at the time, was the 7th largest corporation in the United States, Sarbanes, in his capacity as Chairman of the Senate Banking, Housing, and Urban Affairs Committee, held a series of comprehensive hearings resulting in the passage of a bipartisan bill designed to reform the accounting industry and restore the investor confidence that had been eroded following the collapse of Enron.
>
> "The Public Company Accounting Reform and Investor Protection Act" was signed into law on July 30, 2002, and has been referred to as "the most far-reaching reforms of American business practices since the time of Franklin Delano Roosevelt." The law is now known as the "Sarbanes-Oxley Act," named for the principal sponsors of the legislation. The legislation creates a strong independent oversight board to oversee the auditors of public companies and enables the board to set accounting standards, and investigate and discipline accountants. It addresses conflicts of interest, ensures auditor independence, strengthens corporate governance, by requiring corporate leaders to be personally responsible for the accuracy of their company's financial reports, and establishes safeguards to protect against investment analysts' conflicts.[16]

The results of this natural experiment, juxtaposed with our examination of the entire sample of 32 senators presented earlier, lend strong support to the idea that male and female senators communicate differently with citizens regarding public policy. Overall, women are more likely to discuss an issue as a top accomplishment, they present more issue information on their biography pages, and they are more likely to talk about communal issues on these pages.

SUMMARY AND CONCLUSION

Senators' official websites provide a forum for senators to develop and disseminate representational messages to their constituents. Our analysis of these websites suggests that male and female senators display alternative styles, as well as discussing and emphasizing different topics on their Internet sites. We find men and women often present messages consistent with people's stereotypical views regarding the gender of the senator. For example, male and female senators emphasize their stereotypical strengths regarding issues. However, when gender-role expectations create obstacles for senators (e.g., may create unfavorable images among constituents), senators try to revise potentially damaging stereotypes by demonstrating that they have moved beyond the trappings of a "typical" man or a "typical" woman. In particular, female senators need to overcome stereotypes regarding their lack of leadership and experience. Therefore, female senators often highlight their political qualifications in order to prevail over damaging misconceptions. Similarly, female senators cannot simply reinforce existing stereotypes about their compassion and empathy in their representational messages since agentic traits are weighed more heavily by people when they evaluate politicians. Therefore, female senators try to revise gender-role expectations by highlighting their embodiment of agentic traits like leadership, competence, and experience and by stressing their understanding of policy matters.

Male senators, in contrast, do not need to highlight their agentic traits, given people's adherence to gender stereotypes. Instead, these senators need to convince constituents they are empathetic and care about their constituents, something female senators can take for granted given gender-role expectations. We find that male senators are more likely to emphasize their ties to their state and to highlight their familial connections in their representational messages as a way of shoring up their communal qualities.

In summary, we find evidence consistent with the strategic stereotype theory. Both male and female senators adhere to gender-role expectations when such expectations are likely to be politically advantageous (e.g., female senators emphasizing communal issues; male senators focusing on competitive issues). However, female and male senators try to revise stereotypical views when these stereotypes may be harmful for the senators' political career.

Senators know that citizens, interest groups, and reporters visit their websites. And the number of visitors to their websites is steadily increasing, especially compared to 10 years ago. But to systematically reach large numbers of constituents, senators need stories to appear in the local press highlighting their legislative accomplishments, their symbolic activities, and their success at funneling federal dollars to their states. Consequently, beyond developing important personal relationships with reporters and editors of the local press, senators routinely release to the press stories about their priorities, activities, and accomplishments in the form of press releases.

They send these press releases to reporters and editors and they post them on their websites. Just as with web pages, we expect the senators' press releases to highlight the senators' stereotypical strengths on issue dimensions, while simultaneously revising stereotypical weaknesses on trait dimensions. In chapter 4 we examine the generalizability of the strategic stereotype theory when we look at how the gender of the senator shapes the content of the senators' press releases.

CHAPTER 4

How the Senator's Gender Influences the Content of Press Releases

On March 8, 2012, Senator Kirsten Gillibrand (D-NY) posted a press release on her official website titled, "Gillibrand, Senate Democratic Women Call on Boehner to Abandon Pledge to Continue Contraception Fight." The press release begins, "Senators to Boehner on International Women's Day: 'Women are tired of being targets for a political strategy that endangers their health care and they want it to stop.'" The body of the press release explains, "Today, U.S. Senator Kirsten Gillibrand, along with eleven Democratic women Senators, sent a letter to House Speaker John Boehner calling on him to rescind his pledge to push forward with efforts to restrict women's access to contraception after the Blunt amendment was defeated in the Senate."[1]

On the same day, Senator Gillibrand's colleague from New York, Democrat Charles Schumer, posted a press release with the headline, "Schumer Announces Village of Castorland To Receive $750,000 in Federal Funding—Investment Will Fund Improvements in Village's Sewer System." The press release explains funding will be used to update the village's sewer collection system and build a sewer treatment system for residents and businesses.[2] Schumer explains in the press release, "Efficiently supporting our rural communities with funding for clean water and sewer repairs is pivotal for our community and our economy."

The contrast in the messages is intriguing. Two Democratic senators from New York posted dramatically different messages for the news media on their websites. Are these two press releases illustrative of systematic differences in how men and women senators communicate with the press? We think so. In this chapter, we demonstrate how press releases distributed by male and female senators simultaneously stress their stereotypical strengths along pol-

icy dimensions, while revising potentially damaging views of the traits associated with typical male and female senators. To be sure, we expect the
strategic stereotype theory to explain the content of press releases as well as
it explained the content on the senators' web pages.

Press releases are an important and critical medium employed by U.S.
senators to communicate with the members of the press, and ultimately
with citizens. Similar to the content and links on senators' websites, press
releases are controlled communications projecting specific messages senators wish to communicate to the press. The press releases are nearly unre-
stricted in terms of length and topic. Press releases are convenient; they are
easily presented and readily archived on websites. They can be posted in real
time and messages can be adjusted quickly, effortlessly, and endlessly. Not
surprisingly, all senators display their news releases on their websites.

Even though web pages and press releases are both controlled communications, they perform unique functions. Web pages are a means of introducing senators to constituents across a range of topics. In contrast, press releases are used by senators to advertise specific representational messages.
Senators want to focus reporters, editors, and citizens on messages about
specific issue agendas or positions on particular issues (e.g., Senator Gillibrand's position on women's health issues), on messages highlighting projects they are bringing to the state (e.g., Senator Schumer's sewer project),
and on messages aimed at building confidence and trust with constituents.

Press releases posted on websites are convenient for reporters and editors.
Local media outlets are chronically pressed for resources. Many local news
organizations do not have a reporter dedicated to covering legislative politics. Instead, news outlets often rely on wire services to follow news about
the local representatives (e.g., Arnold 2004; Cook 1989; Schaffner 2006).
And it is not uncommon for local newspapers to simply reprint politicians'
press releases in the news (e.g., Grimmer 2010; Vinson 2003). Grimmer
(2010, 5–8) examined the press releases of ten senate offices in 2007 and
found that, on average, approximately one out of every six press releases was
"quoted, paraphrased, or plagiarized" in local newspapers. Two of the senators had over one-quarter of their press releases appear in local press stories
(Grimmer 2010, 8). The faithful replication of the senators' messages in the
local paper is the goal of every senator's office and every press secretary.

Although senators yearn for press coverage, it is often difficult to isolate
the specific impact that news coverage has on constituents' evaluations of
legislators. However, there is mounting evidence that politicians who adver-

tise their representational messages and activities are able to generate more favorable assessments among constituents. Scholars examining political pamphlets (e.g., Lipinski 2001; Lipinski and Neddenriep 2004; Yiannakis 1982), websites (e.g., Bickers, Evans, Stein, and Wrinkle 2007), and press stories (e.g., Arnold 2004; Druckman 2005; Schaffner 2006) find that constituents know more about legislators and are more likely to think their legislator is doing a good job when they are exposed to media messages. While controlled messages, like direct mail and websites, can be influential, senators strive to influence coverage in the local press. Such coverage is free, it reaches more citizens, and it is viewed as more legitimate by constituents, especially compared to controlled messages (Graber 2010).

Press releases play two important roles in the communication link between representatives and constituents. First, press releases are an important type of controlled message because they provide insights into the substance of representational messages senators decide to disseminate. Second, by comparing press releases to news coverage, we can see whether senators differ in their abilities to garner news attention for their preferred messages.

We illustrate the contours of press releases by presenting some examples in table 4.1. In particular, we look at Democratic senator Pattie Murray of Washington and Republican senator Gordon H. Smith of Oregon. We use these two senators as a way of presenting a picture of a typical press release. In table 4.1, we highlight a few sentences from these senators' press releases, showing similarities in the themes articulated by these two senators.

In this chapter, we are interested in exploring whether men and women differ in the types of messages they deliver to their constituents. In accordance with the strategic stereotype theory, we expect male and female legislators to act strategically. In particular, male and female senators will differ in their policy emphases, with women highlighting communal issues and men focusing on competitive issues. However, when it comes to personal traits, both men and women will try to revise stereotypical disadvantages, with women highlighting their command of agentic traits, while men will demonstrate their possession of communal characteristics.

GENDER DIFFERENCES IN PRESS RELEASES FOR U.S. SENATORS

For the 32 senators in our study, we collected all press releases from the senator's official website for January–April and August–November 2006.[3] We

TABLE 4.1. A Comparison of Press Releases: Senator Gordon Smith versus Senator Patty Murray

Contours of Press Releases	Senator Gordon Smith (R) of Oregon	Senator Patty Murray (D) of Washington
National Issue	*Senator Smith discussing Medicare's prescription drugs benefits in a press release (2/2/2006).* U.S. Senator Gordon Smith, chairman of the Senate Special Committee on Aging, held a hearing on February 2 to examine problems with implementation of the Medicare prescription drug benefit and the step being taken to ensure American seniors are not denied access to medication. The prescription drug benefit became effective January 1.	*Senator Murray focusing on Medicare's prescription drugs benefits in a press release (2/2/2006).* U. S. Senator Patty Murray today spoke on the floor of the U.S. Senate in favor of the Bingaman/Rockefeller/Murray amendment to try and fix the flawed Medicare Prescription Drug law that went into effect on January 1, 2006.
Local Issue	*Senator Smith discusses the lumber industry in Oregon in a press release (2/14/2006).* U.S. Senator Gordon Smith today called for Canada and the United States to resolve their differences regarding lumber systems and to create a shared market that abides by similar rules. "We can continue along the path of a patchwork of tariffs and quotas, or we can seek to resolve the differences in our lumber systems."	*Senator Murray illustrates how national policy affects Washington's tourism in a press release (2/25/2006).* Today at a Senate hearing, U.S. Senator Patty Murray urged the Bush Administration to delay the passport requirements of the Western Hemisphere Travel Initiative (WHTI) until 2008. She also called on the Bush Administration to work closely with the local business and civic leaders in Whatcom Country (WA) to ensure the final plan improves security without hurting cross-border trade and tourism.
Claiming Credit for Projects	*Senator Smith announcing a nanotechnology center for Oregon in a press release (2/6/2006).* U.S. Senators Gordon Smith and Ron Wyden today announced White House approval of a proposed Oregon nano-	*Senator Murray announces a new veterans' health clinic in a press release (2/9/2006).* U.S. Senator Patty Murray today announced that the Department of Veterans. Affairs has approved the establishment of a new

TABLE 4.1.—*Continued*

Contours of Press Releases	Senator Gordon Smith (R) of Oregon	Senator Patty Murray (D) of Washington
	technology center— and $8 million in funding over three years—in the President's 2007 budget, which was released today. Inclusion in the President's budget is a major milestone for the state's burgeoning nanotechnology efforts	Community Based Outpatient Clinic (CBOC) in North Central Washington. The new clinic will provide primary and mental health care for the 26,000 underserved veterans in Chelan, Douglas, Ferry, Grant, Kittitas, and Okanogan counties (WA)
Symbolic Activities	*Senator Smith publicizes a new federal program for suicide prevention. The press release also memorializes Smith's 21 year old son, Garrett, who was a victim of suicide in 2003 (4/20/2006). "It* is hard to imagine the pain of thousands of children who are now suffering in silence and that of their families who just want to help. This grant is especially important to me because it will make a difference in the place where Garrett grew up and the community he loved . . ."	*Senator Murray honored Coretta Scott King, wife of Martin Luther King, following her death (1/31/2006).* "With the death of Coretta Scott King, we have lost a strong and dignified voice for a better America. Despite great personal loss, she remained committed to the belief that our common values of liberty and equality leave no room for discrimination of any kind."

coded 1,920, with an average of 50 press releases per senator. When examining the press releases, we look at whether senators highlight their policy responsiveness, allocation responsiveness, or symbolic responsiveness in their communications. The majority of the press releases discuss policy (58%), almost one quarter of the press releases announce a new or ongoing federal project (24%), and about one-tenth of all the press releases focus on a symbolic action (11%), such as creating National Milk Day or renaming a bridge in honor of a military hero.

When looking at policy discussion in the senators' press releases, we examine the substance of the policy described and we determine whether the senator takes a clear position on the topic. We also examine whether senators claim credit for successful policy outcomes and for bringing projects back to their states. Finally, we assess the number of times senators highlight their leadership positions (e.g., leadership position within the party, committee leadership position) in their press releases.

Consistent with the strategic stereotype theory, we expect men and women to focus on their stereotypical strengths when discussing policy in their representational messages. In particular, male senators will spend more time highlighting their commitment to competitive issues, like the economy and foreign policy, while female senators will showcase their dedication to communal issues, like the environment and child welfare. We expect men and women to focus on these different topics in their press releases because they have campaigned on these issues and they care about these divergent issues. In addition, this strategy provides senators opportunities to raise the salience of specific issues, possibly producing more positive assessments for themselves among constituents.

Senator Blanche Lincoln details the expectations female senators face regarding policy expertise: "I think people do expect women legislators to have a different perspective, particularly on some of the things that have become known as women's issues, children's issues—and I don't have a problem with that. I think it is important for us as women because it did take us longer to get the right to vote, and it has certainly taken us longer to be represented in our body of government. That we as women take on that responsibility and really work towards making sure that we bring about that equality" (Mara 2005).

When it comes to personal traits, we expect men and women to try to dispel concerns about their stereotypical weaknesses. Female senators, therefore, will disseminate messages highlighting their knowledge, experience, and decisiveness as a way of demonstrating their leadership skills. Male senators, in contrast, do not have to work as hard to encourage positive views of their agentic qualities. Instead, these senators need to persuade constituents that they are compassionate and empathetic and care for the people of their state. To promote more positive views of their communal qualities, we expect male senators to advertise their allocation and symbolic responsiveness more frequently in their press releases. We also expect male senators to be more likely than their female colleagues to explicitly claim credit for taking care of the citizens of their state.

Press Releases on Public Policy

We begin by examining policy discussion in press releases. We look at the substance of the issue emphasis in senators' controlled communications.

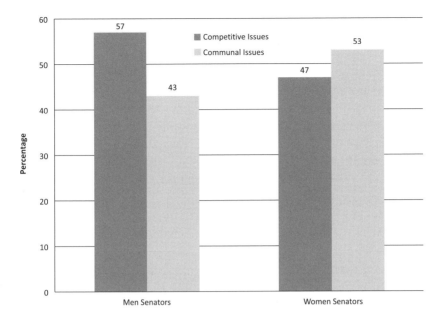

Fig. 4.1. Gender Differences in Policy Emphasis in U.S. Senators' Press Releases. (*Note: Competitive Issues* include defense, foreign policy, business, inflation, economy, budget, energy, farm, and taxes. *Communal Issues* include health care, elderly, welfare, child care, education, and the environment.)

The data in figure 4.1 indicates that male and female senators emphasize their stereotypical policy strengths in press releases. Men mention competitive issues more than communal issues (57% v. 43%, $p < .01$). Similarly, female senators tend to prefer discussing communal issues, compared to competitive issues (53% v. 47%, $p < .01$). Furthermore, male senators are more likely than female senators to discuss competitive issues in their press releases (57% v. 47%, $p < .01$).

While the data in figure 4.1 suggest male and female senators differ in their emphasis on policy matters in their press releases, we need to determine if these gender differences persist when we explore the influence of additional factors. For example, we examine whether the party of the senator influences the content of issue discussion. We expect Democrats will be more likely than Republicans to focus on compassion issues, like health care, the environment, and education. And we want to make sure that women's greater focus on compassion issues is not driven by the fact that female senators are more likely to be Democrats than Republicans.

We also control for three additional factors: the seniority of the senator, the senator's proximity to reelection, and the length of the senators' press releases. Senior senators, who may be "safer" electorally, may be less likely to focus on policy matters—communal or competitive issues—in their press releases. Second, the senator's proximity to the upcoming election could affect how often senators communicate with constituents about issues. In particular, as senators approach election, they may be more likely to discuss issues, both competitive and communal issues, compared to senators whose reelection is two or four years away. Third, we control for the number of paragraphs in each press release so that specific foci are not simply a function of the length of the senators' press releases.[4]

The findings in table 4.2 demonstrate that the gender of the senator does indeed shape the focus of the issue discussion in press releases. Female senators are more likely to talk about communal issues like education, health care, and the environment in their press releases and male senators spend significantly more time focusing on competitive issues like the economy and foreign policy, even when we control for the senator's party, seniority, proximity to election, and the length of the press releases.

In addition, and as expected, the party of the senator influences the issue

TABLE 4.2. Logistic Regression Predicting Discussion of Competitive and Communal Issues in Press Releases[a]

	Communal Issues	Competitive Issues
Female Senator	.22 (.13)*	−.37 (.13)***
Democratic Senator	.24 (.11)**	.40 (.11)***
Election Year	.10 (.13)	.39 (.13)***
Years of Seniority in Senate	−.012 (.009)	−.012 (.008)**
Number of Paragraphs	.025 (.007)***	.02 (.007)***
Constant	−1.56 (.14)***	−1.10 (.13)***
% of Cases Correctly Predicted	76%	71%
N	1,920	1,920

Note: The dependent variable is whether the press release mentioned competitive or communal issues. Competitive issues are defense, foreign policy, business, inflation, economy, budget, energy, farm, and taxes. Communal issues are health care, elderly, welfare, child care, education, and environment. Female Senator is coded 1 for female senators, 0 for male senators. Democratic Senator is coded 1 for Democratic senators and 0 for Republican senators. Election Year is coded 1 for senators up for reelection in 2006, 0 for other senators. Years of Seniority in Senate is coded as years in office. Number of paragraphs is the number of paragraphs per press release.
[a]Unstandardized logit coefficients are followed by standard errors in parentheses.
***$p < .01$; **$p < .05$; *$p < .10$

content of press releases. We find that Democratic senators spend significantly more time focusing on communal issues, compared to Republican senators. Furthermore, Democratic senators are more likely to discuss competitive issues, compared to Republican senators. The greater emphasis on competitive issues may reflect the political context of 2006. One of the most important issues, according to public opinion polls in 2006, was President George W. Bush's handling of the Iraq War (CNN.com 2006). Democratic senators, in their press releases, spent substantially more time focusing on the Bush administration's handling of the war in Iraq, compared to Republican senators. In fact, the difference in attention to the Iraq War is almost five times greater for Democrats than Republicans (an average of .19 paragraphs for Democrats, compared to an average of .05 paragraphs for Republicans).[5]

The electoral context also matters, according to the results in table 4.2. Senators who are approaching reelection (compared to two or four years away) are significantly more likely than other senators to talk about competitive issues. These senators may want to stake out positions on issues or to demonstrate their ability to deal with these salient issues as they approach their reelection bids. In addition, and as expected, senior senators are less likely to mention competitive and communal issues in their press releases. Finally, the probability of discussing competitive and communal issues increases with the length (in paragraphs) of the press releases.[6]

As we did in chapter 3, we look at a natural experiment by examining the subset of men and women senators of the same party and representing the same state. By looking at these seven pairs of senators, we are controlling for the senators' constituency and party affiliation, but varying the senator's gender.[7] If these pairs of senators deviate in their policy priorities, we can reasonably assume that these differences are driven, to a large degree, by the senator's gender.

In six of the seven cases, the female senator spent more time in press releases discussing communal issues compared to male colleagues.[8] For example, in Arkansas, Blanche Lincoln's press releases averaged over two paragraphs (2.29) about communal issues per press release, while Mark Pryor spent less than one paragraph (.81), on average, discussing communal issues in his press releases. We find the same pattern among Republicans. Senator Lisa Murkowski's press releases averaged almost two paragraphs (1.82) about communal issues, while Senator Ted Stevens talked about communal issues less frequently (.36, on average).[9]

In summary, male and female senators prefer to discuss their stereotypical strengths with regard to policy matters. Male senators are more likely to mention competitive issues like the budget and taxes in their press releases, while female senators have a greater likelihood of discussing communal issues, like programs designed to help the poor and the elderly.

Press Releases Highlighting Projects

Senators discuss the federal projects they have brought back to their state in about one-quarter of their press releases. We expect male and female senators to differ in how they advertise their allocation responsiveness. Since men need to revise perceptions that they are less caring and empathetic, male senators may be more likely to advertise their successes at "taking care" of the state as a way of improving constituents' views of their empathy and connections to the state. Highlighting successful projects, such as saving jobs at a local plant or improving the state's water quality, may encourage people to view male senators as more concerned about the lives of their constituents.

We examine the number of projects mentioned in press releases. We find that male senators are significantly more likely to mention projects compared to female senators. In particular, male senators average around two mentions per press release, while their female counterparts average one mention per press release.[10] We explore whether the gender difference in discussion of projects remains statistically significant in a multivariate model. As in the analysis in table 4.2, we control for differences in the senator's seniority, the senator's position in the election cycle, the senator's party, as well as the length of the senator's press releases.

The results of the multivariate analysis are presented in table 4.3.[11] The negative and statistically significant coefficient for the gender of the senator indicates men are significantly more likely than female senators to mention specific federal projects, such as the opening of a new post office or funding aimed at revitalizing an urban community. The greater emphasis on messages about projects may be an attempt by male senators to demonstrate their empathy for citizens of their states. In contrast to the gender of the senators, Democrats and Republicans do not differ in their emphasis on federal projects, senior senators are not more or less likely to focus on these types of projects, and proximity to reelection does not influence the likelihood a senator discussing projects in their controlled messages.

Press Releases on Symbolic Activities and Statements

Symbolic activities and statements are aimed at fostering trust and empathy between citizens and legislators (e.g., Fenno 1978). Since male senators need to improve constituents' views of their empathy and trustworthiness, they may spend more time highlighting their symbolic activities as a way of increasing confidence and rapport with their constituents and ideally revising citizens' stereotypical views of their communal qualities. Women, in contrast, may not want to allocate resources and space on something where they have a natural advantage.[12]

Senators do not advertise their symbolic activities nearly as often as their policy priorities or their distributive activities. Only about one in ten press releases mention the senator's symbolic actions—for example, naming a library after a local hero or cutting a ribbon at a ceremony commemorating the opening of a new federal courthouse. In the bivariate case, we find male senators are somewhat more likely to mention these symbolic activities compared to women senators.[13] However, when we run a multivariate model, we find the gender of the senator is unrelated to whether or not symbolic communications appear in press releases.[14] Therefore, our expectation that male senators would emphasize symbolic statements to shore up their "com-

TABLE 4.3. Negative Binomial Regression Estimates Predicting Allocation Responsiveness in Press Releases[a]

	Mentioning Federal Projects
Female Senator	−.29 (.15)*
Democratic Senator	−.10 (.14)
Election Year	−.23 (.16)
Years of Seniority in Senate	.01 (.01)
Number of Paragraphs	.03 (.01)**
Constant	.12 (.17)
Likelihood Ratio χ^2	23.27***
Degrees of Freedom	5
Number of Observations	1,920

Note: The dependent variable is the number of paragraphs claiming credit for an issue or policy outcome. Female Senator is coded 1 for female senators, 0 for male senators. Democratic Senator is coded 1 for Democratic senators and 0 for Republican senators. Election Year is coded 1 for senators up for reelection in 2006, 0 for other senators. Years of Seniority in Senate is coded as years in office. Number of Paragraphs is the number of paragraphs per press release.

[a]Standard errors are in parentheses, followed by levels of significance.

***$p < .01$; **$p < .05$; *$p < .10$

munal" disadvantage is not supported by the data. Male and female senators are equally unlikely to emphasize these symbolic connections with constituents in their press releases.

Press Releases on Position-Taking and Leadership Credentials

In his classic book, *The Electoral Connection,* Mayhew (1974) discusses the importance of position-taking as a way for representatives to use roll-call votes to stake out popular positions on issues. However, position-taking may also be used to highlight a senator's decisiveness or resolve. By highlighting a specific position on an issue or a set of issues, a senator may be demonstrating his or her ability to make hard decisions, even though these decisions may sometimes be unpopular. In other words, position-taking may signal to constituents that the senator is tough and not afraid of making difficult choices. Given this line of reasoning, we expect that female senators may have a greater desire to take clear positions on issues as way of highlighting their decisiveness and changing people's stereotypes of women as weak.

Female senators may also seek to emphasize their agentic qualities by spending more time discussing their legislative positions (e.g., committee chair, leadership position). By emphasizing their "chairmanship" of an important subcommittee or by discussing their party leadership posts, women attempt to revise potentially damaging stereotypes that constituents may hold about women's leadership abilities. By stressing leadership positions, female senators may also be sending a message about their experience and effectiveness. Since female senators need to dispel worries about their possession of agentic traits, we expect women to be more likely than men to mention their leadership positions in their press releases.

When we compare male and female senators, we find that nearly half (47%) of women's press releases mention their leadership positions, while men cite their positions of power only 37% of the time.[15] Similarly, women are more likely than their male counterparts to take clear positions on policy positions in their press releases. In fact, in more than 25% of their press releases, female senators take a specific stance of an issue; whereas male senators take unambiguous stands on issues 18% of the time.[16]

We rely on binomial regression analysis to examine the impact of gender in multivariate models predicting two dependent variables: (1) the number of times senators mention their leadership positions, and (2) the number of times senators stake out specific positions on issues. The results of this analysis are presented in table 4.4.[17] As with the previous analyses, we control for the party and seniority of the senators, as well as the senator's proximity to election, and the number of paragraphs in the press releases.

The findings in table 4.4 suggest that female senators do indeed emphasize their leadership positions in Congress more than male senators. In particular, female senators are more likely to mention their position on important committees and subcommittees, as well as advertise their leadership position in the chamber. We also find, as expected, that female senators are clearer when talking about matters of public policy than their male counterparts. Female senators are more likely to stake out a clear position on an issue in their press releases, compared to male senators. Even controlling for a series of political factors, the gender of the senator significantly influences how often senators mention their positions of leadership and how often senators take specific positions on policy matters.

Looking at the additional variables in the models, we find that senior senators are more likely to talk about their leadership positions and are more likely to discuss issues in a clear manner, compared to their more junior colleagues. Also, Republican senators, who controlled the Senate in 2006, were

TABLE 4.4. Negative Binomial Regression Estimates Predicting Discussion of Leadership Positions and Clarity of Issue Positions in Press Releases[a]

	Leadership Positions	Clarity of Issue Positions
Female Senator	.37 (.13)***	.35 (.09)***
Democratic Senator	−.68 (.11)***	−.31 (.08)***
Election Year	−.05 (.13)	−.28 (.10)***
Years of Seniority in Senate	.02 (.007)***	.01 (.005)**
Number of Paragraphs	.03 (.006)***	.03 (.005)***
Constant	−2.133 (.15)***	−1.38 (.11)***
Likelihood Ratio χ^2	66.14***	68.11***
Degrees of Freedom	5	5
Number of Observations	1,920	1,920

Note: The dependent variable, leadership position, is measured by the number of paragraphs discussing the senator's leadership positions (e.g., committee or subcommittee chair, party leadership position) in the U.S. Senate in the press release. The dependent variable, clarity of issue positions, is measured by the number of paragraphs in the press release stating an explicit position on an issue. Female Senator is coded 1 for female senators, 0 for male senators. Democratic Senator is coded 1 for Democratic senators and 0 for Republican senators. Election Year is coded 1 for senators up for reelection in 2006, 0 for other senators. Years of Seniority in Senate is coded as years in office. Number of Paragraphs is the number of paragraphs per press release.

[a]Standard errors are in parentheses, followed by levels of significance.

***$p < .01$; **$p < .05$; *$p < .10$

more likely to talk about leadership positions compared to Democrats. These senators are also more likely than their Democratic colleagues to take clear sides on issues. And, not surprisingly, senators who are nearing reelection are less likely to take clear stands on issues compared to senators whose electoral campaigns are two or four years away. As Shepsle (1972) argued in his classic work, candidates (or, in this case, senators facing reelection) take ambiguous positions to avoid offending potential supporters.

In summary, when it comes to revising negative stereotypes, female senators appear to be more likely to focus on topics that encourage people to view female senators as possessing agentic characteristics compared to male senators. That is, women are more likely than men to showcase their decisiveness and leadership positions in their press releases.

Press Releases on Credit Claiming

Mayhew (1974) explains that representatives often engage in credit claiming, where a member of Congress asserts responsibility for desirable policy outcomes (e.g., lower taxes, improved Social Security benefits, better economy) or for bringing a popular project back to the state. As Mayhew explains, credit claiming is such an important activity for members of Congress that "much of congressional life is a relentless search for opportunities to engage in it" (Mayhew 1974, 53).

By claiming credit for helping constituents, senators are trying to demonstrate how much they care for the citizens of their states. Given gender-role expectations, people may view male senators as less caring than female senators. Therefore, male senators may feel more compelled to explicitly claim credit for legislative successes benefitting their constituents. By claiming credit in their press releases, male senators may be trying to revise potentially damaging stereotypes regarding their communal qualities.

However, credit claiming can pay electoral dividends and eschewing such rhetoric may be politically damaging. Therefore, women may be more judicious in their use of credit claiming and may claim credit for projects and proposals highlighting their stereotypical strengths.[18] More specifically, women may be more likely to claim credit on communal issues (e.g., education) or "female" projects (e.g., projects related to the care of children). In contrast, male senators will highlight their successes for all projects and issues, regardless of content.

We begin by examining credit claiming on public policy. We examine the number of paragraphs in a press release where a senator claims credit for an issue or policy outcome. In addition, we distinguish between credit claiming for competitive issues and credit claiming for communal issues. The findings for the three models are presented in table 4.5.[19] Turning to the findings in the first column, male senators are significantly more likely than female senators to claim credit for favorable policy outcomes. Even controlling for the senator's party, seniority, proximity to the election, as well as the number of paragraphs in the press releases, we find men are more likely than women to praise their own accomplishments.

When we look at different types of issues, we find that men are significantly more likely than women to claim credit for competitive issues (see column 2 in table 4.5). Male senators are more likely to tout their policy achievements for issues corresponding to their stereotypical strengths compared to female senators. However, when examining communal issues, we find that male and female senators do not differ in their likelihood of claiming credit. The results in table 4.5 suggest that the content of policy discussion does influence whether male and female senators claim credit for policy outcomes. Women are less likely than men to claim credit in general (for all issues) and they are significantly less likely to claim credit on competitive

TABLE 4.5. Negative Binomial Regression Estimates Predicting Credit Claiming for Policy Outcomes[a]

	Credit Claiming Overall Issues	Credit Claiming Competitive Issues	Credit Claiming Communal Issues
Female Senator	−.47 (.15)***	−.89 (.39)**	−.15 (.29)
Democratic Senator	−.003 (.13)	−.63 (.31)**	.70 (.25)***
Election Year	.74 (.15)***	.91 (.38)**	1.06 (.28)***
Years of Seniority in Senate	.007 (.009)	−.03 (.03)	.009 (.02)
Number of Paragraphs	.009 (.008)	.02 (.01)*	.001 (.01)
Constant	−1.62 (.15)***	−3.82 (.41)***	−2.25 (.25)***
Likelihood Ratio χ^2	26.19***	16.06***	37.55***
Degrees of Freedom	5	5	5
Number of Observations	1,920	1,920	1,920

Note: The dependent variable is the number of paragraphs claiming credit for an issue or policy outcome. Competitive issues are defense, foreign policy, business, inflation, economy, budget, energy, farm, and taxes. Communal issues are: health care, elderly, welfare, child care, education, and environment Female Senator is coded 1 for female senators, 0 for male senators. Democratic Senator is coded 1 for Democratic senators and 0 for Republican senators. Election Year is coded 1 for senators up for reelection in 2006, 0 for other senators. Years of Seniority in Senate is coded as years in office. Number of Paragraphs is the number of paragraphs per press release.

[a]Standard errors are in parentheses, followed by levels of significance.

***$p < .01$; **$p < .05$; *$p < .10$

issues. However, women are not more or less likely than men to claim credit for issues that correspond to women's stereotypical strengths.

An examination of the rival explanations in the three models indicates senators approaching reelection are much more likely to claim credit for policy successes than senators two and four years away from their next reelection bid. Proximity to reelection is powerfully related to credit claiming in each of the three models in table 4.5.

We also see that Democrats and Republicans are equally likely to claim credit on policy matters in general. However, the substance of the issues is important for Democratic and Republican senators. Republican senators are more likely to claim credit on competitive issues, and Democratic senators are more likely to stress communal issues. This is an interesting finding and resonates with the theory of "issue-ownership" (Petrocik, Benoit, and Hansen 2003/2004). Republicans are seen as able to keep taxes low, government small, and maintain a strong national defense, while Democrats are expected to help the elderly, protect Social Security and the environment, and provide health care for citizens.

Senators also claim credit for bringing popular projects back to their states. Therefore, we replicate the analysis in table 4.5, but we examine press releases mainly about federal projects. We look at credit claiming overall and then distinguish between credit claiming on projects corresponding to "male" policy domains (e.g., a project creating jobs by building a new highway) and "female" policy domains (e.g., funding a methamphetamine task force).[20]

The results presented in table 4.6 demonstrate that the gender of the senator does indeed shape credit claiming on federal projects. Just as with issues, men are more likely to claim credit for projects, generally, and they are more likely than women to claim credit for projects corresponding to their stereotypical strengths. However, with regard to projects relating to "female" issues, there is no relationship between the gender of the senator and claiming credit for federal projects related to women's stereotypical strengths.

We also find that party and seniority are related to credit claiming on projects, with senior senators and Republican senators spending more time claiming credit for bringing projects back to their states, compared to junior and Democratic senators. Republicans, who were in the majority in 2006, and senators with more seniority are more likely to have the clout and political power required to bring more projects back to their states.

TABLE 4.6. Logistic Regression Predicting Credit Claiming for Federal Projects[a]

	Credit Claiming for Overall Projects	Credit Claiming for "Male" Projects	Credit Claiming for "Female" Projects
Female Senator	−.86 (.39)**	−2.36 (1.26)*	.29 (.60)
Democratic Senator	−.90 (.37)**	−.49 (.87)	−1.25 (.67)*
Election Year	.46 (.43)	1.62 (.99)	−1.75 (1.08)
Years of Seniority in Senate	.06 (.02)**	−.10 (.09)	.08 (.04)**
Number of Paragraphs	.03 (.03)	.12 (.05)**	.02 (.04)
Constant	−2.44 (.37)***	−3.73 (.72)***	−3.94 (.67)***
% of Cases Correctly Predicted	91%	98%	97%
N	463	463	463

Note: The dependent variable is the number of paragraphs claiming credit for a federal project. "Male" projects are related to the following areas: defense, jobs, farm, and business. "Female" projects are related to the following areas: health care, the poor and elderly, child care, education, and the environment. Female Senator is coded 1 for female senators, 0 for male senators. Democratic Senator is coded 1 for Democratic senators and 0 for Republican senators. Election Year is coded 1 for senators up for reelection in 2006, 0 for other senators. Years of Seniority in Senate is coded as years in office. Number of Paragraphs is the number of paragraphs per press release.

[a]Unstandardized logit coefficients are followed by standard errors in parentheses.

***$p < .01$; **$p < .05$; *$p < .10$

SUMMARY AND CONCLUSION

Consistent with the senators' introductory messages on their web pages, male and female senators produce press releases that highlight positive gender stereotypes about issues while simultaneously acting to revise potentially damaging gender stereotypes about their personal traits. We find that the gender of the senator predicts the types of issues senators discuss in their press releases. Men play to their strengths and focus on competitive issues, while women provide more information on communal issues.

Male and female senators also use their press releases to encourage constituents to revise their stereotypical trait views of men and women. Female senators produce press releases telling citizens they are experienced and decisive by focusing on the important leadership roles they hold in the U.S. Senate and by pronouncing clear positions on matters of public policy. Male senators work diligently to display their communal characteristics, showcasing their ability to deliver federal projects for their state and by claiming credit for positive policy outcomes.

Still, at the end of the day, senators' efforts to develop and deliver their communications via their websites and press releases will have limited reach unless these messages are transmitted by the local press. Local newspapers are delivered to the homes of tens of thousands of constituents and local media coverage is one click away on home television sets, laptops, and smartphones. Senators hope their controlled communications will be picked up by news media and delivered to busy constituents who are searching for news about local events, sports, and weather.

In chapter 5 we turn to a full investigation of the amount, tone, and content of local news coverage about U.S. senators. We look at whether the news media's coverage of politicians varies with the gender of the senator. Do the news media devote systematically more coverage to certain types of senators while ignoring other senators? Are male senators more likely to be covered favorably by the press than female senators? Are the news media more faithfully mirroring the messages of female senators compared to male senators? These are the questions that drive the analyses in chapter 5.

CHAPTER 5

Coverage of Senators in the Local Press

IN 1872, AN EDITORIAL in the *New York Times* described presidential candidate Victoria Woodhull as wearing "dainty high-heeled boots" (Falk 2010). More than 100 years later, in 2010, the *New York Times* published an article with the headline "Blazing Campaign Trails in a Certain 3-Inch Heel." In the article, the reporter explains that "Reshma Saujani has a lot to say about her bid to challenge Representative Carolyn B. Maloney in the Sept. 14 Democratic primary . . . But as Ms. Saujani, a 34-year-old lawyer, described some of her passions, I found myself increasingly, and in spite of myself, wondering about her shoes" (Dominus 2010).[1] The article, 15 paragraphs long, continues with 13 more paragraphs discussing Saujani's shoes. We learn the costs of the shoes ($300), their fit ("comfy"), and their color (black patent leather), among other things. The article does not appear in the style section of the paper but in the metro section. During the same election cycle, a *Boston Globe* journalist wrote a column about Martha Coakley, a Democrat running for a U.S. Senate seat in Massachusetts.[2] The columnist writes, "Martha Coakley is a very good-looking woman, and by far the handsomest candidate among the four Democrats running for Ted Kennedy's seat. Call it the babe factor." He concludes his column by saying, "Right now, Martha Coakley is a slightly better-looking version of Senator Maria Cantwell of Washington. It may not be enough to win, but it is certainly not going to hurt."

In *Nine and Counting* (2000), the women in the U.S. Senate describe similar treatment in the news media. For example, Kay Bailey Hutchison, elected to the U.S. Senate in 1993, had been a state representative, state treasurer, banker, and small businesswoman. But, when she won her senate election, the headline in the newspaper read "Former University of Texas Longhorn Cheerleader Elected" (Mikulski et al. 2000, 43). Similarly, former senator Carol Moseley Braun was a lawyer, a former federal prosecutor, and a state senator before winning election to the U.S. Senate in 1992. However, after her election to the U.S. Senate, the *New York Times* described her as a "den mother with a cheerleader's smile" (Mikulski et al. 2000, 43).

News stories highlighting women's appearance, their roles as mothers, and other stereotypical traits are commonplace in press treatment of female politicians. In a 2003 front-page article in the *New York Times,* the reporter writes about female senators balancing work with family. The reporter explains, "Senator Lisa Murkowski, Republican of Alaska, missed Thursday's child tax credit vote, a definite no-no for a freshman lawmaker who faces accusations of nepotism for having been appointed to her seat by her father. But Ms. Murkowski's oldest son, Nicolas Martell, 12, was graduating from sixth grade, and she was scheduled to speak at the ceremony. The plane ride to Anchorage would take 11 hours, so she left early. Senator Kay Bailey Hutchison, Republican of Texas, was late to the Senate's prayer breakfast this week because her 2-year-old daughter, Bailey, slept late. Senator Mary Landrieu, Democrat of Louisiana, brought her children, Connor Snellings, 11, and Mary Shannon Snellings, 5, to a fund-raiser on Wednesday night" (Stolberg 2003, 1).[3] In this news article, the juggling of the dual responsibilities of senator and parent was not discussed for any male senators.

The news media's coverage of female politicians has long been criticized for treating female politicians differently than their male counterparts (e.g., Braden 1996; Falk 2010; Heldman, Carroll, and Olson 2005; Kahn 1996; Larson 2001). If the news media is biased in their coverage of female politicians, then the press may act as an obstacle for women in elective office. U.S. senators need the help of the news media to communicate their representational messages to hundreds of thousands or millions of constituents. The local news media are an essential conduit of information for U.S. senators as they present themselves to their constituents and try to explain their Washington activity (Arnold 2004; Fenno 1978; Fenno 1996).

Although senators try to influence the media coverage by disseminating press releases and presenting a plethora of information on their official websites (Lipinksi and Neddenriep 2004), journalists are selective in what they report about the senators' actions. Reporters and editors do not have the resources to report every bill introduced, every vote taken, or every speech a senator makes on the floor of the chamber or in the senator's home state. Instead, journalists and editors rely on specific criteria of newsworthiness when deciding what to cover and what to publish in the newspaper (Graber 2010; Vinson 2003). Stories that are conflictual or have the potential to influence a great number of readers are more likely to be covered by the local news organizations (Arnold 2004; Kahn and Kenney 1999).

The relationship between journalists and senators is an adversarial one (Cook 1989). Senators want coverage highlighting their positive contributions to constituents. Reporters and editors, on the other hand, want stories generating interest among readers. While these distinct goals will sometimes converge on the same story (e.g., senator helps enact legislation that will help generate significant job growth in the state), often the divergent goals lead to critical or scant coverage for the senator.

How does the news media cover senators in the local press? Most of the research examining this question has focused on election coverage. Researchers have found the closeness of the race influences the type of coverage given to senators. In noncompetitive races, senators receive less coverage. However, this coverage is generally positive. In competitive races, senators are covered much more extensively, with more articles focusing on their legislative record and their issue positions and policy priorities. While coverage of senators in competitive races is more substantive, it is also more critical (e.g., Kahn and Kenney 1999; Westlye 1991).

Examination of news coverage during non-campaign periods is less prevalent (Arnold 2004; Vinson 2003). Arnold's (2004) study of the 1993–1994 period shows small local newspapers often produce more coverage of House members than large metropolitan dailies. Arnold also shows that coverage tends to focus on position taking more than coverage of other legislative actions, like bill sponsorship or committee work.

Coverage of representatives in their local newspapers are influenced by a number of factors, including the representative's leadership position and seniority, with more senior representatives and representatives holding leadership positions generating more coverage (e.g., Vinson 2003). In addition, the fit between the media market and the congressional district influences coverage (Arnold 2004; Goldenberg and Traugott 1983; Schaffner and Sellers 2003; Vinson 2003).

Scholars have suggested that news coverage is produced in a way that tends to favor incumbents (Cook 1989; Schaffner 2006; Vinson 2003). One reason is because local reporters often lack the necessary time to initiate and research their political stories (Kaniss 1991). Therefore, reporters often rely on representatives for information, using their press releases or websites for details about the representatives' activities. As Paletz and Entman (1981) explain, local reporters do not have the necessary resources to pursue in-depth and independent coverage of congressional members, leading reporters to be strongly influenced by actions of legislators when covering Congress or congressional elections.

We are interested in understanding how the gender of the senator influences news media coverage. We have spent the last two chapters exploring the representational messages generated by male and female senators. We know that senators' messages are aimed at highlighting their stereotypical strengths on issues and revising their stereotypical weaknesses on traits.

In this chapter, we are interested in exploring whether the gender of the senator influences the nature and content of news coverage of sitting U.S. senators. In particular, are male and female senators covered differently in terms of the amount of news coverage, the tone of coverage, and the substance of coverage? These are important questions that have been ignored by previous scholars. Furthermore, an examination of the nature of press coverage of U.S. senators helps us understand whether the representational messages of male and female senators are likely to reach the senators' constituents. We have strong theoretical reasons to expect that the gender of the senator will play a key role in influencing press patterns.

WILL THE NEWS MEDIA DIFFERENTIATE
BETWEEN MALE AND FEMALE SENATORS?

Journalists, like all citizens, hold gender stereotypes about men and women. In particular, news personnel are likely to associate agentic traits (e.g., decisive, assertive, knowledgeable) with male senators and communal traits (e.g., compassionate, empathetic) with female senators. These stereotypical views of men and women are likely to influence how male and female senators are treated by the news media. Adherence to these gender stereotypes, for example, may lead news personnel to view male senators as stronger leaders and more knowledgeable. Therefore, male senators may receive more news attention since gender stereotypes encourage reporters and editors to view male senators as authoritative sources who are knowledgeable about a wide range of issues.

In addition, gender role expectations may influence the tone of coverage devoted to male and female senators in their state newspapers. Gender differences in the tone of coverage may reflect the greater congruity between stereotypical agentic traits and the leadership prototype.

Female senators, in contrast to their male colleagues, are violating prescriptive stereotypes by simply being a U.S. senator. Differences in the overlap between leadership traits and senators' stereotypical traits may produce more positive coverage for male senators, compared to their female colleagues.

While gender-role expectations will influence how male and female senators are covered in the news, the senators' own messages will also affect patterns of press attention. When gender stereotypes are reinforced by the behavior of male and female senators, we expect greater correspondence between the senators' preferred messages and coverage of the senators in the press. For example, since senators highlight their stereotypical policy strengths in their representational messages, we expect coverage in the news will largely mirror the senators' preferred themes.

Senators' messages about traits, unlike policy messages, contradict prevailing gender stereotypes. Therefore, it is unlikely than news coverage of senators will simply mirror the messages disseminated by these senators. Instead, the news media's coverage may ignore the senators' own messages and reinforce common gender stereotypes in coverage. That is, news coverage of senators may highlight agentic traits for male senators, while focusing on communal traits of female senators.

Overall, we expect gender stereotypes will lead news personnel to cover male and female senators differently, with women receiving less coverage and less positive coverage. Furthermore, when male and female senators emphasize themes resonating with common gender stereotypes, the news media coverage will reflect these messages. However, when male and female senators try to revise negative trait stereotypes with their representational messages, news media coverage may not portray these messages faithfully.

GENDER DIFFERENCES IN AMOUNT AND TONE OF
NEWS COVERAGE FOR U.S. SENATORS

To assess how the news media cover U.S. senators in the news, we conducted an extensive content analysis of coverage in the largest circulating newspaper in each senator's state (see chapter 2 for details on the research design). In conducting the content analysis of news coverage, we attempt to capture how the news media portray the senator, as well as assess how closely news coverage matches the senator's messages.

Amount of Coverage

We expect that male senators will receive more coverage than female senators. Journalists and editors, who are likely to hold gender stereotypes about "proper" male and female roles, are likely to consider male senators to be more authoritative because they are more likely to exemplify the leadership prototype. This will lead journalists to identify male senators in headlines and quote their reactions more readily than their female counterparts.

Our expectation is supported by prior studies investigating gender differences in press treatment. In the campaign setting, Kahn (1996) found that female candidates for statewide office receive less attention than their male counterparts, controlling for incumbency and the competitiveness of the race (e.g., Heldman, Carroll, and Olson 2005; Kahn 1996; Kittilson and Fridkin 2008).[4] In a more recent study exploring press treatment of men and women in the U. S. Congress, Niven (2005) looked at newspaper coverage of all women serving in the U.S. Senate and in the U.S. House between 2001 and 2003. Niven found that female politicians received significantly less coverage than their male counterparts in statewide and national newspapers. In a related study, Niven and Zilber (2001b) interviewed press secretaries of male and female members of Congress in 1998 to see how these staffers viewed news coverage of their bosses. Press secretaries for female members overwhelmingly complained about a lack of press coverage for their members, compared to the press secretaries working for male members.

In addition, women are also less likely than men to be used as sources in the news (Armstrong 2004; Freedman and Fico 2205; Rogers, Thorson, and Antecol 2000; Zoch and Turk 1998), reducing the amount of attention they receive in the press. For example, a study conducted by the Project for Excellence in Journalism in 2005 found significant gender differences in the use of women as expert sources in newspapers, television, and online. Researchers examined 16 newspapers, 4 nightly newscast programs, 3 network morning news programs, 9 different cable news programs, and 9 websites. Across these various media outlets, three-quarters (76%) of the stories contained at least one male source, while only a third (33%) contained a female source.

Does the gender of the senator affect the amount of media coverage senators receive in their local newspapers? When we examine the bivariate relationship between quantity of coverage and the gender of the senator, we find some support for our expectation that women receive less press attention than their male counterparts. For example, men are mentioned in the headline of a story 16% of the time, while women are mentioned in the headline only 13% of the time.[5] Similarly, male senators are more likely to be quoted than their female counterparts. Indeed, an average of about three-quarters of a paragraph is devoted to direct quotes of male senators per article, compared to an average of about a half of a paragraph quoting female senators directly.[6]

However, before concluding that female senators receive less press attention than male senators, it is necessary to consider alternative explanations that may influence media coverage. For example, it is necessary to consider the seniority of the senator since senior senators often receive more coverage and more prominent coverage than more junior members (e.g., Kahn and Kenney 1999). In addition, senators facing reelection may be covered more extensively than their colleagues, since the upcoming election may make the senator more newsworthy. And senators facing reelection may seek out news coverage as a way of generating favorable impressions among their constituents.

Also, the amount of coverage devoted to a senator may be related to the size of the newspaper. Newspapers with higher circulation are likely to be serving larger metropolitan areas and the competition for news is likely to be more intense (Arnold 2004; Vinson 2005). Therefore, we expect as the circulation size of the paper increases, the amount of press attention given to senators will decrease.

We also need to consider whether the senator's own press releases influence news coverage. We control for the number of press releases issued by a senator when examining the amount and prominence of press attention. We know from previous scholars that reporters are often overworked and have limited resources. Therefore, they may rely on the senator's press releases when deciding whether to write a story about the sitting senator (e.g., Arnold 2004; Grimmer 2010; Schaffner 2006; Vinson 2010).[7]

Finally, the party of the senator may influence the amount of news coverage. In 2006, Republicans were the majority party in the U.S. Senate. Therefore, Republican senators may have been considered more newsworthy than their Democratic counterparts and Republicans may have enjoyed more press attention. With these rival factors identified, we turn to an analysis of the amount of coverage.

We begin by looking at the prominence of coverage. In particular, we examine whether the gender of the senator influences the probability that a senator is mentioned in a headline of a news article.[8] The findings in table 5.1

suggest that female senators are significantly less likely to be mentioned in a headline compared to male senators. In fact, the gender of the senator is one of the most powerful variables in the model. The size of the coefficient for gender of the senator can be compared directly to the size of the coefficient for the party of senator and the senator's proximity to election since each of these are binary variables. Surprisingly, the gender of the senator is even larger than the senator's proximity to election, with both variables easily reaching statistical significance.

The remaining variables in the model do not reach statistical significance. For example, junior and senior senators do not differ in their likelihood of being mentioned in the headline. Similarly, Democratic and Republican senators are just as likely to get their names in news headlines. Furthermore, the size of the senator's hometown newspaper does not affect the probability that the senator will be mentioned in headlines. Finally, the senator's efforts at obtaining press attention, as measured by the number of press releases the senator disseminates, does not alter the likelihood that the senator is mentioned in the headline of a news story.

TABLE 5.1. Logistic Regression Predicting
Headline Mentions in News Articles[a]

	Headline Mentions
Female Senator	−.36 (.11)***
Democratic Senator	−.11 (.12)
Election Year	.33 (.12)***
Years of Seniority in Senate	.01 (.005)
Log of Newspaper Circulation	.04 (.17)
Log of Press Releases	−.08 (.15)
Constant	−1.72 (.91)*
% of Cases Correctly Predicted	85%
N	3,822

Note: The dependent variable is whether the senator is mentioned in the headline (1) or not (0). Female Senator is coded 1 for female senators, 0 for male senators. Democratic Senator is coded 1 for Democratic senators and 0 for Republican senators. Election Year is coded 1 for senators up for reelection in 2006, 0 for other senators. Years of Seniority in Senate is coded as years in office. Log of Newspaper Circulation is log to base 10 of the newspaper's circulation size. Log of Press Releases is log to base 10 of the number of press releases posted on the senator's website.

[a]Unstandardized logit coefficients are followed by standard errors in parentheses.

***$p < .01$; **$p < .05$; *$p < .10$

We turn next to examining the number of paragraphs published about senators and the number of times senators are directly quoted in the news. The results from these two analyses are presented in table 5.2.[9] In the equation predicting number of paragraphs published about the senator, the sign of the coefficient measuring gender of the senator is in the predicted direction (i.e., negative, indicating that female senators receive less coverage), but the relationship fails to reach statistical significance. Gender is statistically significant in the equation predicting the number of times a senator is quoted in the news. We find that female senators are significantly less likely to be quoted in their local newspaper compared to men, even controlling for rival factors. This finding resonates with the more general finding that women are less likely than men to serve as sources for newsworthy stories (Project for Excellence in Journalism 2005). Furthermore, the size of the gender coefficient is sizeable. For example, the gender of the senator is more important than the senator's party and proximity to election when predicting how often senators are quoted in the news.

Considering the remaining variables in the models, we find that senators facing reelection garner more press attention. We also find that newspapers

TABLE 5.2. Binomial Regression Predicting Number of Paragraphs and Number of Quotes in News Articles[a]

	Number of Paragraphs	Number of Quotes
Female Senator	−.02 (.03)	−.22 (.08)***
Democratic Senator	.03 (.03)	.16 (.09)*
Election Year	.14 (.03)***	−.004 (.09)
Years of Seniority in Senate	.001 (.001)	−.01 (.004)***
Log of Newspaper Circulation	−.18 (.05)***	−.25 (.13)**
Log of Press Releases	−.15 (.05)***	−.09 (.12)
Constant	2.06 (.30)***	1.15 (.80)
Likelihood Ratio χ^2	37.84***	31.34 ***
Degrees of Freedom	6	6
Number of Observations	3,821	3,814

Note: The dependent variables are (1) the number of paragraphs published about the senator per news article and (2) the number of times the senator is quoted per news article. Female Senator is coded 1 for female senators, 0 for male senators. Democratic Senator is coded 1 for Democratic senators and 0 for Republican senators. Election Year is coded 1 for senators up for reelection in 2006, 0 for other senators. Years of Seniority in Senate is coded as years in office. Log of Newspaper Circulation is log to base 10 of the newspaper's circulation size. Log of Press Releases is log to base 10 of the number of press releases posted on the senator's website.

[a]Standard errors are in parentheses, followed by levels of significance.

***$p < .01$; **$p < .05$; *$p < .10$

with larger circulations, typically serving larger metropolitan areas, allocate less news space to their hometown senators. Finally, the results in table 5.2 suggest that the dissemination of press releases does not positively influence the amount of paragraphs published about the senator or the number of times the senator is quoted in the local paper.

Tone of Coverage

We hypothesize that female senators will receive more negative coverage than male senators. Women seeking and holding offices typically associated with male politicians (e.g., the U.S. Senate) face the "double bind." If they behave like male politicians (e.g., confident, assertive, strong-minded), they are violating "prescriptive" stereotypes. Acting in nonstereotypical ways may lead to negative treatment by reporters and editors. However, if female senators act in ways reinforcing gender stereotypes (e.g., indecisive, shy, weak leadership skills), then they may receive negative coverage for not acting like strong leaders.

Studies examining media coverage of female candidates running for president show that female candidates often receive more critical coverage than their male counterparts. Elizabeth Dole, campaigning for the GOP presidential nomination in 2000, received more negative coverage than her male counterparts. For example, the press criticized her campaign more often than her rivals' for fundraising difficulties. However, many of her male counterparts were also having similar problems raising campaign financing for their electoral campaigns (e.g., Aday and Devitt 2000; Heldman, Carroll, and Olson 2005).

Similarly, research examining presidential candidate Hillary Clinton and vice presidential candidate Sarah Palin in 2008 found that these candidates were often the subject of negative treatment in the news. Lawrence and Rose (2009), in their ambitious study of Hillary Clinton's presidential bid, demonstrated that Hillary Clinton received significantly more negative news coverage than Barack Obama, especially early in the nominating campaign.[10] Similarly, Carroll (2009) found a significant amount of discussion about Clinton in 2008 was negative in tone.

Researchers also document a similar pattern of coverage in the news media's portrayal of Sarah Palin during her vice presidential bid in 2008 (Fridkin, Carle, and Woodall 2011; Harris and Frerking 2008; Heldman, Oliver, and Conroy 2009). For example, a great deal of attention focused on Sarah

Palin's role as a mother, leading to critical comments by reporters (Fridkin, Carle, and Woodall 2011; Harris and Frerking 2008; Heldman, Oliver, and Conroy 2009). Furthermore, a comparison of media coverage of Sarah Palin in 2008 and Geraldine Ferraro in 1984 indicated that both candidates received more critical coverage than their male counterparts (Fridkin, Carle, and Woodall 2011; Heldman, Oliver, and Conroy 2009).

Finally, researchers have found that these negative depictions of female candidates running for president are not new. For example, Falk (2010), in her book *Women for President: Media Bias in Nine Campaigns,* analyzed media coverage of women running for president from 1872 to 2008. Falk reports little progress in the tone of coverage devoted to women's candidacies. Instead, Falk found the press often portrays female candidates as incompetent and lacking electoral viability.

We systematically examine whether the gender of the senator affects the tone of coverage given to senators in the local press. We look at several measures of tone, including the number of criticisms about the senators, the balance of positive versus negative traits published about the senators, and the proportion of articles crediting the senator with positive policy outcomes. The data in figure 5.1 shows that female senators do not always receive more negative coverage compared to their male counterparts. While more criticisms are published about female senators compared to their male counterparts, there is no difference in the number of negative traits written about male and female senators.[11] Furthermore, more positive traits are published about female senators and female senators are more often credited with favorable policy outcomes, when compared to their male colleagues.[12] These bivariate results do not produce a clear pattern regarding the valence of coverage devoted to male and female senators. We turn to a multivariate analysis to see if controlling for rival factors (e.g., characteristics of the senators and characteristics of the newspaper) produces a more consistent picture regarding gender and the tone of coverage.

We begin by looking at the number of criticisms published about male and female senators in news articles. The results, presented in table 5.3, suggest that female senators do not receive more press criticisms than their male counterparts.[13] In fact, we find statistically fewer criticisms are published about female senators compared to male senators, showing the value of controlling for important rival factors. Put simply, female senators receive less critical coverage than male senators.

We also find senators up for reelection face greater press scrutiny than

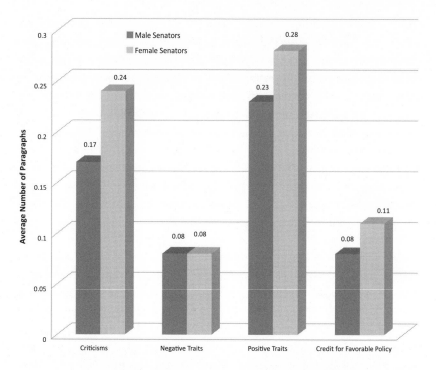

Fig. 5.1. Gender Differences in the Tone of Coverage

senators who are two and four years away from their next reelection bids. And criticisms are more common in large circulating newspapers and for senior senators who may have a longer and more controversial record to defend.

Turning to the tone of issue coverage, we look at the likelihood of reporters crediting a senator for a positive policy outcome in their news reports.[14] According to the results presented in table 5.4, women continue to receive more favorable press treatment than their male colleagues. This is consistent with the bivariate results presented in figure 5.1. The positive and significant logit coefficient for gender of the senator indicates, holding all things equal, the probability that a female senator will be credited for a positive policy outcome is significantly higher than the probability that a male senator will receive similar praise in the press.

Furthermore, the gender of the senator is the only characteristic of the senator that significantly influences the probability of the press crediting a senator for a positive outcome. That is, the senator's party, seniority, and proximity to the next election fail to influence whether the senator is lauded for favorable policy outcomes in the news. Crediting female senators for successful policy outcomes does not reflect the senators' own emphases. As we showed in the last chapter, male senators are significantly more likely than their female colleagues to claim credit for favorable policy consequences in their press releases.

Our final measure capturing the tone of coverage reflects the senator's personality characteristics. As we know, almost one-third of all news articles about senators discuss issues, while 20% of news articles mention the senator's personality. While press attention to issues is more common than news coverage of the senator's personal traits, positive and negative trait coverage is, nevertheless, an important aspect of coverage. We look at the balance of trait coverage by subtracting the number of positive trait mentions from the number of negative trait mentions in a given article. We recode the resulting score to –1 (negative traits outnumbered positive traits), 0 (the number of

TABLE 5.3. Negative Binomial Regression Estimates Predicting Number of Criticisms per Article[a]

	Number of Criticisms
Female Senator	−.29 (.11)***
Democratic Senator	.13 (.11)
Election Year	1.45 (.10)***
Years of Seniority in Senate	.02 (.005)***
Log of Newspaper Circulation	.31 (.15)**
Log of Press Releases	−.27 (.15)*
Constant	−2.318 (.89)***
Likelihood Ratio χ^2	301.69***
Degrees of Freedom	6
Number of Observations	3,821

Note: The dependent variable is the number of criticisms published in each article. Female Senator is coded 1 for female senators, 0 for male senators. Democratic Senator is coded 1 for Democratic senators and 0 for Republican senators. Election Year is coded 1 for senators up for reelection in 2006, 0 for other senators. Years of Seniority in Senate is coded as years in office. Log of Newspaper Circulation is log to base 10 of the newspaper's circulation size. Log of Press Releases is log to base 10 of the number of press releases posted on the senator's website.

[a]Standard errors are in parentheses, followed by levels of significance. ***$p < .01$; **$p < .05$; *$p < .10$

positive and negative trait mentions are equal), or 1 (positive traits outnumbered negative traits).[15] With this dependent variable in place, we can determine if the gender of the senator is related to trait coverage in the news media. The findings are presented in table 5.5. The gender of the senator is
positive and highly significant, indicating that female senators receive more
favorable coverage of their personality traits.

While female senators receive more positive coverage of their personalities, the negative coverage of personality traits increases dramatically for
senators up for reelection. Senators nearing reelection are much more likely
to receive negative trait attention in the news compared to their counterparts who are two or four years away from their next election.

Overall, across the three different measures of tone of newspaper coverage, we find that female senators receive significantly more positive coverage
compared to their male colleagues. This is true even controlling for potentially confounding factors. Contrary to our expectation that women will be
viewed more critically by the press because they do not fit the "senatorial"

TABLE 5.4. Logistic Regression Predicting
Giving Senator Credit on Issues in News Story[a]

	Credit on Issues
Female Senator	.57 (.12)***
Democratic Senator	−.17 (.14)
Election Year	−.11 (.14)
Years of Seniority in Senate	.001 (.007)
Log of Newspaper Circulation	.38 (.20)*
Log of Press Releases	−.60 (.18)***
Constant	−3.43 (1.09)**
% of Cases Correctly Predicted	90%
N	3,822

Note: The dependent variable is whether the senator is given
credit for a positive policy outcome or not. Female Senator is coded
1 for female senators, 0 for male senators. Democratic Senator is
coded 1 for Democratic senators and 0 for Republican senators.
Election Year is coded 1 for senators up for reelection in 2006, 0 for
other senators. Years of Seniority in Senate is coded as years in
office. Log of Newspaper Circulation is log to base 10 of the
newspaper's circulation size. Log of Press Releases is log to base 10
of the number of press releases posted on the senator's website.
[a]Unstandardized logit coefficients are followed by standard
errors in parentheses.
***$p < .01$; **$p < .05$; *$p < .10$

prototype, we find that the press allocates more favorable coverage to these senators. The gender of the senator, compared to rival hypotheses, is the most stable and consistent variable across the three measures of tone.

So far in this chapter, we have seen that the news media do cover male and female senators differently in the local newspaper. Female senators receive less coverage than their male colleague, they are quoted less often, and they are less likely to be mentioned in the headlines than male senators. Yet, overall, coverage of women is more favorable; they attract fewer criticisms, receive more credit for positive policy outcomes, and receive more positive trait mentions. We turn now to examining differences in the substance of coverage given to male and female senators.

TABLE 5.5. Logistic Ordinal Regression Predicting Tone of Trait Coverage[a]

	Tone of Trait Coverage
Female Senator	.51 (.10)***
Democratic Senator	−.19 (.11)*
Election Year	−.91 (.12)***
Years of Seniority in Senate	.007 (.005)
Log of Newspaper Circulation	−.20 (.16)
Log of Press Releases	.21 (.14)
Threshold −1	−4.15 (.88)***
Threshold 0	1.14 (.88)
Model χ^2	106.63***
−2 Log Likelihood	440.19
Degrees of Freedom	6
Pseudo R^2 (Cox and Snell)	.03
N	3,822

Note: The dependent variable is the balance of positive and negative trait mentions about the senator in a news article. The dependent variable has been recoded to −1 (more negative traits than positive traits), 0 (same number of positive and negative traits), or 1 (more positive traits than negative traits) in a news article. Female Senator is coded 1 for female senators, 0 for male senators. Democratic Senator is coded 1 for Democratic senators and 0 for Republican senators. Election Year is coded 1 for senators up for reelection in 2006, 0 for other senators. Years of Seniority in Senate is coded as years in office. Log of Newspaper Circulation is log to base 10 of the newspaper's circulation size. Log of Press Releases is log to base 10 of the number of press releases posted on the senator's website.

[a]Unstandardized logit coefficients are followed by standard errors in parentheses.

***$p < .01$; **$p < .05$; *$p < .10$

GENDER DIFFERENCES IN SUBSTANCE OF
NEWS COVERAGE FOR U.S. SENATORS

In the spring of 2006, the following two articles were published in the *Herald Sun* of Durham, North Carolina, and *The Oregonian,* of Portland, Oregon, respectively: "Dole Accepts Mikulski Double or Nothing Challenge" and "Wyden Says It's 'Crunch Time' for Baghdad." The first article is five paragraphs long and explains that "Maryland Senator Barbara Mikulski issued a challenge Wednesday to North Carolina Senator Elizabeth Dole. Mikulski bet her crab cakes against Dole's barbeque that Maryland will defeat UNC" in the Final Four in the NCAA women's basketball tournament. Dole responded by saying, "I accept your challenge and predict the Tar Heels will be triumphant in what is sure to be another classic ACC contest" (Hayes 2006).

The second article was fifteen paragraphs long and discusses Senator Wyden's reaction to the situation in Iraq after a recent fact-finding trip. Senator Wyden explains that his trip "convinced him that helping the rival Iraqi populations form a government is the linchpin to national security, and in turn, to economic development." The article mentions Senator Wyden's position as a member of the Senate Intelligence Committee, describes his views on the Iraq War, and discusses his 2002 voting against giving President Bush authority to wage war in Iraq (Barnet 2006).

These two articles demonstrate important differences in how senators' activities are described in the press. The first article focuses on symbolic responsiveness by describing a friendly wager between two female senators regarding an upcoming women's NCAA basketball game. The article, published in one of Senator Dole's hometown newspapers, showcases the senator's support of the local team. In contrast, the article about Senator Wyden focuses on policy matters, highlights the senator's recent visit to Iraq, mentions the senator's vote on the Iraq War resolution, and cites Senator Wyden's position on the Senate Intelligence Committee. The latter article is more detailed and more substantive than the former article. Is this pattern generalizable; does the press systematically differentiate between male and female senators with regard to the substance of news coverage?

We expect the press to devote more substantive coverage to male senators (e.g., providing more press attention to their policy priorities) since men are considered more authoritative and are more likely to be viewed as exemplifying the classic leadership prototype. Female senators, in contrast, may not be treated as seriously by news media personnel, resulting in less substantive coverage and more attention to their personal characteristics. Scholarship examining press treatment of male and female candidates indicates that the news media are more likely to focus on female candidates' personal lives, appearances, and personalities, while male candidates receive more news attention for their policy positions and policy priorities (e.g., Bystrom, Banwart, Kaid, and Robertson 2004; Devitt 1999; Kahn 1996).

We also believe that the content of coverage will follow prescribed stereotypes. For example, when covering policy, male senators will receive more attention to competitive or "male" issues (e.g., defense, business, the economy), while issue coverage of female senators will focus on compassion or "female" issues (e.g., health care, welfare, and the environment). Similarly, news coverage of candidates' personal traits will conform to existing stereotypes, with men capturing attention on agentic traits (e.g., experienced, strong leader) and women garnering more coverage on communal traits (e.g., compassionate, empathetic). Research on candidates for the Senate and governor find that the news media continue to associate male candidates with competitive issues as well as agentic traits and female candidates with communal issues and traits (e.g., Kahn 1996).

Studies of news coverage of female representatives in a non-campaign context find similar patterns. Niven (2005) found that men received more issue-oriented coverage, while women were more likely to be characterized by their sex, their families, and their personality. Carroll and Schreiber's (1997) study, relying on in-depth interviews and an extensive content analysis of the 103rd Congress in almost 30 newspapers in 1994, found that coverage of female legislators focused on women's health and abortion. This was true even though women were working on legislation or serving on committees in "traditional" male arenas, such as foreign affairs, international trade, regulatory reform, and appropriations. Finally, journalists' preferences regarding the gender of the source in stories correspond to issue stereotypes. Journalists rely almost exclusively on male sources for stories about defense and foreign affairs and turn to women for comments related to stories about social issues (Project for Excellence in Journalism 2005).

NEWS ATTENTION TO ISSUES AND TRAITS

We turn first to an examination of the variance in the amount of coverage dedicated to issues and personal traits. Specifically, we look at whether male

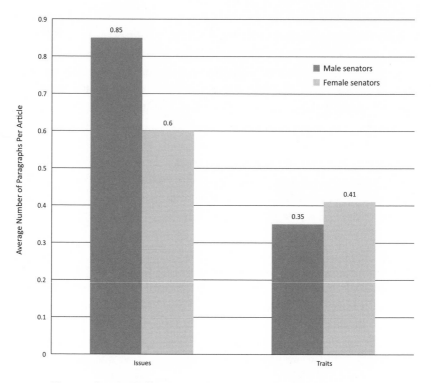

Fig. 5.2. Gender Differences in News Coverage of Issues and Traits

senators receive more substantive coverage (i.e., coverage focusing on issues) compared to female senators. Conversely, we examine whether the
focus on personality is more prevalent when the news media is covering female senators.

The data in figure 5.2 reveals that both male and female senators receive
more press attention for their views on issues compared to coverage of their
personality characteristics. For male senators, issue coverage is more than
twice as prevalent as trait coverage. Male senators receive, on average, almost
one paragraph (.85) focused on issues per article. In contrast, these male senators receive only .35 of paragraph, on average, about their trait characteristics. Coverage of issues is also more common than trait coverage for female
senators, although the difference is not as large (.60 on issues versus .41 on
traits). In addition, consistent with our expectations, we find that male senators receive more substantive coverage while female senators receive more

coverage of personal traits. The gender difference in issue attention is more striking than the difference in trait attention for male and female senators.[16]

We present a multivariate analysis examining the amount of trait and issue coverage, controlling for characteristics of the senator and characteristics of the local newspaper. The results in table 5.6 indicate that female senators receive significantly less press attention for their policy priorities than their male colleagues.[17] This is an interesting and important finding since our analysis in earlier chapters indicates that female senators actually emphasize policy matters more than their male colleagues in their controlled communications. For example, when we examined the senators' official websites, we found that female senators were significantly more likely to mention issues as a top accomplishment on their biography page and they devoted more paragraphs to issues on their websites compared to men. Despite these efforts, we find that women receive significantly less issue attention in the news than men.

Regarding personal traits, we were unable to find a statistically significant difference in trait coverage for male and female senators. The coefficient measuring the gender of the senator, while positive, is far from statistically

TABLE 5.6. Negative Binomial Regression Estimates Predicting Number of Issue Paragraphs and Number of Trait Paragraphs per Article[a]

	Number of Issue Paragraphs	Number of Trait Paragraphs
Female Senator	−.70 (.08)***	.06 (.10)
Democratic Senator	.12 (.09)	−.14 (.11)
Election Year	.63 (.09)***	.22 (.11)**
Years of Seniority in Senate	.001 (.004)	.007 (.005)
Log of Newspaper Circulation	−1.18 (.12)***	0.16 (.16)
Log of Press Releases	.25 (.12)**	.25 (.14)*
Constant	5.60 (.77)***	−.50 (1.0)
Likelihood Ratio χ^2	198.33***	16.04**
Degrees of Freedom	6	6
Number of Observations	3,814	3,814

Note: The dependent variables are (1) the number of issue paragraphs and (2) the number of trait paragraphs. Gender of the Senator is coded 1 for female senators, 0 for male senators. Party of the Senator is coded 1 for Democratic senators and 0 for Republican senators. Election Year is coded 1 for senators up for reelection in 2006, 0 for other senators. Seniority is coded as years in office. Log of Newspaper Circulation is log to base 10 of the newspaper's circulation size. Log of Press Releases is log to base 10 of the number of press releases posted on the senator's website.

[a]Standard errors are in parentheses, followed by levels of significance.

***$p < .01$; **$p < .05$; *$p < .10$

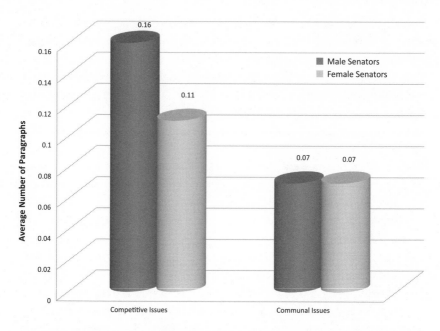

Fig. 5.3. Gender Differences in the Substance of Issue Coverage. (*Note: Competitive Issues* include defense, foreign policy, business, inflation, economy, budget, energy, farm, and taxes. *Communal Issues* include health care, elderly, welfare, child care, education, and the environment.)

significant. Male and female senators receive about the same amount of attention to their personal traits in the press.

Looking at additional factors in the model, we find that press coverage of senators facing reelection is more extensive; senators facing reelection receive more policy and more trait coverage compared to senators two and four years away from their next campaign. Similarly, we find that larger newspapers dedicate less space to the senators' policy views compared to smaller papers.

We turn next to examining the actual content of coverage given to the senators' policy views and personality characteristics. That is, we look at what types of issues and what types of personal traits reporters talk about when covering male and female senators. In figure 5.3, we present bivariate results indicating that competitive issues are covered more often than communal issues. We also find, as expected, that competitive issues receive significantly more attention for male senators than for female senators.[18] However, female senators do not receive more coverage of communal issues compared to their male counterparts. Even though women are more likely to highlight these issues on their web pages and in their press releases, the coverage by the news media does not echo this preference.

These gender differences in coverage persist in a multivariate model, controlling for characteristics of the senator as well as the size of the local newspaper (see table 5.7).[19] Newspapers focus significantly more coverage on competitive issues when covering male senators compared to female senators. The results of the logistic regression indicate that gender is one of the most important variables in the model. This greater emphasis on issues like the economy and defense for male senators resonates with the communications stressed by male senators.

However, the news media coverage does not reinforce the female senators' choice of issues. While female senators prefer to talk about issues like health care and education, the press does not stress these issues when reporting on female senators. The coefficient measuring the gender of the senator in the model predicting communal issues is negative and statistically insignificant. That is, press coverage of communal issues does not vary by the gen-

TABLE 5.7. Logistic Regression Predicting the Content of Issue Coverage[a]

	Competitive Issues	Communal Issues
Gender of Senator	−.59 (.17)***	−0.15 (.18)
Party of Senator	.07 (.18)	1.39 (.25)***
Election Year	.57 (.17)***	.67 (.20)***
Seniority	.03 (.006)***	−.007 (.01)
Log of Newspaper Circulation	−.82 (.27)***	−2.14 (.37)***
Log of Press Releases	−.18 (.23)	−.59 (.26)**
Constant	1.66 (1.46)	−1.96 (1.17)
% of Cases Correctly Predicted	94%	96%
N	3,822	3,822

Note: The dependent variable is whether a competitive (or communal) issue is mentioned in a news story. Competitive issues include defense, foreign policy, business, inflation, economy, budget, energy, farm, and taxes. Communal issues include health care, elderly, welfare, child care, education, and environment. Female Senator is coded 1 for female senators, 0 for male senators. Democratic Senator is coded 1 for Democratic senators and 0 for Republican senators. Election Year is coded 1 for senators up for reelection in 2006, 0 for other senators. Years of Seniority in Senate is coded as years in office. Log of Newspaper Circulation is log to base 10 of the newspaper's circulation size. Log of Press Releases is log to base 10 of the number of press releases posted on the senator's website.

[a]Unstandardized logit coefficients are followed by standard errors in parentheses.

***$p < .01$; **$p < .05$; *$p < .10$

der of the senator, once rival explanations are taken into account. Although female senators choose to talk about communal issues, press coverage does not mirror their preferences.

While the gender of the senator does not influence the amount of communal issue coverage, the party of the senator is important. Democratic senators receive more attention regarding communal issues compared to Republican senators. The party difference in news coverage resonates with studies suggesting that Democrats, in general, are expected to help the elderly, protect Social Security and the environment, and provide health care for citizens (Petrocik, Benoit, and Hansen 2003/2004). However, we do not find that competitive issues are more likely to be covered for Republican senators, at least in 2006, despite research suggesting Republicans are seen as able to keep taxes low, government small, and maintain a strong national defense (Petrocik, Benoit, and Hansen 2003/2004).

The seniority of the senator influences attention to "competitive" issues, with senior senators receiving more attention to these types of issues. Seniority, in contrast, is not related to coverage of communal issues. Coverage of both competitive and communal issues increases for senators up for reelection, while newspapers with larger circulations provide less attention to both types of issues.

Coverage of issues mirrors the preferred messages of male senators more faithfully than the messages of female senators. If reporters and editors regard male senators are more authoritative sources, the press may also portray the trait messages of male senators more accurately than the trait messages disseminated by female senators. When looking at the senators' official websites, we found communal traits, like compassion and integrity, are discussed much less often by senators, regardless of the senator's gender. In particular, agentic traits are three times more likely to be mentioned than communal traits on senators' websites. In addition, female senators are significantly more likely than their male colleagues to talk about their leadership abilities (e.g., competence, independence) in their controlled messages.

When we look at the pattern of press coverage devoted to the personalities of the senators, we find a disconnect between the senators' messages and the news media's messages. Senators, especially female senators, prefer to focus on agentic traits; however, the news media favor communal traits like honesty and trustworthiness. In particular, only 7% of the articles about senate candidates mention agentic traits when describing the senators, while 12% of the articles relied on communal traits when discussing the senators' personalities.[20]

While the news media prefer to focus on communal traits in their coverage of U.S. senators, do reporters follow the senators' own emphasis and cover agentic traits more frequently for female senators? The answer is a resounding no. According to the multivariate analysis in table 5.8, the news attention to agentic traits like experience, leadership, and competence is not significantly different for male and female senators. The coefficient for gender, while positive, is far from statistically significant. When we look at news coverage of communal traits like compassion and honesty, we find that women do receive somewhat more attention for communal traits in their news coverage compared to men. Overall, the news media's coverage of the senators' personalities is not strikingly different for male and female senators.

These results indicate that senators and reporters have divergent views regarding the coverage of important senatorial traits. U.S. senators, and especially female senators, prefer to discuss how they embody agentic traits. However, news reports of these senators focus more often on their possession of communal traits. It is possible that the news media's preference for communal traits may help female senators since women are advantaged over men on these personality dimensions. However, since female senators are not given media attention regarding agentic traits, female senators may not

TABLE 5.8. Logistic Regression Predicting the Content of Trait Coverage

	Agentic Traits	Communal Traits
Female Senator	.23 (.14)	.20 (.12)*
Democratic Senator	.38 (.17)**	−.31 (.13)**
Election Year	.38 (.16)**	−.28 (.14)**
Years of Seniority in Senate	.01 (.007)	.004 (.006)
Log of Newspaper Circulation	−.67 (.23)***	.24 (.18)
Log of Press Releases	−.08 (.21)	.11 (.18)
Constant	.62 (1.25)	3.38 (1.02)**
% of Cases Correctly Predicted	93%	88%
N	3,822	3,822

Note: The dependent variable is whether an agentic (or communal) trait is mentioned in a news story. Agentic traits include experience, strong leader, competent, accomplished, hardworking, aggressive, independent, consistent, and ambitious. Communal traits include caring, advocate, moral, compassionate, and honest. Female Senator is coded 1 for female senators, 0 for male senators. Democratic Senator is coded 1 for Democratic senators and 0 for Republican senators. Election Year is coded 1 for senators up for reelection in 2006, 0 for other senators. Years of Seniority in Senate is coded as years in office. Log of Newspaper Circulation is log to base 10 of the newspaper's circulation size. Log of Press Releases is log to base 10 of the number of press releases posted on the senator's website.

[a]Unstandardized logit coefficients are followed by standard errors in parentheses.

***$p < .01$; **$p < .05$; *$p < .10$

be successful in overcoming potentially damaging gender expectations regarding their competence and leadership abilities.

The remaining variables in the models demonstrate agentic traits are more likely to appear in press reports for senators nearing an election, while communal traits are more often reported for senators two or four years away from reelection. This may signify that agentic traits like leadership and knowledge are considered more important by the press for senators facing reelection.

Press Attention to Representational Style

While policy and personal traits are important aspects of coverage, we conclude our examination of news by looking at four additional dimensions of the senators' representational styles: press attention devoted to the senators' (1) positions on issues; (2) leadership positions; (3) symbolic activities; and (4) allocation activities. We have shown that senators strategically emphasize aspects of their representational styles as a way of revising potentially harmful stereotypes. Female senators, on their websites and in their press releases, try to demonstrate their possession of agentic qualities by taking clear positions on issues and by highlighting their leadership positions on committees and in the chamber. Male senators, on the other hand, often emphasize their communal skills in their controlled communications by talking about their allocation and symbolic activities.

In figure 5.4, we look at the bivariate relationship between the gender of the senator and news attention for these four types of representational messages. The data in figure 5.4 illustrate that news coverage follows gender stereotypes more closely than the senators' own messages. For example, newspapers are significantly more likely to discuss the senators' stands on issues and the senators' leadership posts for male senators compared to female senators.[21] These messages, illustrating decisiveness and leadership for male senators, clearly contradict the senators' own emphasis. Similarly, news stories are more likely to highlight the symbolic and allocation responsiveness of female senators than male senators.[22] Again, the news attention to these types of representational activities corresponds to women's stereotypical strengths (i.e., empathy, connectedness), ignoring the male senators' own emphasis on these activities in their own representational messages.

These stereotypical differences in press attention are robust, according to the multivariate results presented table 5.9. Although female senators are

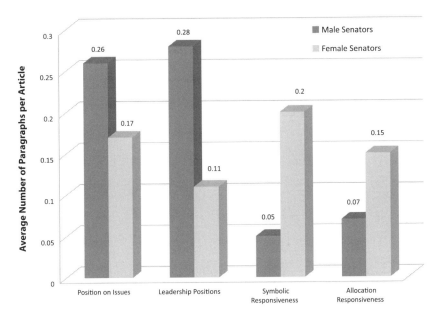

Fig. 5.4. Gender Differences in News Coverage of Issue and Leadership Position and Symbolic and Allocation Responsiveness

significantly more likely than their male colleagues to mention their issue positions in their press releases and on their official websites, female senators receive significantly *less* attention to their issue positions. To illustrate the substantive significance of these findings, we rely on the logit coefficients to calculate the probability that a news story will mention a male senator or a female senator's position on an issue.[23] We find that the probability that a male senator's issue position is mentioned in a news story is .15. In contrast, a similarly situated female senator (e.g., same party, same proximity to election) has only a .05 probability of having her positions on an issue mentioned in her news coverage.

Similarly, even though women are more likely than men to mention their leadership positions in their controlled communications, female senators receive far *less* media attention focused on their leadership positions compared to male senators. Again, relying on the logistic coefficients to estimate probabilities, we find that male senators have a .17 probability of having their leadership position mentioned in a given news story. In comparison, female senators (e.g., same party, same seniority, from a state with the same size of newspaper) have only a .08 probability of having their leadership position discussed in their news stories.

Turning to symbolic responsiveness, coverage of female senators is more likely to emphasize this style of representation. This difference in coverage conforms more closely to gender-role expectations than to the messages disseminated by male and female senators. Finally, with regard to allocation responsiveness, the press spends about the same amount of time discussing male and female senators' efforts at providing federal projects for their states. While the press is not differentiating between male and female senators when discussing allocation responsiveness, we know from the senators' own press releases that men spend more time than women highlighting projects benefitting their states.

Across these four key aspects of the senators' representational records, the gender of the senator is one of the most consistent and powerful factors

TABLE 5.9. Logistic Regression Predicting Gender Difference in News Coverage: Issue Responsiveness, Leadership Positions, Symbolic Positions, and Allocation Responsiveness

	Issue Responsiveness	Leadership Positions[a]	Symbolic Positions	Allocation Responsiveness
Female Senator	−.89 (.12)***	−1.12 (.17)***	91 (.17)***	.08 (.19)
Democratic Senator	−.08 (.12)	.28 (.19)	.69 (.23)***	.76 (.24)***
Election Year	.22 (.13)*	.82 (.16)***	−.32 (.22)	.07 (.23)
Years of Seniority in Senate	.008 (.005)	.002 (.007)	−.005 (.10)	.009 (.009)
Log of Newspaper Circulation	−.53 (.19)***	−1.84 (.27)***	−1.46 (.33)***	−1.33 (.34)***
Log of Press Releases	−.14 (.17)	.54 (.23)**	−.22 (.26)	.29 (.27)
Constant	1.34 (1.06)	6.15 (1.55)**	4.33 (1.79)**	2.78 (1.84)
% of Cases Correctly Predicted	87%	93%	96%	96%
N	3,822	3,822	3,822	3,822

Note: The dependent variables are whether (1) the senator's position on issues is mentioned in a news story, (2) the senator's leadership position is mentioned in a news story, (3) the senator's efforts at symbolic responsiveness are mentioned in a news story, and (4) the senator's efforts at allocation responsiveness are mentioned in a news story. Female Senator is coded 1 for female senators, 0 for male senators. Democratic Senator is coded 1 for Democratic senators and 0 for Republican senators. Election Year is coded 1 for senators up for reelection in 2006, 0 for other senators. Years of Seniority in Senate is coded as years in office. Log of Newspaper Circulation is log to base 10 of the newspaper's circulation size. Log of Press Releases is log to base 10 of the number of press releases posted on the senator's website.
[a]Unstandardized logit coefficients are followed by standard errors in parentheses.
***$p < .01$; **$p < .05$; *$p < .10$

influencing coverage patterns. In addition to gender, we find that the party of the senator influences coverage, with Democratic senators receiving more coverage of their symbolic and allocation responsiveness. The greater news attention to these representational activities of Democrats is consistent with the "trait ownership" expectation that Democrats are seen as more compassionate and empathetic than Republicans (Hayes 2005). The proximity to election also influences coverage patterns, with senators nearing reelection receiving more attention to their policy positions and more coverage of their leadership positions in the chamber. We also find that larger circulating newspapers spend less time covering each aspect of the senators' representational style, suggesting that competition for space is more intense in these larger daily newspapers, compared to smaller newspapers.

SUMMARY AND CONCLUSION

The gender of the senator is among the most consistent and powerful forces influencing the amount, tone, and content of coverage. Consistent with earlier research on campaigns, we find that female senators receive less coverage than their male counterparts. Female senators are mentioned significantly less often in the headlines of news stories and they are quoted less often in news articles in their hometown newspapers. However, unlike previous research, we find that female senators receive more positive press attention. Female senators receive fewer press criticisms, they are credited more often for favorable policy consequences, and reporters are more likely to use positive traits when describing female senators.

While women receive more positive coverage, the content of press coverage does not echo their preferred messages. Instead, news treatment of male and female senators reinforces common gender stereotypes. Female senators stress issues in their controlled communications. Yet reporters spend significantly less time focusing on issues for female senators, compared to their male colleagues. Similarly, female senators are more likely than their male colleagues to take clear positions on issues and highlight their leadership credentials in their own messages. Yet, the news media actually focus on these topics *less* often for female senators.

Male senators are somewhat more successful in controlling the news media's agenda. Men talk about competitive issues more than women and they receive more press attention to these issues. Women, in contrast, focus on communal issues in their own messages, but news coverage for communal issues is not significantly greater for female senators. Men, nevertheless, are not uniformly effective in garnering attention for their messages, especially when these messages conflict with gender stereotypes. Men, for instance, are more likely than women to illustrate how they take care of the state by bringing home federal projects. But the news media do not focus on allocation responsiveness more when covering male senators.

We have documented and analyzed the representational messages flowing from U.S. senators and we have identified and examined how these messages are covered in the local news. We show that both controlled and uncontrolled messages vary dramatically by the gender of the senator. Furthermore, we find the news media do a poor job representing the messages disseminated by the senators, especially female senators. News coverage of U.S. senators is a critical step in the representative relationship between elected officials and the public. The distortion of the senators' messages may serve to inhibit the senators' ability to successfully disseminate their messages to constituents.

How do the messages disseminated by the senators and the news media influence citizens' knowledge and assessments of U.S. senators? Do constituents systematically know more about male senators than female ones? Do potential voters rely on gender stereotypes when evaluating senators? Do the senators' messages and the news media's coverage affect how citizens' view their senators? Answers to these questions will shed light on the nature of representation in the U.S. Senate and will open a discussion about whether the quality of representation depends on the gender of the senator. In the next chapter, we begin to explore these questions.

CHAPTER 6

Citizens' Understanding of
Their U.S. Senators

THE IRAQ WAR began in the spring of 2003 with almost three-quarters of
Americans supporting the invasion. However, by the spring of 2006 approximately half of U.S. citizens believed the United States had made the wrong
decision using military force against Iraq.[1] A national debate was underway
during the 2006 congressional elections, partly focused on the question of
how long should America stay in Iraq. Some members of Congress were
working on legislation to force the Bush administration to make plans to
leave Iraq by a specific date. One piece of legislation, known as the Levin
Amendment, proposed troop withdrawals to begin by late 2006, but with no
specified data for complete withdrawal. The Levin Amendment was soundly
defeated by a vote of 60-39 in the U.S. Senate. The vote on the amendment
was covered in newspapers and newscasts across the country.[2]

Although the Iraq War dominated the hearts and minds of millions of
U.S. citizens in the summer of 2006, there is a great deal of evidence compiled over more than 50 years suggesting that most Americans, most of the
time, do not follow the specifics and details of politics (e.g., Converse 1964;
Kinder 2003). To be sure, this includes people's ability to identify their legislators' positions on issues, as well as the far more difficult task of identify the
legislators' votes on specific pieces of legislation (e.g., Bartels 2010).

Consequently, when we examined the Cooperative Congressional Election Study (CCES) we did not expect a majority of respondents (54%) to be
able to correctly identify their senator's vote on the Levin Amendment. This
level of knowledge for a specific vote in Congress undoubtedly reflects the
intensity of the public's feelings about U.S. war policy in Iraq in the summer
of 2006. In addition, we found respondents were better able to accurately

recall the votes of female senators compared to male senators on the Levin Amendment (60% vs. 52%). And, the greater accuracy of roll-call voting for female senators was not limited to the issue of the Iraq War. For instance, when respondents were asked to recall how their senators voted on a proposal to increase the minimum wage, almost two-thirds (63%) of the respondents accurately recalled their female senators' votes on the proposal, while less than half (43%) could accurately recall how their male senator had voted. Similarly, on a vote proposing to ban partial-birth abortions, more than half of the respondents (53%) accurately reported how their female senators voted on the potential ban, while only about four out of ten respondents (41%) could correctly report their male senators' vote on the proposed ban. This pattern did not disappear when respondents were asked for more rudimentary information about their senators, such as their senator's party affiliation. In particular, 85% of respondents could correctly identify the party of their female senator, while less than three-quarters of respondents (74%) gave the correct party affiliation of their male senator.

In this chapter, we seek to understand why information levels are higher for female senators compared to their male colleagues. We know of no prior work examining differences in people's level of knowledge about male and female senators. This gender difference in knowledge levels raises questions about the nature of the representational relationship between constituents and male and female senators. If people have a better understanding of female legislators' actions, is the quality of representation enhanced for constituents represented by women? What drives this variance in people's level of information about men and women senators? Is the difference the result of messages presented by senators and transmitted by the news? Or, are citizens simply more interested in female senators than male senators? In this chapter, we explore answers to these questions. We begin by offering a theoretical explanation for the gender gap in citizens' knowledge about their U.S. senators.

WHY DO PEOPLE KNOW MORE ABOUT FEMALE SENATORS?

We have some theoretical expectations regarding why the senator's gender influences what citizens know about their senators. Although women gained the right to vote nearly 100 years ago, politics continues to be seen as a man's game and people expect senators to be men (e.g., Verba, Burns, and Schlozman 1997).

In other words, people's prototypes or stereotypes lead them to view the typical senator as male. While the number of female senators has increased almost ten-fold since late the 1980s, male senators continue to outnumber female senators by a ratio of approximately 5 to 1. During the period of our study, the U.S. Senate included 14 female senators among 86 male senators.

Since norms about gender roles (i.e., gender stereotypes) lead people to expect men to be senators, female senators stand out as unique or unusual. According to research in social psychology, salient stimuli are given "figural emphasis not because of their own properties per se, but because of the contrast between them and the current context or the perceiver's temporary or long-term expectancies" (Bargh 1984, 18). In other words, people pay attention to objects that are different. These objects may be noticed because they are different from all the other objects in the setting (e.g., a few women among a large group of men). Or these objects may be noticed because they conflict with one's expectations (e.g., senators are expected to be men).

Information that is salient, because it is unexpected or novel, cannot be processed automatically. Instead, unexpected information requires a greater degree of attention in order to be understood. Since people are expending more effort when processing unexpected stimuli, they are more likely to re-call this information (Hastie and Kumar 1979). Social psychologists have consistently demonstrated that unique information is more memorable, producing the so-called Von Restorff Effect (e.g., Hastie 1981; Hunt 1995).

Extrapolating to citizens' knowledge about male and female senators, citizens cannot rely on automatic processing to understand incoming information about female senators. Instead, people need to engage in conscious processing and expend more effort when trying to interpret news about female senators. This behavior will produce greater recall of processed information about female senators compared to information obtained about less salient male senators. Therefore, we expect people to know more about female than male senators.

Scholars have not explored whether citizens know more about female than male politicians. In an earlier study examining senate candidates, we found that potential voters were more likely to say they have been exposed to the messages of incumbent women seeking reelection compared to incumbent men (Kahn and Kenney 2004). In addition, we found that constituents were more willing to rate the performance of female incumbents. However, we know of no study examining differences in the amount of information constituents hold about male and female legislators.

Of course, the gender of the senator is only one force that may shape what citizens know about their representatives. The characteristics of citizens play a key role in understanding people's knowledge about politics. For example, Delli Carpini and Keeter (1993), in their classic book, *What Americans Know about Politics and Why It Matters,* identify a series of demographic factors related to political knowledge, including education, age, and gender. In particular, Delli Carpini and Keeter find that people with less education, younger people, and women had lower levels of knowledge about politics.

The fact that women know less about politics than men is of particular interest to us (e.g., Burns, Schlozman, and Verba 2001; Kenski and Jamieson 2000; Mondak and Anderson 2004). Research by Mondak and Anderson (2004) suggest that gender differences in political knowledge are partially explained by a gender difference in the "propensity to guess" by survey respondents answering questions. In particular, men are much less likely than women to choose a "don't know" response and are more likely than women to guess when offering an answer.

However, while gender differences in the willingness to answer survey questions probably exaggerate the gender gap in political knowledge, it does not eliminate the gap. Burns, Schlozman, and Verba (2001) suggest that political socialization leads women to view politics as "belonging" to men, leading to lower levels of political interest and political engagement. Since women historically have been excluded from political life, politics and government is seen as an arena dominated by men. Therefore, women are less motivated to seek out information about politics and government (see also Delli Carpini and Keeter 1996).

In certain circumstances, gender differences in political knowledge diminish or disappear. For example, Delli Carpini and Keeter (1996) fail to find a gender gap in political knowledge when looking at local political issues (e.g., people's ability to name the head of the local school board) and issues more directly relevant to women, such as health care and abortion policy (see also Stolle and Gidengil 2010; Kenski and Jamieson 2000). In a more recent study, Dolan (2011) compares traditional measures of political knowledge with a "gender-relevant" measure of political knowledge. The gender-relevant measure of political knowledge includes questions asking respondents to correctly identify the percent of women in Congress or to correctly identify the number of women on the Supreme Court. Dolan finds that male respondents are more likely to score higher than women on the traditional measure of political knowledge (i.e., "do you happen to know which party holds a majority of the seats in the U.S. House of Representatives?"). In contrast, gender differences disappear or are even reversed for the gender-relevant measures of political knowledge. For example, significantly more women than men are able to correctly identify the percentage of women serving in Congress. Dolan's research also demonstrates the importance of political knowledge by showing that "gender-relevant" political knowledge and "traditional" political knowledge influence levels of participation, political interest, and political efficacy for both male and female respondents.

In a related vein, several researchers find that when the political landscape features female politicians or female candidates, political interest, political knowledge, and political engagement increases among female respondents (e.g., Atkeson 2003; Campbell and Wolbrecht 2006; Hansen 1997; Karp and Banducci 2008; Koch 1997). For example, Verba, Burns, and Schlozman (1997) find that living in a state with a female senator or female Senate candidate increases a woman's ability to identify the female politician. However, the presence of a female politician in a state does not affect men's ability to name their senator or identify the Senate candidates in their state. Similarly, Koch (1997) and Hansen (1997), looking at the 1992 election, find that women's political engagement increases significantly when a female Senate candidate is on the ballot.

Women senators understand that they act as role models for women, and especially younger women. Senator Olympia Snowe explains, "Our goal is to reach young woman and let them know we didn't just get dropped here from the sky. It is our hope that, by telling our individual stories, we can help make it clear to others that it is within their ability to get involved and succeed" (Mikulski et al. 2000, 180). Similarly, Senator Barbara Mikulski remarked, "I'm so proud that the women of the Senate work together, act as role models and mentors for other women, and make a difference by standing up for a variety of issues important to women and families. Together, we are opening doors for the next generation of leadership" (Mara 2005, xv). In this chapter, we examine whether female constituents continue to lag behind their male counterparts in their level of information about their senators. And more importantly, we examine whether the presence of female senators help reduce this gender gap in political knowledge.

Beyond demographic characteristics, scholars have identified a series of additional factors that are related to levels of political knowledge. For instance, media usage is related to people's understanding about politics, with people who pay attention to the news displaying higher levels of knowledge about politics (e.g., Brians and Wattenberg 1996; Zhao and Chaffee 1995). Furthermore, people who are more interested in politics and are more strongly attached to the political parties tend to be more informed about politics (e.g., Dolan 2011; Dow 2009; Galston 2001). Finally, researchers have shown that the political context can affect levels of political information about the electorate. For instance, when campaigns are more competitive and when the news media is covering the candidates more extensively, people's understanding about politics increases (Kahn and Kenney 1999).

In the end, we expect that people will have greater levels of information about female senators compared to male senators because we expect that the novelty of female senators will encourage people to pay more attention to these senators. We also anticipate that gender differences in constituents' level of political knowledge will be reduced when people are exposed to female senators. Understanding the determinants of information levels about politics is important because political knowledge can stimulate and facilitate political participation (Palfrey and Poole 1987; Junn 1991). People with higher levels of political knowledge feel more attached to the political system and are more willing to pay attention to politics (Delli Carpini and Keeter 1993). In addition, politically savvy citizens are better able to process political information and may be more resistant to political manipulation (e.g., Fiske, Lau, and Smith 1990; Lodge, McGraw, and Stroh 1989). Also, at election time, citizens need rudimentary information about legislators in order to hold them accountable, such as recognizing the senator's name or the senator's party affiliation. We turn now to an examination of what people know about their senators.

CONSTITUENTS' KNOWLEDGE OF THEIR U.S. SENATORS

To examine citizens' understanding of U.S. senators, we rely on the 2006 Cooperative Congressional Election Survey (CCES). As discussed in chapter 2, the CCES was conducted by Polimetrix, Inc., during the 2006 election. The 2006 CCES contained a large sample of 36,500 respondents. In our analysis, we restrict our attention to the 32 senators examined in our study, resulting in a survey sample of about 18,000 respondents in 17 states.

We develop a series of measures to assess how much respondents know about the senators serving their states. We assess rudimentary information, as well as more sophisticated information about incumbent politicians. We begin by looking at citizens' willingness to answer simple questions about their senator. In particular, we examine whether people are willing to answer three questions about their senator: (1) a question assessing the respondents' approval of the senator's job performance; (2) a question asking respondents to volunteer the party identification of the senator; and (3) a question asking respondents to identify the senator's ideological position on a scale ranging from extremely liberal to extremely conservative. For our initial analysis, we create an index ranging from 0 to 3, measuring people's willingness to answer these three questions.[3] Respondents answered, on average, two questions, with 10% of the sample answering none of the three questions and 37% of the respondents answering all of the questions.

To explore whether the gender of the senator significantly influences people's willingness to answer questions about the senators, we rely on logistic ordinal regression since the dependent variable can take on one of four values. In the regression equation, the primary independent variable of interest is the senator's gender. However, we also assess additional factors that may influence people's level of information about the senator. We are interested in examining whether the information environment influences what constituents know about their senator. We expect when more information about the senators is published in local news outlets and more information is disseminated by the legislator, people will know more about their sitting senator. To capture the information environment, we create an index measuring the amount of news published about the senator in the state newspaper, as well as the amount of information written about the senators in their own press releases.[4]

We also include a control variable for the election year, since people may be more aware of senators who are approaching election. Senators nearing reelection may be engaging in more media-oriented activities in anticipation of their reelection campaign and people may be more motivated to seek out information about these senators as Election Day nears.[5]

In addition, it is important to control for individual level differences in people's predisposition to learn about politics in general, and their U.S. senators, in particular. The literature on political knowledge points to a number of demographic factors, including the respondent's gender, age, and education level. We also include a series of political variables, including how often a respondent pays attention to the national evening news since people who watch the national news are likely to be more informed about politics. We include a measure of political interest, where respondents are asked whether they are very much interested, somewhat interested, or not much interested in politics and current affairs. We expect people with high levels of political interest will be more informed about their senators.[6]

We develop a measure of political sophistication by creating an index based on whether respondents could correctly identify the party identification of their sitting governor, as well as correctly identify the political ideology of the Democratic Party and the Republican Party. For the ideology questions, respondents received a correct score for the Democratic Party if they placed the Democratic Party to the left of the middle and they received a correct score for the Republican Party if they placed the Republican Party to the right of the middle. The political sophistication scale ranges from 0 (no questions answered correctly) to 3 (each of the three questions answered correctly).

Finally, we include a measure of strength of partisanship for respondents, with strong Democrats and strong Republicans receiving a score of 3, weak Democrats or weak Republicans receiving a score of 2, leaning Democrats and leaning Republicans scoring a 1 and pure Independents receiving a score of 0. We expect strong identifiers to be more aware of their political surroundings, including knowing pertinent facts about their sitting senators.

With the control variables in hand, we examine whether the gender of the senator significantly influences people's willingness to answer questions about their senator. In each of the analyses in this chapter, it is necessary to examine "Senator 1" and "Senator 2" (the senior and junior senator from each state) separately since each respondent is asked to make assessments of both senators serving their state. The findings in table 6.1 demonstrate the gender of the senator significantly and powerfully influences people's willingness to answer questions about their senior and junior senator, holding key rival hypotheses constant.[7] In both equations, the coefficient for the gender of the senator is large and statistically significant, indicating people are much more likely to answer questions about female senators as opposed to male senators.[8]

Compared to the gender of the senator, the senator's proximity to reelection is less important. Since both of these variables are binary, we can compare the size of the coefficients directly. We see the coefficient for the gender of the senator is more than three times larger than the election year coefficient in each of the equations. The final measure of the political context, the variable assessing the information environment, is highly significant. The positive and significant coefficient indicates that as the amount of news at-

TABLE 6.1. Logistic Ordinal Regression Predicting Respondents'
Willingness to Answer Questions about Their Senators[a]

	Senator 1	Senator 2
Political Context		
Female Senator	.66 (.06)**	.58 (.07)**
Information Environment	.12 (.02)**	.32 (.02)**
Election Year	−.17 (.06)**	.17 (.09)
Citizen Characteristics		
Strength of Party Identification	.20 (.03)**	.20 (.03)**
Political Interest	.97 (.04)**	.88 (.05)**
Political Sophistication	.59 (.04)**	.57 (.03)**
Education	.17 (.02)**	.15 (.02)**
Age	.03 (.003)**	.02 (.002)**
Female Respondent	−.66 (.07)**	−.51 (.07)**
Attention to News	.16 (.03)**	.14 (.03)**
Threshold 0	4.39 (.19)**	4.90 (.21)**
Threshold 1	5.41 (.20)**	5.81 (.22)**
Threshold 2	6.54 (.20)**	6.89 (.22)**
Model χ^2	2,377.68**	2,232.33**
−2 Log Likelihood	10,636.79	10,746.06
Degrees of Freedom	10	10
Pseudo R^2 (Cox and Snell)	.36	.34
N	5,329	5,434

Note: The dependent variable is citizens' willingness to answer three questions about their senator: a question assessing the respondent's approval of the senator's job performance, a question asking respondents to volunteer the party identification of the senator, and a question asking respondents to identify the senator's ideological position. Female Senator is coded 1 for female senators, 0 for male senators. Information Environment is measured by an index assessing the amount of news published about the senator in the state newspaper and the amount of information written about the senators in their own press releases. Election Year is coded 1 for senators up for reelection in 2006, 0 for other senators. Strength of Party ranges from Independent (0) to strong Republican or Democrat (3). Political Interest ranged from "not at all" interested (1) to "very interested" (3). Political Sophistication ranges from 0 to 3. Education is coded on a six-point scale ranging from no high school to postgraduate education, and Age is coded in years. Female Respondent is coded 1 for female and 0 for male. Attention to News is based on a four-point scale indicating that the respondent watched the national evening news: not at all (1); once or twice a week (2); a few times a week (3); almost every day (4).

[a]Unstandardized logit coefficients are followed by standard errors in parentheses.
**$p < .01$; *$p < .05$

tention increases and as the amount of information disseminated by the senator increases, people are more willing to answer questions about their sitting senators.

Turning to the citizen characteristics, our findings resonate with prior research examining the determinants of political knowledge. For instance, people's willingness to answer questions about the senators is related to citizens' level of education, age, and gender. In particular, more educated respondents, older respondents, and male respondents are significantly more willing to answer questions about their senators, compared to less educated, younger, and female respondents. In addition, people who pay more attention to the news are more willing to answer questions about their U.S. senators. We also find that standard political variables powerfully influence the respondents' willingness to answer questions about sitting senators. More specifically, we find that people's level of political interest, their strength of partisanship, and their level of political sophistication are important predictors in both of the models.

We turn next to examining citizens' willingness to answer more demanding questions about their sitting senators. In particular, respondents are asked to identify each senator's vote on seven roll-call votes on the following topics: (1) withdrawing of force from Iraq (i.e., the Levin Amendment), (2) late-term abortion, (3) stem cell research, (4) immigration reform, (5) raising the minimum wage, (6) capital gains tax cut, and (7) the free trade agreement with Central America (CAFTA).[9] We sum up the number of roll-call vote questions that respondents were willing to answer. On average, respondents answered four of the seven vote questions, with about 18% of the people unable to answer any of the questions and about 30% of the respondents willing to answer each of the seven roll-call questions. Relying on the same independent variables introduced earlier and utilizing OLS regression, we look to see whether people are more willing to answer challenging questions about female senators, compared to male senators.

The findings in table 6.2 demonstrate respondents are significantly more likely to answer questions about female senators' roll-call behavior compared to their male colleagues.[10] In fact, according to the standardized regression coefficients, the gender of the senator is more important than the information environment and the election year when predicting citizens' willingness to answer questions about their senators' voting records. In both models, the gender of the senator produces almost a half-a-point advantage for female senators on the eight-point index. These results, consistent with the findings presented in table 6.1, indicate that female senators draw people's attention and citizens are more likely to process information about female senators compared to male senators.

We continue to find that respondent's demographic and political predispositions powerfully influence their willingness to answer roll-call questions. Political interest is the most important political variable, followed by political sophistication. Among the demographic characteristics, education and gender are the most consequential. As education increases, people are more able to offer answers to questions about the senators' voting records. Female respondents are also significantly less likely than male respondents

TABLE 6.2. OLS Regression Predicting Respondents' Willingness to Answer Roll-call Questions[a]

	Senator 1		Senator 2	
Political Context				
Female Senator	.44 (.07)**	.08	.33 (.08)**	.06
Information Environment	.05 (.02)**	.03	.09 (.03)**	.05
Election Year	−.14 (.7)	−.02	.07 (.10)	.01
Citizen Characteristics				
Strength of Party Identification	.14 (.03)**	.06	.15 (.03)**	.06
Political Interest	1.2 (.06)**	.30	1.10 (.05)**	.28
Political Sophistication	.34 (.04)**	.11	.33 (.04)**	.11
Education	.21 (.02)**	.11	.22 (.02)**	.12
Age	.01 (.003)**	.05	.008 (.003)**	.04
Female Respondent	−.63 (.07)**	−.11	−.62 (.07)**	−.11
Attention to News	.13 (.03)**	.06	.13 (.03)**	.05
Constant	1.84 (.21)**		−1.80 (.23)**	
R^2	.24		.23	
N		5,339		5,450

Note: The dependent variable is citizens' willingness to answer questions about the senator's roll-call vote on seven different votes. Female Senator is coded 1 for female senators, 0 for male senators. Information Environment is measured by an index assessing the amount of news published about the senator in the state newspaper and the amount of information written about the senators in their own press releases. Election Year is coded 1 for senators up for reelection in 2006, 0 for other senators. Strength of Party ranges from Independent (0) to strong Republican or Democrat (3). Political Interest ranges from "not at all" interested (1) to "very interested" (3). Political Sophistication ranges from 0 to 3. Education is coded on a six-point scale ranging from no high school to postgraduate education, and Age is coded in years. Female Respondent is coded 1 for female and 0 for male. Attention to News is based on a four-point scale indicating that the respondent watched the national evening news: not at all (1); once or twice a week (2); a few times a week (3); almost every day (4).

[a]Unstandardized OLS coefficients, with standard errors in parentheses, followed by standardized coefficients.

**p < .01; *p < .05

to offer answers to questions about their senators. The tendency for women to respond less frequently to answering questions (i.e., roll-call questions, as well as more generic questions about the senators) may reflect women's disinclination to guess when they are not certain, documented by Mondak and Anderson (2004).

Our results thus far demonstrate people's willingness to answer questions varies with characteristics of their senator, the media environment, as well as by the demographic and political characteristics of the respondents. We now turn to exploring whether these same factors are important when we examine the *accuracy* of people's perceptions of their senators. We start with rudimentary information (i.e., the senator's party identification) and move to progressively more challenging information (i.e., ideology, roll-call votes). We begin by looking at whether a senator's gender influences citizens' ability to identify the party of the senator. We rely on logistic regression to estimate people's ability to correctly recall their senators' party identification since the dependent variable is dichotomous (i.e., correctly recall senator's party identification or not). We utilize the same independent variables introduced in our earlier analyses. As before, the findings in table 6.3 indicate that the gender of the senator powerfully influences people's ability to accurately identify the party of their sitting senator.[11]

In figure 6.1, we illustrate graphically the impact of the gender of the senator by converting the logit coefficients to probabilities, relying on a procedure described by King (1989).[12] The figure shows, all else equal, that people have a higher probability of recalling a female senator's party correctly compared to a male senator's party. More specifically, people have a .79 probability of knowing the party identification of a female senator, but only a .63 probability of correctly identifying the party of a male senator, representing a .16 change in probability.

The remaining variables in the model in table 6.3 reveal similar patterns to those discussed earlier. We again find that people are significantly more likely to know the party identification of their senator when the political climate is rich with information, when the news coverage is abundant, and the senators' offices actively disseminate substantive press releases. We also continue to see that the respondents' political and demographic characteristics influence their knowledge about their senator; for example, well-educated people who are interested and sophisticated about politics are more knowledgeable about their senators. In addition, women and young people are less likely than men and older people to correctly recall the party identification of their senator.

We turn next to a slightly more complicated task for citizens: can respondents correctly identify the political ideology of their senator? We use a relatively easy standard to assess the accuracy of the respondent's answer. If a respondent places their Republican senator to the right of moderate on the ideological scale, the respondent is coded as correctly identifying their senator's ideology. Similarly, if a respondent places their Democratic senator to the left of moderate of the ideological scale, the respondent is coded as correctly identifying their senator's ideology. All other respondents are coded as unable to correctly identify their senator's ideology.[13]

Placing senators on an ideological scale, even simply placing them to the left or the right on a liberal-conservative continuum, is difficult for most re-

TABLE 6.3. Logistic Regression Predicting Ability to Identify Senator's Party Affiliation[a]

	Senator 1	Senator 2
Political Context		
Female Senator	.88 (.08)**	.61 (.08)**
Information Environment	.09 (.02)**	.43 (.03)**
Election Year	−.12 (.08)	.31 (.11)**
Citizen Characteristics		
Strength of Party Identification	.27 (.03)**	.32 (.03)**
Political Interest	.95 (.06)**	.93 (.06)**
Political Sophistication	.82 (.04)**	.88 (.04)**
Education	.26 (.03)**	.34 (.03)**
Age	.04 (.003)**	.03 (.003)**
Female Respondent	−.49 (.08)**	−.36 (.08)**
Attention to News	.04 (.03)	.05 (.03)
Constant	−7.00 (.26)**	−8.88 (.31)**
% of Cases Correctly Predicted	77%	78%
N	4,288	4,378

Note: The dependent variable is the citizens' ability to correctly identify the party of the senator. Female Senator is coded 1 for female senators, 0 for male senators. Information Environment is measured by an index assessing the amount of news published about the senator in the state newspaper and the amount of information written about the senators in their own press releases. Election Year is coded 1 for senators up for reelection in 2006, 0 for other senators. Strength of Party ranges from Independent (0) to strong Republican or Democrat (3). Political Interest ranged from "not at all" interested (1) to "very interested" (3). Political Sophistication ranges from 0 to 3. Education is coded on a six-point scale ranging from no high school to postgraduate education, and Age is coded in years. Female Respondent is coded 1 for female and 0 for male. Attention to News is based on a four-point scale indicating that the respondent watched the national evening news: not at all (1); once or twice a week (2); a few times a week (3); almost every day (4).
[a]Unstandardized logit coefficients are followed by standard errors in parentheses.
$**p < .01; *p < .05$

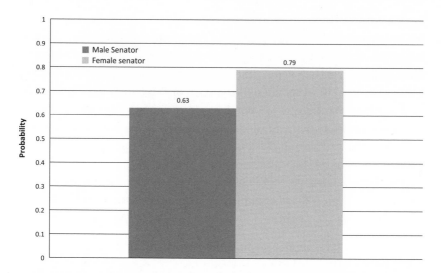

Fig. 6.1. Correctly Recalling Senator's Party by Gender of the Senator and Gender of the Respondent. (*Note:* This figure shows the impact of the gender of the senator on the probability of correctly recalling the senator's party identification. These probabilities are based on the unstandardized estimates presented in table 6.3. We calculate the probability by varying the gender of the senator while holding all remaining variables at their means [see King 1989, 105]. For ease of presentation, we average the probabilities for Senator 1 and Senator 2.)

spondents. While about two-thirds of respondents can correctly identify their senator's party affiliation, only about half of the respondents can accurately place their senator on the correct side of the ideological scale.[14] We again rely on logistic regression to examine how the gender of the senator, holding rival forces constant, influence people's ability to place the senator's ideological standings. The results of this analysis are presented in table 6.4. We continue to find that people give more accurate answers about female senators, with respondents much more likely to place female senators correctly on the ideological scale compared to male senators.[15]

However, some of the factors that significantly influenced knowledge of senators in previous analyses are less important here. For instance, the information environment does not encourage people to accurately identify their senators' ideological leanings. Even when newspapers allocate a lot of coverage to the state's sitting senators and the senators are presenting a great deal of information to their constituents, constituents do not become more knowledgeable about the ideological leanings of their senators. Similarly, citizens who pay attention to the news are not more likely to know the ideological leanings of their senators. This is not surprising given our examination of the substance of news coverage and press releases. We know from assessing the content of press coverage that reporters rarely discuss ideological information when covering senators. In particular, less than 10% of all the articles examined in our study mention the senators' ideology, with an average of less than .10 paragraphs per article. Similarly, only *one* press release out of almost 2,000 explicitly mentioned a senator's ideology.

We continue to find that certain types of political and demographic

TABLE 6.4. Logistic Regression Predicting Ability to Correctly Identify the Senator's Ideology[a]

	Senator 1	Senator 2
Political Context		
Female Senator	.73(.07)**	.37 (.08)**
Information Environment	−.009 (.02)	.02 (.03)
Election Year	−.15 (.08)	−.12 (.10)
Citizen Characteristics		
Strength of Party Identification	.12 (.03)**	.04 (.03)
Political Interest	.62 (.06)**	.52 (.05)**
Political Sophistication	.92 (.05)**	1.04 (.05)**
Education	.07 (.02)**	.09 (.02)**
Age	.01 (.003)**	.01 (.003)**
Female Respondent	−.36 (.07)**	−.30 (.07)**
Attention to News	−.02 (.03)	−.009 (.03)
Constant	−5.06 (23)**	−4.94 (.25)**
% of Cases Correctly Predicted	73%	72%
N	4,288	4,378

Note: The dependent variable is the citizens' ability to correctly identify the ideology of the senator. Female Senator is coded 1 for female senators, 0 for male senators. Information Environment is measured by an index assessing the amount of news published about the senator in the state newspaper and the amount of information written about the senators in their own press releases. Election Year is coded 1 for senators up for reelection in 2006, 0 for other senators. Strength of Party ranges from Independent (0) to strong Republican or Democrat (3). Political Interest ranged from "not at all" interested (1) to "very interested" (3). Political Sophistication ranges from 0 to 3. Education is coded on a six-point scale ranging from no high school to postgraduate education, and Age is coded in years. Female Respondent is coded 1 for female and 0 for male. Attention to News is based on a four-point scale indicating that the respondent watched the national evening news: not at all (1); once or twice a week (2); a few times a week (3); almost every day (4).
[a]Unstandardized logit coefficients are followed by standard errors in parentheses.
**$p < .01$; *$p < .05$

qualities enhance people's likelihood of possessing ideological information about their senators. For example, as age, education, political interest, and political sophistication increase, people are significantly more aware of their senators' political proclivities. And controlling for all other factors, men continue to outpace women in their ability to offer accurate ideological information about their senators.

We conclude our examination of the impact of the gender of the senator on people's knowledge about their senators with a difficult test for respondents. We look at people's ability to accurately recall their senator's vote on several different roll-call votes. To measure respondents' knowledge of the senators' voting records, we constructed an index by comparing the senator's actual vote with the respondent's recollection of how the senator voted on the seven ballot measures presented earlier. On average, respondents correctly reported three of the seven roll-call votes for their senator, with one out of five respondents not able to accurately recall any of their senator's votes and only 7% of the respondents able to correctly answer each of the seven roll-call questions.

We examine how the gender of senator influences people's familiarity with the senator's voting record with OLS regression, controlling for the political context and citizen characteristics. The findings in table 6.5 once again demonstrate the importance of the senator's gender: the gender of the senator powerfully influences people's ability to recall their senator's votes on important legislative matters. In the model predicting Senator 1, the unstandardized OLS coefficient suggests that being a female senator, controlling for all other factors, increases a respondent's score on the eight-point scale by almost a half of a point. In the model predicting Senator 2, the unstandardized OLS coefficient indicates that people's scores for female senators are, on average, are almost three-quarters of a point higher than people's scores for male senators, all else being equal.[16] Furthermore, the impact of the gender of the senator is substantial relative to the other variables in the model. The standardized coefficients indicate that the senator's gender is more important than the respondent's age and strength of partisanship when predicting people's ability to accurately recall the senators' voting record.

The remaining variables in the models perform as expected. For instance, we find that states with more information available about the senators encourage respondents to more accurately recall their senators' roll-call votes. Similarly, people who pay more attention to the news are more likely to score higher on the roll-call index. And the political and demographic characteristics of the respondent continue to be important, with political interest powerfully influencing people's recall of their senators' actions in office. To illustrate, the unstandardized coefficient for political interest in the model for Senator 1 suggests that a one-point change on the interest variable (e.g., moving from somewhat interested to very interested in politics) produces almost a one-point increase in people's score on the roll-call index, holding all rival hypotheses constant.

The results of our analysis thus far are strikingly consistent. People are more willing to answer questions about female senators and people have much more accurate information about female senators compared to their

TABLE 6.5. OLS Regression Predicting Accuracy of Respondents' Knowledge of Senators' Roll-call Votes[a]

	Senator 1		Senator 2	
Political Context				
Female Senator	.40 (.06)**	.09	.68 (.07)**	.15
Information Environment	.090(.01)**	.08	.09 (.02)**	.05
Election Year	−.35 (.06)**	−.08	−.006 (.08)	−.01
Citizen Characteristics				
Strength of Party Identification	.12 (.02)**	.06	.12 (.02)**	.06
Political Interest	.99 (.04)**	.31	.88 (.04)**	.28
Political Sophistication	.39 (.03)**	.16	.38 (.03)**	.15
Education	.21 (.02)**	.14	.22 (.02)**	.14
Age	.01 (.002)**	.06	.01(.002)**	.05
Female Respondent	−.61 (.06)**	−.13	−.52(.06)**	−.11
Attention to News	.04(.02)*	.02	.06 (.02)*	.03
Constant	−2.32 (.16)**		−2.28 (.18)**	
R^2	.29		.28	
N		5,329		5,450

Note: The dependent variable is the number of roll-call votes that citizens correctly answer about the senator across seven different roll-call votes. Female Senator is coded 1 for female senators, 0 for male senators. Information Environment is measured by an index assessing the amount of news published about the senator in the state newspaper and the amount of information written about the senators in their own press releases. Election Year is coded 1 for senators up for reelection in 2006, 0 for other senators. Strength of Party ranges from Independent (0) to strong Republican or Democrat (3). Political Interest ranges from "not at all" interested (1) to "very interested" (3). Political Sophistication ranges from 0 to 3. Education is coded on a six-point scale ranging from no high school to postgraduate education, and Age is coded in years. Female Respondent is coded 1 for female and 0 for male. Attention to News is based on a four-point scale indicating that the respondent watched the national evening news: not at all (1); once or twice a week (2); a few times a week (3); almost every day (4).

[a]Unstandardized OLS coefficients, with standard errors in parentheses, followed by standardized coefficients.

**p < .01; *p < .05

male counterparts. In addition, when people are living in states rich with political information, people are more likely to answer questions more accurately (with the exception of ideology). People who are more interested and informed about politics have higher levels of information about their senators and are more willing to offer this information when asked. Finally, older and educated respondents score higher on the information measures examined in this chapter than younger and less educated individuals.

One of the most powerful and unwavering findings in this chapter is the fact that female respondents score significantly lower on *every* measure of senator knowledge. Given findings from previous studies suggesting that women's level of political knowledge is often enhanced when they are exposed to female candidates and female officeholders (Atkeson 2003; Campbell and Wolbrecht 2006; Hansen 1997; Karp and Banducci 2008; Koch 1997), we wanted to determine if women's understanding of their senators increases when they are represented by a female senator. That is, we expect that a woman's level of information about a senator depends on or is conditioned by the gender of their senator.

To explore the conditional relationship between female respondents' awareness of their senators and the gender of the senator, we examine the statistical interaction between gender of the senator and gender of the respondent in a series of OLS regression equations. We develop two dependent variables. The first dependent variable is an index created by summing people's *willingness* to answer basic questions about their senator. We simply combine responses to the first two dependent variables examined in this chapter (e.g., tables 6.1–6.2), creating an index that ranges from 0 to 10. The second dependent variable is an index created by summing people's *accuracy* in answering the following questions: (1) party identification of the senator, (2) ideology of the senator, and (3) roll-call vote of the senator. We combine responses to these last three dependent variables (e.g., tables 6.3–6.5) to create an "accuracy" index ranging from 0 to 9.

We present the results of the multiplicative analyses in table 6.6. We are particularly interested in the interaction coefficients at the top of the table. As the positive interaction (i.e., multiplicative) coefficients indicate, female respondents are more willing to answer questions about their senator and are more accurate in these responses when they are evaluating a female senator compared to a male senator. In three of the four cases, the interaction coefficient is large and statistically significant.

To aid in the interpretation of the interaction effects, we rely on the OLS

TABLE 6.6. OLS Regression Estimating the Interaction Effect of Senator Gender and Respondent Gender on Willingness and Accuracy in Answering Questions

	Willingness to Answer		Accuracy in Answering	
	Senator 1	Senator 2	Senator 1	Senator 2
Interaction				
Female Senator*Female Respondent	.53 (.14)**	.28 (.14)*	.35 (.11)**	.13 (.11)
Political Environment				
Female Senator	.07 (.12)	.14 (.12)	.16 (.10)	.59 (.10)**
Information Environment	.05 (.02)**	.10 (.03)**	.09 (.01)**	.09 (.02)**
Election Year	−.13 (.07)	.06 (.10)	−.35 (.06)**	−.01 (.08)
Citizen Characteristics				
Strength of Party Identification	.14 (.03)**	.15 (.03)**	.11 (.02)**	.12 (.02)**
Political Interest	1.18 (.06)**	1.10 (.05)**	.99 (.04)**	.88 (.04)**
Political Sophistication	.35 (.04)**	.33 (.04)**	.40 (.03)**	.38 (.03)**
Education	.21 (.02)**	.22 (.03)**	.21 (.02)**	.21 (.02)**
Age	.01 (.003)**	.008 (.003)**	.01 (.002)**	.008 (.002)**
Female Respondent	−.86 (.10)**	−.76 (.10)**	−.76 (.07)**	−.58 (.08)**
Attention to News	.13 (.03)**	.13 (.03)**	.04 (.02)	.06 (.02)*
Constant	−1.68 (.21)**	−1.71 (.23)**	−2.21 (.16)**	−2.24 (.18)**
R^2	.24	.23	.29	.28
N	5,339	5,450	5,339	5,450

Note: "Willingness to Answer" is an index composed of the dependent variables utilized in Tables 6.1–6.3, and "Accuracy in Answering" is an index composed of the dependent variables utilized in Tables 6.4–6.5 (see text for more information). Female Senator is coded 1 for female senators, 0 for male senators. Information Environment is measured by an index assessing the amount of news published about the senator in the state newspaper and the amount of information written about the senators in their own press releases. Election Year is coded 1 for senators up for reelection in 2006, 0 for other senators. Strength of Party ranges from Independent (0) to strong Republican or Democrat (3). Political Interest ranges from "not at all" interested (1) to "very interested" (3). Political Sophistication ranges from 0 to 3. Education is coded on a six-point scale ranging from no high school to postgraduate education, and Age is coded in years. Female Respondent is coded 1 for female and 0 for male. Attention to News is based on a four-point scale indicating that the respondent watched the national evening news: not at all (1); once or twice a week (2); a few times a week (3); almost every day (4).

[a]Unstandardized OLS coefficients are followed by standard errors in parentheses.

**$p < .01$; *$p < .05$

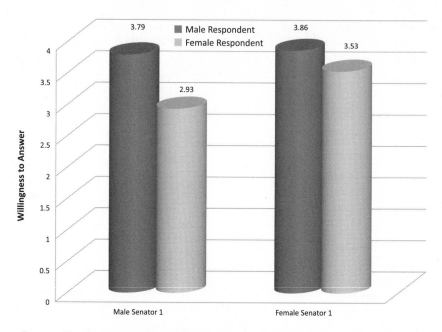

Fig. 6.2. The Interaction Effect of Senator's Gender and Respondent's Gender on Willingness to Answer Questions about Senators. (*Note:* These estimates are based on the OLS coefficients presented in table 6.6. The point estimates are derived by varying the gender of the respondent and the gender of the senator while holding all remaining variables at their means [Lewis-Beck 1980].)

coefficients in table 6.6 to estimate male and female respondents' willingness to answer questions as well as the accuracy of their answers about male and female senators. In particular, we derive point estimates by varying the gender of the respondent and the gender of the senator, while holding all remaining variables at their means (Lewis-Beck 1980).[17]

We begin by looking at people's willingness to answer questions about their senators. The data in figure 6.2 show that the gender gap in citizens' willingness to answer questions about their senators is substantially wider when the citizens are evaluating a male senator. In particular, male respondents answer, on average, about four questions about male senators, while female respondents answer, on average, less than three questions about male senators. In comparison, when evaluating female senators, the gender gap among respondents is much narrower, with both male and female respondents answering almost four questions about their female senator.

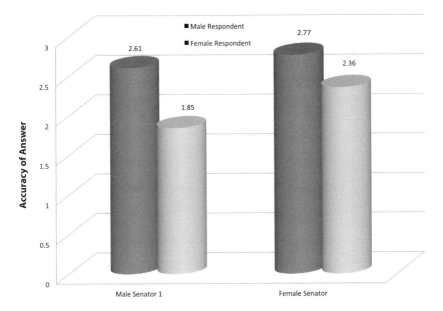

Fig. 6.3. The Interaction Effect of Senator's Gender and Respondent's Gender on Accuracy of Answers about Senators. (*Note:* These estimates are based on the OLS coefficients presented in table 6.6. The point estimates are derived by varying the gender of the respondent and the gender of the senator while holding all remaining variables at their means [Lewis-Beck 1980].)

Furthermore, male respondents are less affected by the gender of their senator. These respondents answer about four questions about their senator, regardless of the gender of the senator. Female respondents, in contrast, are more affected by their senator's gender, answering more than three and a half questions, on average, when they are evaluating a female senator, compared to less than three questions when evaluating a male senator.

Turning to the accuracy of people's answers about the senators, we find a similar pattern. Female respondents give more accurate answers when assessing a female senator compared to a male senator (see figure 6.3). We find, on average, more than a half of a point difference in the accuracy of answers when women are answering questions about a female senator than when women are answering questions about a male senator (2.36 vs. 1.85). For male respondents, the gender of the senator is less consequential; producing little change in male respondents' accuracy scores (2.77 vs. 2.61). Similarly, we find that the gender difference in respondents' answers is more dramatic when respondents are targeting a male senator (i.e., more than three-fourths of a point on the accuracy index, 2.61 vs. 1.85) than when respondents are answering questions about a female senator (less than half a point on the accuracy index, 2.77 vs. 2.36).

These results indicate that the gender of the senator is more consequential for female respondents than for male respondents. While both male and female respondents are more likely to answer questions and are more accurate in answering questions about female senators, female respondents are more affected by the senator's gender. The presence of a female senator may stimulate women to pay more attention to their political environment and learn more about their representatives. Female senators, in other words, may act as a symbol for women in the electorate. As Olympia Snowe noted when she successfully lobbied for the commissioning of a portrait of former Maine senator Margaret Chase Smith to hang in the Capitol, "the portrait of this woman, who served with such dignity and honor, is a testimony to the possibilities that exist for all women" (Mikulski et al. 2000, 191).

SUMMARY AND CONCLUSION

We began this chapter examining whether people's level of information about their sitting senators varies with the senator's gender. Our findings are strong and consistent, regardless of the complexity of the questions examined. Citizens are much more informed about female senators than their male colleagues. Furthermore, the importance of the gender of the senator in predicting levels of information remains influential in spite of stiff controls, such as measures assessing the respondents' party attachment, interest in politics, consumption of news, and sophistication about politics. The power and uniformity of our results are consistent with our theoretical expectations. We reasoned that female senators remain unique, especially across the arc of U.S. history. Therefore, because female senators are salient, citizens need to expend time and energy to process information about these senators. This additional cognitive effort produces higher levels of information recall for female senators compared to male senators. Despite the fact that female senators receive less press attention and less prominent attention, as we reported earlier in the book, citizens know more about these senators.

We also document a stubborn and persistent gender gap in citizens' understanding about their political figures. On average, across each of the dependent variables examining knowledge about hometown senators, we find that female respondents are less informed than male respondents. However, we also demonstrate that this gender gap among citizens is diminished when people are assessing female senators. This finding resonates with recent research suggesting that women's interest in politics is piqued by the presence of female leaders. Women's interest and involvement in the political system appears to be enhanced by the existence of female political leaders, providing additional justification for the need for "descriptive" representation.

In the next chapter, we examine senators as they run for reelection to see if female senators face different constraints than their male colleagues. We examine a sample of 21 senators running for reelection in 2006, examining their campaign communications, the campaign coverage, as well as voters' evaluations of their candidacies. We look at whether gender differences in representational messages present during the governing period are also evident when senators run for reelection. We look at the senators' own campaign messages, as well as coverage of these senators in the news, as they run for reelection. Finally, we examine how citizens evaluate these female and male senators on a range of personal traits and issue assessments to examine how gender stereotypes, along with messages presented by the senators and the news media, influence citizens' evaluations of senators during campaigns.

CHAPTER 7

The Impact of the Senator's Gender during Reelection Campaigns

THE FUNDAMENTAL MECHANISM for holding legislators accountable to the people of the United States is frequent elections. This has always been the case for members of the U.S. House of Representatives. But for U.S. senators, the U.S. Constitution granted state legislatures power to select and hold senators accountable. In the midst of a nationwide movement to further democratize many of America's political institutions in the early decades of the 20th century, Congress passed and the states ratified the 17th Amendment in 1913. This allowed citizens to select and remove senators via direct elections. The first elections for U.S. senators took place in 1914. Many generations later, the idea that citizens choose their senators every six years is ensconced in the legal foundations and political culture of the United States.

This chapter is about senatorial elections. We examine the campaign messages disseminated by male and female senators running for reelection. We compare the gender differences in representational messages found earlier in this book with gender differences in campaign rhetoric. We look at whether female and male senators continue to emphasize the same themes and messages during campaigns or whether they alter their communications in response to the electoral context. In addition, we determine how the news media cover male and female senators running for reelection, investigating whether the gender differences in media treatment discovered during the governing period are also evident during electoral campaigns. Finally, we examine whether the news media change the content and the tone of their coverage as the governing phase gives way to the election season.

Once we have a clear understanding of the consistency of messages from governing to campaigning, we turn to exploring how citizens react to the campaign messages about male and female senators. Specifically, we examine how citizens evaluate male and female senators seeking reelection. We examine several questions. For example, do the senators' messages or the news media's messages influence how people evaluate male and female senators during campaigns? Do gender stereotypes influence the attitudes and actions of citizens as they make decisions on Election Day? Locating answers to these questions will allow us to understand more clearly the relationship between representational messages and electoral accountability in the U.S. Senate.

THE ELECTORAL CONTEXT

There are national and local forces at play in senatorial elections (Jacobson 2009). In 2006, the national forces were trending in favor of the Democratic Party. President Bush's approval rating among the American electorate, as measured by the classic Gallup Poll question, was 42% in mid-August 2006 and had dropped to 37% by early October 2006.[1] The Iraq War was a pressing concern for most Americans. In general, the vast majority of U.S. citizens were tired of the war, felt the war had been a mistake, believed the war was not worth pursuing, felt less safe vis-à-vis a terrorist threat, and wanted U.S forces to come home.[2] The Democratic Party, sensing possible victory in the fall 2006 midterm elections, was mobilizing strong candidates with a significant amount of funding.

Against this backdrop, Senator Debbie Stabenow, a Democrat from Michigan, was seeking her first reelection. She had captured her senatorial seat in 2000 by a narrow margin. Over four million voters went to the polls in 2000 and she won by approximately 43,000 votes, slightly less than 1%. In 2006, Republican Michael Bouchard was trying to take her seat. He had been a state senator in Michigan, he was the sheriff of Oakland County, and he won the GOP primary with 60% of the vote. Senator Stabenow campaigned aggressively to hold her seat. She spent over $12 million, more than doubling Bouchard's spending.[3] One of her top financial contributors was EMILY's List (i.e., $189,375), an organization that seeks to support pro-choice Democratic women. In addition, when we categorize campaign funds by "industry," groups focused on women's issues contributed over $600,000 to Stabenow's campaign. This was second only to law-related organizations, which gave over $1.4 million.[4] Senator Stabenow had a significant lead in polls through the fall, leading by as many as 19% on the eve of the election.[5] In the end, she defeated Bouchard 57% to 41%, a winning margin of 16%. Still, even with a comfortable lead, she concentrated a sizeable amount of her campaign resources on TV commercials encouraging Michigan voters to support her reelection. Below is an example of one of Senator Stabenow's 30-second ads. The commercial is titled "Leader."

> DEBBIE STABENOW: Times are tough in Michigan, but so are we. With a level playing field, our workers can compete with anybody.
> That's why I'm fighting for a U.S. trade prosecutor—to crack down on countries that violate our trade laws.
> To reduce health care costs—to help Michigan businesses compete.
> And to invest in education—so our children have a chance to get ahead.
> I'm Debbie Stabenow, and I approve this message because we've got a great future here in Michigan and I'm fighting for it every day.

Six hundred miles to the east, appointed Democratic Senator Robert Menendez of New Jersey was also seeking his first reelection. Senator Menendez was appointed to the U.S. Senate in December 2005 by Governor Jon Corzine. The appointment left Senator Menendez less than a year to communicate with and explain to constituents why he should be reelected. Senator Menendez had been a successful member of the U.S. House of Representatives since 1992, winning reelections by wide margins year after year. His opponent in 2006 was Republican Thomas Kean Jr., the minority whip in the New Jersey Senate. Kean's father had been New Jersey's governor from 1983 to 1990.

Senator Menendez, knowing he was challenged by a quality candidate with ample resources, raised significant sums of money and outspent Kean approximately $13 million to $7.5 million.[6] Polls in New Jersey showed Senator Menendez leading in early November by approximately eight percentage points.[7] While Senator Menendez won by a vote margin of nine points, 53% to 45%, his electoral prospects were uncertain during the length of the campaign. In the weeks leading up to Election Day, Senator Menendez blasted the airwaves with a number of commercials in the expensive New Jersey media market. Below is an example of one of Senator Menendez's 30-second advertisements. The commercial is titled "Put."

> ROBERT MENENDEZ: Some pretty strong New Jersey people work here.
> Standing up for them means you better be strong, too.

So when George Bush tried to sell our ports to a foreign country and
threatened our security, I led the fight to stop him. And we won.
Five years after 9/11, President Bush still doesn't get it—homeland security starts here. And if he won't stand up for New Jersey, I will.
I'm Sen. Bob Menendez, and I approved this message.

The Stabenow and Menendez commercials, when juxtaposed side by
side, provide interesting comparisons. Both senators were seeking their first
reelections, both were Democrats from historically Democratic leaning
states, both faced quality challengers, and both had significant advantages
in terms of resources. To be sure, there are similarities in their messages. Both
senators emphasized agentic traits: Senator Stabenow is a "fighter" and Senator Menendez is "strong" and will "stand up" for New Jersey. We know from
our exploration of the senators' representational messages that agentic traits
are much more likely to be mentioned by senators on their official websites.
The senators, however, emphasized different types of issues. In particular,
Senator Stabenow emphasized the need to reduce health-care costs and invest in education (as well as improve trade fairness), while Senator Menendez
focused on homeland security. The gender difference in political priorities is
consistent with our earlier findings where we show that male senators prefer
to focus on competitive issues, like defense, homeland security, and the
economy, while women are more likely to discuss communal issues like education, health care, and the environment.

These two examples suggest that the topics and foci of representational
and campaign messages may mirror one another. We explore the relationship between these two types of messages in the first section of the chapter.
Once we have a solid understanding of the correlation between governing
and campaign messages, we turn to an examination of news coverage during
reelection contests. Finally, with controlled and uncontrolled campaign
messages in hand, we examine how voters form impressions of incumbents
running for reelection.

MEASURING THE CONTENT AND IMPACT OF
MESSAGES IN SENATE CAMPAIGNS

This chapter is focused on campaigns; thus, we need to revise our sample of
senators and look exclusively at senators running for reelection. As discussed
in chapter 2, we selected 21 senators running for reelection in 2006, stratify-

ing our sample by the competitiveness of the race and the party of the senator. We included 15 male senators and 6 female senators in our sample. All female senators running for reelection are included in our sample and we have included 65% of the male senators seeking reelection.[8]

To measure the senators' campaign messages, we rely on two complementary datasets: (1) the senators' campaign websites and (2) the senators' political advertisements.[9] The data on campaign websites were collected by Druckman, Kifer, and Parkin (2009). Campaign websites for all 21 senators in our sample are included in the Druckman et al. data set. We also completed an original content analysis of televised campaign advertisements; we examined 131 advertisements for 16 of the 21 incumbents in our sample. To measure the news media's coverage of the 21 incumbents seeking reelection, we conducted a content analysis of campaign coverage in the largest circulating newspaper in the senator's state from October 1 through Election Day. We coded over 2,000 articles for the 21 incumbents running for reelection.

Finally, to measure citizens' attitudes during campaigns, we rely on the 2006 Cooperative Congressional Election Study (CCES). We created a unique module as part of the CCES data-collection effort. For our module, approximately 75 respondents were sampled in each of the 21 states featuring an incumbent running for reelection, for a total of 1,045 respondents. We asked respondents a battery of questions related to messages generated by the senators and the news media. For example, we asked citizens to assess their senators on four traits (i.e., honesty, caring, experience, and leadership) and two issues (i.e., the economy and health care).[10] In addition, we included questions intended to capture additional forces known to influence people's evaluations of senatorial candidates, such as party identification, ideology, and assessments of national conditions. We rely on this survey in the final section of the chapter to explore how citizens evaluate incumbent senators during reelection campaigns. These distinct data sets allow us to explore a range of questions related to how gender influences campaign communications and their impact on citizens during senate elections. We turn first to examining the types of messages male and female incumbents choose to emphasize as they run for reelection.

THE CONTENT OF INCUMBENT MESSAGES DURING CAMPAIGNS

We expect senators' strategies during reelection campaigns will match their governing strategies to a large degree. Consistent with theorizing in earlier

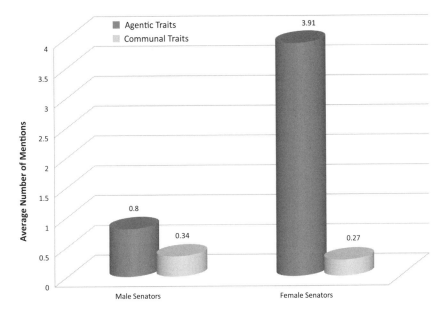

Fig. 7.1. Gender Differences in Trait Emphasis in Political Advertisements. (*Note: Agentic Traits* include experience, strong leader, competent, accomplished, hardworking, aggressive, independent, consistent, and ambitious. *Communal Traits* include caring, advocate, moral, compassionate, and honest.)

chapters, male and female senators will try to revise potentially damaging stereotypes regarding their personal traits, with women focusing more extensively on their embodiment of agentic traits, and men demonstrating their possession of communal traits, like empathy. However, since agentic traits, like competence and leadership, are salient to voters during a campaign (e.g., Funk 1999; Hayes 2005; Hayes 2010), both male and female senators are expected to focus on these dimensions more than personal characteristics like compassion and integrity.

We begin our exploration into campaign messages by looking at the personal characteristics that senators emphasize on the campaign trail.[11] The data in figure 7.1 demonstrates that incumbent senators, male and female, mention "male" or agentic traits more frequently than "female" or communal traits.[12] However, the preference for agentic traits is much more dramatic for female senators. Women highlight traits like experience more than four times as often as men.[13] We explore the relationship between the senator's gender and their emphasis on traits in a multivariate model. In the multi-

138 THE CHANGING FACE OF REPRESENTATION

variate analysis, we control for the party and seniority of the senator. In addition, since we are looking at rhetoric during a campaign, we control for the closeness of the race since senators may emphasize different traits depending on the competitiveness of the contest (e.g., Kahn and Kenney 1999). We also include a measure assessing whether a senator's opponent criticizes the senator's agentic traits in the opponent's advertisements.

The results, presented in table 7.1., indicate the gender of the senator is significantly related to the likelihood of emphasizing agentic traits in campaign advertisements. Female senators emphasize these trait dimensions significantly more often than their male colleagues.[14] Converting logit coefficients to probabilities (King 1989), we find that female senators have a .77 probability of mentioning agentic traits in their commercials, while the probability for male senators falls to only .27. Furthermore, the gender of the senator is the only variable in the model that significantly influences the reliance on agentic traits in the senators' political advertisements.[15]

TABLE 7.1. Logistic Regression Predicting Mentioning Agentic Traits in Political Advertisements[a]

Senator Characteristics	
Female Senator	2.22 (.84)***
Years of Seniority in Senate	−.17 (.22)
Democratic Senator	−.37 (.73)
Campaign Characteristics	
Competition	.02 (.02)
Opponents' Trait Emphasis	.73 (1.0)
Constant	−.94 (.58)
Likelihood Ratio χ^2	87.3***
Degrees of Freedom	5
Number of Observations	135

Note: The dependent variable is whether the senator mentions agentic traits in a political advertisement. Female Senator is coded 1 for female senators, 0 for male senators. Years of Seniority in Senate is coded as years in office. Democratic Senator is coded 1 for Democratic senators and 0 for Republican senators. Competition is measured by subtracting incumbent support from challenger support based on preelection polling data published in the 2006 New York Times Election Guide. Opponents' Trait Emphasis is whether the opponent mentioned the senator's lack of agentic traits (e.g., the senator is a weak leader) in the opponent's own commercial. Agentic traits include experience, strong leader, competent, accomplished, hardworking, aggressive, independent, consistent, and ambitious.

[a]Standard errors are in parentheses, followed by levels of significance.
***$p < .01$; **$p < .05$; *$p < .10$

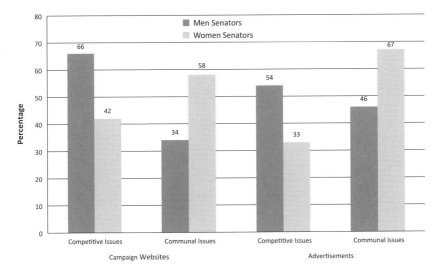

Fig. 7.2. Percentage of Issues about Competitive or Communal Issues on Campaign Websites and in Political Advertisements. (*Note: Competitive Issues* include defense, foreign policy, business, inflation, economy, budget, energy, farm, and taxes. *Communal Issues* include health care, elderly, welfare, child care, education, and the environment.)

We turn next to the substance of issue discussion in the senators' campaign propaganda. While we expect women to be more likely to focus on "compassion" issues compared to men, the differences may be less dramatic during the 2006 campaign given the dominance of the Iraq War. Beginning with the senators' campaign websites, we examine the content of the issue discussion on the candidates' biography pages.[16] As expected, the data in figure 7.2 shows that female senators are more likely to focus on communal issues on their campaign websites, while male senators prefer to highlight their commitment to competitive issues. Almost two-thirds of the issue discussion on the male senator's biography page focuses on issues such as homeland security and the economy. In contrast, almost 60% of the issue content on the female senators' biography page emphasizes communal issues, like helping the elderly and protecting the environment.[17] Furthermore, we find the same pattern when we look at the senators' political advertisements. Female senators emphasize communal issues more than their male colleagues (67% vs. 46%), while men favor "male issues" over "female issues" (54% vs. 46%).[18]

In summary, gender differences found in representational messages are evident in senators' campaign communications as well. Female incumbents are more likely to discuss communal issues compared to male incumbents running for reelection. We also find that male and female senators prefer to highlight their agentic traits in campaign messages, with women talking almost exclusively about "agentic" traits. We turn next to examining the content of the news media's messages about male and female senators during their reelection campaigns.

THE CONTENT OF THE NEWS MEDIA'S MESSAGES DURING CAMPAIGNS

Do the gender differences in news coverage discovered during the governing period persist when senators run for reelection? We focus on the substance of coverage given to male and female senators pursuing reelection. When journalists cover senators in the non-electoral arena, they consistently represent the messages of male senators more accurately than female senators. While women prefer to emphasize communal issues in their controlled messages, the news media does not represent this preference in their coverage. Similarly, women focus more extensively on agentic traits in their governing messages; however, this emphasis is not represented in news coverage. During the campaign, do reporters and editors more accurately mirror the messages of female senators?

To answer this question, we begin by comparing the issues incumbents are talking about in their campaign messages with the news media's coverage of the incumbents' issue priorities. We compare the content on the incumbent senators' campaign websites with the content of campaign news coverage.[19] This analysis yields two key findings, presented in figure 7.3. First, the content of issue coverage in the campaign news is identical for male and female senators. In particular, about 70% of their coverage is devoted to competitive issues, while only about 30% percent of their coverage is devoted to communal issues, regardless of the senator's gender.

Second, the data in figure 7.3 suggests that the pattern of press coverage more faithfully represents the policy messages of male senators compared to the preferred issue messages of female senators.[20] For instance, men emphasize issues like foreign policy and the economy two-thirds of the time on their websites and the news coverage largely reflect this emphasis.

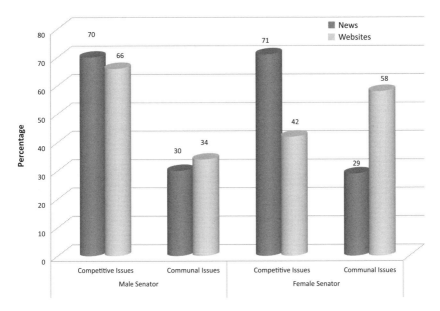

Fig. 7.3. Comparison of Issue Content on Senators' Campaign Webpage versus Coverage in the News. (*Note: Agentic Traits* include experience, strong leader, competent, accomplished, hardworking, aggressive, independent, consistent, and ambitious. *Communal Traits* include caring, advocate, moral, compassionate, and honest.)

For female senators, in contrast, the news media do a poorer job reflecting the senators' preferred issue agenda. Women discuss communal issues more often than competitive issues (i.e., 58% vs. 42%). However, news coverage of female senators does not reflect this preference. In particular, less than one-third of the stories written about female senators discuss communal issues.

We turn to a more systematic investigation of the link between the senators' issue messages and the news media's coverage of issues in table 7.2. We look at coverage of competitive and communal issues in the news, controlling for the characteristics of the senator (i.e., gender, seniority, party), characteristics of the newspaper (i.e., the number of paragraphs published about the senator, the circulation of the newspaper), and characteristics of the campaign (i.e., the closeness of the race). In these models, we include a variable assessing whether senators mentioned competitive or communal issues on the front page of their campaign websites. We also include a variable measuring whether challengers mentioned competitive or communal issues on the front page of the challengers' campaign websites. With these additional measures, we can see if the candidates are influencing the campaign news agenda by emphasizing certain policy matters in their campaigns.

Turning to the first two columns in table 7.2, the findings from the additive model are largely consistent with the pattern presented in figure 7.3. More specifically, coverage of competitive and communal issues does not

TABLE 7.2. Logistic Regression Predicting Issue Coverage in the News[a]

	Additive Models		Multiplicative Models	
	Competitive Issues	Communal Issues	Competitive Issues	Communal Issues
Senator Characteristics				
Female Senator	.49 (.26)*	.19 (.43)	1.26 (.33)***	.73 (.42)*
Democratic Senator	−.58 (.20)***	−.97 (.28)***	−.46 (.19)***	−.83 (.26)***
Years of Seniority in Senate	.20 (.06)***	.38 (.09)***	.23 (.06)***	.44 (.09)***
Campaign Characteristics				
Senator's Webpage	.98 (.23)***	1.35 (.38)***	1.14 (.23)***	1.34 (.38)***
Female Senator*Senator Webpage			−1.50 (.41)***	−2.92 (.74)***
Challenger's Webpage	.46 (.23)**	.82 (.26)***	.59 (.23)**	0.86 (.25)***
Competition	−.02 (.008)***	−.03 (.01)***	−.02 (.008)***	0.02 (.01)***
Campaign Spending	.08 (.28)	−.26 (.38)	.65 (.32)*	0.46 (.40)
Newspaper Characteristics				
Newspaper Circulation	−.19 (.30)	.87 (.48)*	−.21 (.33)	1.91 (.55)***
Senator Paragraphs	.14 (.01)***	.12 (.01)***	.14 (.01)***	.12 (.01)***
Constant	−2.23 (1.74)	−8.87 (2.68)***	−4.91 (1.91)***	15.11 (3.14)***
Correctly Predicted	86%	93%	86%	93%
Number of Observations	2,077	2,077	2,077	2,077

Note: The dependent variable is whether competitive or communal issues are mentioned in the news article. Female Senator is coded 1 for female senators, 0 for male senators. Democratic Senator is coded 1 for Democratic senators and 0 for Republican senators. Years of Seniority in Senate is coded as years in office. Senator Webpage is whether competitive or communal issues are mentioned on the front page of the senator's campaign website. Challenger's Webpage is whether competitive or communal issues are mentioned on the front page of the challenger's campaign website. Competition is measured by subtracting incumbent support from challenger support based on preelection polling data published in the 2006 *New York Times Election Guide.* Campaign Spending is divided by voting population and is logged to base 10. The campaign spending data comes from the 2006 *New York Times Election Guide.* Newspaper Circulation is logged to base 10 of the newspaper's circulation size. Senator Paragraphs is the number of paragraphs about the senator in each article. "Male" issues include defense, foreign policy, business, inflation, economy, budget, farm, and taxes. "Female" issues include health care, elderly, welfare, child care, and education.

[a]Standard errors are in parentheses, followed by levels of significance.

***$p < .01$; **$p < .05$; *$p < .10$

differ dramatically with the gender of the senator. Male and female senators receive the same amount of coverage for communal issues. For competitive issues, female senators actually receive somewhat more issue attention than male senators, despite the preference of female senators to discuss alternative issues.

In addition, the findings indicate senators and challengers influence the news media's agenda. When incumbents highlight competitive or communal issues on the front page of their campaign websites, senators receive significantly more attention regarding these particular policy matters. Challengers, too, are able to influence the coverage of senators by focusing on certain types of topics on their campaign websites.

We also find that the party and seniority of the senator significantly influences the content of issue coverage, with senior senators and Republicans receiving substantially more coverage of competitive and communal issues compared to more junior senators and Democratic senators. Furthermore, and as expected, the coverage of issues, both competitive and communal, increases with the closeness of the senate contest.

Finally, given the disconnect between the issue messages of female senators and the coverage of issues in the news, we estimate a multiplicative model to see whether female senators are less effective at garnering coverage for their preferred issue agendas. In particular, in the last two columns of table 7.2, we include an interaction term, multiplying the gender of the senator with the issue message on the senator's campaign webpage. The results of the multiplicative analysis (i.e., the negative and significant interaction coefficient) indicate that female senators are significantly *less* effective at generating coverage for their preferred messages.

Relying on the logit estimates in table 7.2 to estimate probabilities (King 1989), we find that when male senators emphasize competitive issues like the economy or foreign policy on the front page of their campaign website, male senators have a .19 probability of receiving coverage of these issues in the news. In comparison, when these same senators refrain from highlighting these issues on their webpages, the probability that these issues will be mentioned for male senators drops to a .07 probability. Male senators, by focusing on competitive issues on their webpages, can more than double the probability that the news media will mention these issues in coverage of the senator's campaign.

For female senators, coverage of issues is less responsive to their campaign emphasis. When female senators discuss competitive issues on their campaign websites, the probability that women will receive coverage of

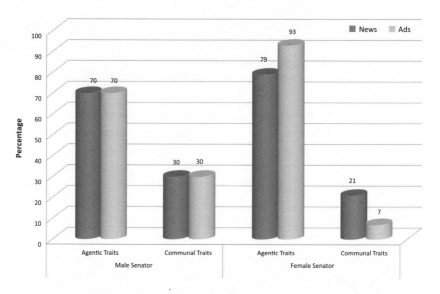

Fig. 7.4. Comparison of Trait Content Senators' Advertisements versus Coverage in the News. (*Note: Agentic Traits* include experience, strong leader, competent, accomplished, hardworking, aggressive, independent, consistent, and ambitious. *Communal Traits* include caring, advocate, moral, compassionate, and honest.)

these issues is .21. However, when female senators do not discuss competitive issues on their campaign websites, the probability of news coverage drops only slightly to a probability of .16.[21] Overall, the multiplicative models in table 7.2 illustrates that female senators are significantly less successful than male senators at attracting news coverage for their preferred issue agendas.

Turning to the campaign coverage of personal traits, we know that both male and female incumbents prefer to focus on "agentic" traits when running for reelection. However, female senators highlight traits like competence and leadership more so than their male counterparts in their political communications. Does campaign coverage mirror these differences? In figure 7.4, we compare the incumbents' preferred messages about traits, as represented in their political advertisements, to campaign coverage of the senators' personal traits.[22] The results reveal that the news media, once again, represent the trait emphasis of male incumbents while misrepresenting the preferred messages of female incumbents. Although female senators talk almost exclusively about agentic traits in their commercials, the campaign coverage does not reflect this preference.[23] For example, the proportion of attention to communal traits is three times larger in the news than in the female senators' own campaign messages (i.e., 21% in the newspapers versus 7% in their own advertisements). For male senators, the news coverage of agentic and communal traits *perfectly* represents the senators' own preferences.[24]

Overall, we find that patterns of coverage frequently lead to inequities for women running for reelection. The coverage for female senators seeking reelection is less likely to represent their preferred messages, compared to the press attention given to male senators running for reelection.

CITIZENS' VIEWS OF INCUMBENT SENATORS
DURING REELECTION CAMPAIGNS

Senators and the press disseminate messages in an attempt to influence constituents' impressions of their representatives. Senators hope their controlled communications will cultivate positive views among citizens leading voters to reelect them. The press has a different objective, though—reporters and editors want to produce interesting stories citizens will read. Sometimes these two different motivations converge to produce similar messages, but often the messages of candidates and the press conflict. While both sets of communications are available to constituents, consistent messages across divergent mediums will be more influential than messages that are splintered in terms of topic and focus.

During all elections, potential voters, distracted by the details of daily life, are bombarded with hundreds of campaign messages. Senate campaigns are no different. Citizens need to rely on cognitive shortcuts to help digest the abundance of campaign information; people often turn to stereotypes to organize and simplify their political environment (e.g., Bodenhausen and Macrae 1998; Fiske and Neuberg 1990). People use all types of stereotypes, including party stereotypes, stereotypes about incumbents, and gender stereotypes (Kahn 1993; Rahn 1993).

Gender stereotypes, like other types of stereotypes, influence how information is processed and retained. In particular, when people have little time and little motivation to interpret political information, they are more likely to remember stereotypically consistent information (e.g., Macrae, Hewstone, and Griffiths 1993). However, when people are exposed to incongruent information, they need to spend time reconciling the incongruent information with their existing stereotypes. For example, the typical stereotype is that women are weak leaders; yet, potential voters are receiving information where female senators are acting as strong leaders. Since it is necessary for people to expend more cognitive energy processing inconsistent information, memory is enhanced (Scrull and Wyer 1989). But interpreting inconsistent information is a difficult task and occurs when people have sufficient time, energy, and resources (Bodenhausen and Wyer 1985).

In general, then, people may rely on gender stereotypes when interpreting and assimilating political messages about senators. The reliance on gender stereotypes will produce enhanced memory for stereotypically consistent information when people have limited resources, while these same stereotypes will produce better recall of stereotypically inconsistent information when people have sufficient time and energy. Information that is unrelated to the gender stereotype (e.g., issues that are not linked to the competitive-communal dimension or traits that are orthogonal to the agentic-communal dimension) will be less likely to be remembered by potential voters.

We turn to an examination of how citizens evaluate U.S. senators as they run for reelection. In our analysis, we look at how the messages presented by the senators and the news media, as well as common gender stereotypes, influence people's views of their senators.

We begin by assessing how citizens evaluate their senators' abilities to deal with health care and the economy.[25] Given common gender stereotypes, we expect that people will view female senators as more competent at dealing with health-care issues, while male senators will be seen as better able to deal with economic issues (e.g., Huddy and Capelos 2002; Kahn 1996; Sapiro 1981/1982). Furthermore, messages presented by senators in their representational and campaign communications reinforce these stereotypes. In particular, we have shown that female senators are more likely to emphasize "communal" issues, like health care, while male senators focus more heavily on competitive issues, like the economy.

While we expect the gender of the senator will influence people's views of the senator's ability to deal with health care and the economy, additional factors may also be important. We control for three sets of forces that may influence people's perceptions of a senator's ability to deal with specific issues: characteristics of the senators, characteristics of the campaign, and characteristics of the respondents.

Beginning with the senator's characteristics, we assess the senator's seniority, the senator's electoral vulnerability, and the senator's party. Senior senators may be viewed as more competent, generally, because of their wealth of experience. In contrast, senators who are vulnerable, because they are embroiled in a scandal or appointed to office, may be viewed as less competent by citizens.[26] Finally, given research on party ownership, we expect the party of the senator will influence assessments of issue competency, with people viewing Democrats at better able to deal with health issues and Republicans being more adept at dealing with the economy (Petrocik, Benoit, and Hansen 2003/2004).

We also expect the campaign setting will influence people's evaluations of their senators. We expect that senators running in competitive races may be evaluated more critically than senators running in lopsided races. In competitive races, senators are facing a quality challenger who is more adept at critiquing the incumbent. In addition, in these races, the news attention is more abundant and more negative (e.g., Kahn and Kenney 1999). Similarly, campaign spending is likely to influence evaluations of the senator (Westlye 1989; Jacobson 2007; Herrnson 1995). In particular, as the incumbent senator's advantage in campaign spending increases, we expect that impressions of the senator will become more positive.

The messages presented during the campaign may also influence people's views of the senators' competence for handling economic and health issues. We rely on the campaign website data and measure whether the economy or health care is mentioned on the front page of the senator's campaign website. We expect that when senators highlight their commitment to these issues in their campaign materials, voters will view them as better able to deal with these issues.[27] We also look at the number of paragraphs published about economic and health care in the news coverage of the senator during the campaign. If senators receive more press attention for these specific issues, people may view these senators as more competent at dealing with these policy matters.

Finally, we know that people's views about politicians are strongly influenced by their partisan attachments and their ideological views (e.g., Campbell, Converse, Miller, and Stokes 1960; Miller 1991; Wright and Berkman 1986). Therefore, we include measures assessing party proximity and ideological proximity between the senator and the respondent.[28] We expect people to view senators as better able to deal with economic and health issues when they share the same party and ideological positions as their senator.

With these control variables in place, we turn to examining how the gen-

TABLE 7.3. OLS Estimates Predicting Issue Evaluations of Senators Running for Reelection[a]

	Health Care		Economy	
Senator Characteristics				
Female Senator	.24 (.12)**	.08	.13 (.10)	.04
Vulnerable	−.41 (.12)***	−.11	−.48 (.13)***	−.13
Years of Seniority in Senate	.07 (.04)*	.06	.02 (.03)	.01
Democratic Senator	.44 (.12)***	.14	.31(.09)***	.09
Campaign Characteristics				
Competition	−.001 (.005)	−.01	.003 (.004)	.03
Difference in Campaign Spending	.13 (.03)***	.09	.14 (.04)***	.10
News Paragraphs about Specific Issue	−1.71 (1.72)	−.03	−1.1 (2.02)	−.01
Campaign Website on Specific Issue	.32 (.17)*	.08	.06 (.11)	.01
Respondent Characteristics				
Party Proximity	.22 (.02)***	.28	.20 (.03)***	.25
Ideological Proximity	.36 (.03)***	.45	.38 (.03)***	.46
Constant	3.39 (.10)***		3.68 (.11)***	
R^2	.52		.48	
N	896		932	

Note: The dependent variable is respondents' ratings of senator's ability to deal with health care or the economy. See Appendix I for exact question wording. Female Senator is coded 1 for female senators, 0 for male senators. Vulnerable senators are senators who have been appointed senators and senators involved in scandals. Years of Seniority in Senate is coded as years in office. Democratic Senator is coded 1 for Democratic senators and 0 for Republican senators. Competition is measured by subtracting incumbent support from challenger support based on preelection polling data published in the 2006 *New York Times Election Guide*. Difference in Campaign Spending is the difference in spending between the senator and the challenger (campaign spending is divided by vote age population for each state to account for states of varying population and then logged to account for diminishing returns). Campaign spending data comes from the 2006 *New York Times Election Guide*. News Paragraphs about Specific Issue is the proportion of paragraphs about health (or the economy) divided by the total number of paragraphs about the senator in the state's largest circulating newspaper. Campaign Website on Issues is whether health care (or the economy) is mentioned on the front page of the senator's campaign website. Party Proximity is the distance between the respondent's placement on the seven-point party identification measure and the party affiliation of the senator. Ideological Proximity is measured by comparing the respondent's self-placement on the ideology scale with the respondent's placement of the incumbent on the same ideological scale. See the text for more details about measurement.

[a]Standard errors are in parentheses, followed by levels of significance and standardized coefficients.

***$p < .01$; **$p < .05$; *$p < .10$

der of the senator influences people's issue assessments during reelection campaigns. The findings in table 7.3 indicate that female senators are given significantly higher ratings on their ability to deal with health care compared to male senators. Even controlling for a host of rival factors, we find the gender of the senator influences people's assessment of the senator's ability to deal with this crucial "communal" issue. In contrast, male senators are not significantly advantaged on the issue of the economy. People do not differ in their views of male and female senators' competence for dealing with economic issues, controlling for potentially confounding factors.

Turning to the remaining variables in the models, we find that the senator's party and the senator's vulnerability powerfully predict people's evaluations of the senator's competence to deal with economic and health care issues. More vulnerable senators are viewed more negatively in both equations. Similarly, Democratic senators are viewed more positively; people view Democratic senators as significantly better equipped to deal with economic and health-care issues. The party effect is especially pronounced for health care, an issue traditionally linked to the Democratic Party. The unstandardized coefficient for party in the health-care model indicates that Democratic senators receive, on average, almost a half point gain on the six-point competence scale compared to Republican senators, holding all other variables constant.

Campaign messages about issues appear to be less consequential, with one exception. Measures assessing the amount of news coverage devoted to health care and economic issues in the local press do not influence people's views of the senator's ability to deal with these issues.[29] The senators' own emphasis on issues is somewhat important for health care but not for the economy. When senators focus on health care, as illustrated by placing health care on the front page of their campaign website, people are somewhat more likely to view the senators' competence on health care more favorably. We also find differences in campaign spending powerfully influence evaluations of senators' abilities to deal with health care and the economy. As senators increase their advantage in campaign spending, senators receive significantly more favorable views of their ability to deal with issues.

Finally, the respondents' own political predispositions are important predictors of their issue assessments. In particular, when respondents and senators share the same party attachment and the same ideological positions, the respondents are significantly more likely to give senators more positive ratings on their ability to deal with health care and economic issues.

According to the standardized coefficients, party and ideological proximity are by far the most powerful factors in the two models.

We turn next to determine whether gender stereotypes influence people's views of the senators' personality characteristics. With issues, senators' emphasize their stereotypical strengths on policy matters. However, regarding to personal traits, senators try to revise views about their stereotypical weaknesses. Therefore, the senators' own messages clash with common gender stereotypes. Furthermore, the news media do not always represent the senators' preferred trait messages. Given the inconsistency of trait information in the campaign environment, we expect gender stereotyping to be less pronounced for traits than issues.

We examine citizens' assessments along four trait measures: leadership, honesty, caring, and experience. As we did with issues, we develop a model including characteristics of the senator (e.g., party, seniority), characteristics of the citizens (i.e., ideological and party proximity), and characteristics of the campaign (e.g., competition). We also develop a measure to assess the content of trait discussion during the campaign. In particular, we operationalize the tone of trait coverage in the press for each of the four trait dimensions. For example, we calculate the tone of news coverage concerning the senator's honesty by subtracting the number of negative press mentions about the senator's honesty from the number of positive press mentions about the incumbent's honesty and then dividing the sum by the total number of paragraphs published about the senator. The product indicates the proportion of positive (relative to negative) coverage published about the senator's honesty. We calculate similar measures for the tone of trait coverage about the senator's leadership, empathy, and experience.[30]

We predict people's assessments of the senator's personality on the four trait dimensions in table 7.4. The results indicate the gender of the senator is not a powerful predictor of citizens' assessments of the senators' personality. Across the four models, the gender of the senator never reaches statistical significance. People do not develop distinct views of the personality of male and female senators once we control for rival factors.

While the gender of the senator does not consistently or powerfully influence citizens' views of their senators' personality, we find the vulnerability and party of the senator are more consequential. Vulnerable senators, who may have been involved in scandals or who have been appointed to office, are viewed as weaker leaders, less honest, less caring, and less experienced than other senators.

TABLE 7.4. OLS Estimates Predicting Trait Evaluations of Senators Running for Reelection[a]

	Leadership		Honesty		Caring		Experience	
Candidate Characteristics								
Female Senator	.11 (.07)	.05	.07 (.09)	.03	.08 (.08)	.03	-.01 (.07)	-.01
Vulnerable	-.30 (.09)***	-.12	-.40 (.15)**	-.16	-.31 (.10)***	-.12	-.16 (.09)*	-.08
Years of Seniority in Senate	.04 (.02)**	.05	.03 (.03)	.04	.01 (.02)	.02	-.004 (.02)	-.01
Democratic Senator	.09 (.06)	.04	.23 (.09)***	.10	.26 (.07)***	.12	.10 (.07)	.06
Campaign Characteristics								
Competition	.009 (.003)***	.13	.003 (.004)	.04	.001 (.003)	.01	.005 (.003)*	.09
Difference in Campaign Spending	.06 (.02)**	.06	-.031 (.03)	-.03	.04 (.03)	.04	.05 (.02)*	.06
Tone of Trait Coverage in News	.06 (.06)	.03	.07 (.12)	.03	.01 (.06)	.01	.05 (.10)	.02
Respondent Characteristics								
Party Proximity	.14 (.02)***	.25	.11 (.02)***	.19	.11 (.02)***	.21	.02 (.02)	.05
Ideological Proximity	.25 (.02)***	.44	.22 (.02)***	.39	.23 (.02)***	.41	.13 (.02)***	.30
Constant	2.22 (.06)***		2.89 (.11)***		2.19 (.07)***		3.31 (.08)***	
R^2	.48		.33		.36		.14	
N	927		834		924		901	

Note: The dependent variable is respondents' assessments of the senator's leadership, honesty, caring, and experience. See Appendix 1 for exact question wording. Female Senator is coded 1 for female senators, 0 for male senators. Vulnerable senators are senators who have been appointed senators and senators involved in scandals. Years of Seniority in Senate is coded as years in office. Democratic Senator is coded 1 for Democratic senators and 0 for Republican senators. Competition is measured by subtracting incumbent support from challenger support based on preelection polling data published in the 2006 *New York Times Election Guide.* Difference in Campaign Spending is the difference in spending between the senator and the challenger (campaign spending is divided by vote age population for each state to account for states of varying population and then logged to account for diminishing returns). Campaign spending data comes from the 2006 *New York Times Election Guide.* Tone of Trait Coverage is the number of positive trait mentions published about the senator minus the number of negative trait mentions published about the senator in the state's largest circulating newspaper divided by the total number of paragraphs published about the senator. Party Proximity is the distance between the respondent's placement on the seven-point party identification measure and the party affiliation of the senator. Ideological Proximity is measured by comparing the respondent's self-placement on the ideology scale with the respondent's placement of the incumbent on the same ideological scale. See the text for more details about measurement.

[a]Standard errors are in parentheses, followed by levels of significance and standardized coefficients.

***$p < .01$; **$p < .05$; *$p < .10$

The party of the senator is also important, leading people to view Democrats as more honest and more caring than Republicans. The advantage for Democratic senators on the dimension of caring is predicted by Hayes's (2005) theory of trait ownership. Hayes argues that because Democrats are seen as owning social-welfare issues, people view Democratic politicians as more compassionate than their Republican colleagues. However, the Democratic advantage on honesty may also be driven by the political climate. In 2006, the Republican Party was struggling because of the unpopularity of President George W. Bush, as well as scandals involving Republicans, such as the Jack Abramoff lobbying scandal, the campaign-finance investigation of Republican Tom Delay, and the congressional page scandal involving Republican Mark Foley. The Republican Party's involvement in a range of scandals may have produced the higher ratings of honesty for Democratic senators.

The context of the campaign plays a less influential role. We find that senators cruising to victory in lopsided races (i.e., ahead in the polls, outspending their rivals) are viewed as stronger leaders and more experienced than senators involved in closer reelection bids. However, the tone of trait coverage in the news does not influence people's evaluations of the senators' personality.

Finally, as with health care and the economy, the citizens' political proclivities strongly influence their views of the senators' personality. When people share their senator's party or when people are closer ideologically to their senator, they view their senator as a stronger leader, more honest, more caring, and more experienced. Political proximity powerfully predicts how people will feel about their senator's possession of personal traits.

Overall, citizens do not rely heavily on gender stereotypes when forming impressions of their senators' personality or issue abilities. Across the six models examined, gender influences evaluations in only one of the six models. People view women as better able to deal with health issues, a view consistent with both gender stereotypes and the female senators' own messages.

Ultimately, it is important to examine whether citizens rely on gender as a cue when voting in senate elections. We develop a model predicting whether respondents indicate voting for their incumbent senator or the challenger.[31] In the model, we include the gender of the senator. We also continue to include additional characteristics of the senator, such as the seniority of the senator, the party of the senator, and the vulnerability of the senator.

We also include measures assessing the context of the campaign, including the competitiveness of the race and the differences in campaign spending. As the incumbents' advantage in the polls and in campaign spending increases, we expect that people will be more likely to vote for the senator. In addition, we include two indicators of the negativity of the campaign. First, we include a measure assessing whether the challenger criticized the incumbent on the front page of the challenger's campaign website. Second, we measure the number of critical paragraphs published about the incumbent in the major newspaper in the state. As negative information increases, we expect the incumbent's share of the vote will decline.

Based on decades of research on senate elections (e.g., Abramowitz 1988; Kahn and Kenney 1999; Westlye 1991; Wright and Berkman 1986), we include attitudinal factors known to influence voting decisions in Senate elections. We measure trait assessments of the Senate incumbent since political psychologists and political scientists have demonstrated that citizens use trait information to develop impressions of candidates during campaigns (e.g., Bartels 2002; Fridkin and Kenney 2009; Funk 1996; Lodge, McGraw, and Stroh 1989; Lodge, Steenbergen, and Brau 1995; Markus 1982). We also look at citizens' views regarding the senator's ability to deal with economic and health-care issues since such assessments may influence decisions to support the incumbent senator (e.g., Abbe, Goodiffe, Herrnson, and Patterson 2003; Druckman 2004).[32]

In addition, it is important to examine the impact of national conditions on voting decisions in Senate elections (e.g., Abramowitz 2006; Jacobson and Kernell 1983; Westlye 1991). First, given the salience of the Iraq War during the 2006 campaign, we include a measure assessing whether the respondent and the senator share the same view regarding the Iraq War.[33] Second, we consider whether respondents' views of the national economy affect their impressions of their incumbent senator.[34] Third, given the unpopularity of President George Bush, we measure presidential approval, linking respondents' approval ratings with the party of their senator running for reelection.[35] Finally, the respondents' own political profile is likely to influence their likelihood of voting for the incumbent senator (Abramowitz and Segal 1992; Kahn and Kenney 1999; Wright and Berkman 1986). Therefore, we include the measures of party and ideological proximity introduced earlier.

The results of our analysis, presented in table 7.5, indicate that the gender of the senator does not have an independent influence on people's likelihood of voting for the sitting senator.[36] The coefficient for gender is far from statistically significance. In fact, none of the measures tapping characteristics of the senator achieve statistical significance. The party of the senator, the seniority of the senator, and the vulnerability of the senator fail to significantly influence vote choice, once we control for attitudinal assessments.

Similarly, the context of the campaign fails to influence voting decisions in Senate elections. The closeness of the campaign and differences in campaign spending do not affect people's likelihood of voting for the senator versus the challenger. And, the negativity of the campaign, whether mea-

TABLE 7.5. Logistic Regression Predicting
Likelihood of Voting for Incumbent Senator[a]

Candidate Characteristics

Gender of Senator	−.17 (.91)
Vulnerable	.31 (1.28)
Democratic Senator	.57 (1.04)
Years of Seniority in Senate	.04 (.23)

Campaign Characteristics

Competition	−.03 (.05)
Difference in Campaign Spending	−.23 (.32)
Negativity of Opponent's Campaign	1.19 (1.17)
Criticisms in the News	−.01 (.02)

Citizens' Attitudes about Senator

Leadership	.39 (.48)
Honesty	1.52 (.53)***
Empathy	.07 (.50)
Experience	.81 (.49)*
Competence on Economy	1.02 (.56)*
Competence on Health Care	.72 (.55)
Iraq War Proximity	.42 (.40)
Sociotropic Economic Evaluation	−.11 (.32)
Presidential Approval	1.30 (.38)***
Party Proximity	1.34 (.34)***
Ideology Proximity	1.00 (.32)***
Constant	−17.17 (4.0)***
Number of Observations	593
Correctly Predicted	97%

Note: The dependent variable is a postelection measure of vote choice (1 = incumbent, 0 = other). See Appendix E for exact question wording and see text and previous tables for details about measurement of the independent variables.

[a]Logistic coefficients are followed by standard errors in parentheses.

***$p < .01$; **$p < .05$; *$p < .10$

sured by challenger's decision to "go negative," or the amount of critical press attention given to incumbent, is inconsequential.

Turning to the attitudinal measures, we see people's evaluations of the senator's personality shape citizens' voting decisions. For example, as ratings of an incumbent's honesty and experience increase, people are significantly more likely to vote for the sitting senator. People's views of their senator's ability to deal with economic issues are also consequential. However, general views of the economy are less important. People's assessments of the state of the economy do not affect their senatorial vote decision.

We find that people's views on the Iraq War are unrelated to their vote decision. Citizens who share their senator's position on the Iraq War are no more likely to vote for the senator, compared to citizens who disagree with their senator's position. However, more general views about President Bush's performance as president powerfully affect vote choice. For example, people who approve of President Bush's performance as president are significantly more likely to vote for Republican incumbents than people who disapprove of President Bush's performance. Turning to partisanship and ideology, we find that citizens' own political predispositions influence their probability of voting for their senator. In particular, people are more likely to vote for their senator when they share their senator's party affiliation and their senator's ideological views.[37]

CONCLUSION

We began this chapter by comparing the senators' representational messages with the messages that senators disseminate when they are campaigning for reelection. We found that senators are remarkably consistent over time regarding the topics they choose to emphasize. Looking across diverse data sets, including campaign and official websites, political advertisements, and press releases, we found that female incumbents prefer to talk about communal issues, while men are more likely to focus on competitive issues. We also find that men and women prefer to highlight their agentic traits in their campaign and governing messages. Also, women emphasize these traits more frequently than male senators in both settings.

We turned next to examining how the press covers male and female senators as they run for reelection. We found the gender differences in press treatment uncovered during the governing period persist when senators campaign for reelection. In particular, the news media often distorts the messages of female senators. During campaigns, the news media do a particularly poor job of accurately representing the preferred trait and issue messages of female senators.

While the gender of the senator significantly and consistently influences the content of campaign messages as well as shaping the news media's coverage of male and female candidates, we found that citizens are less likely to use gender as a cue when evaluating senators running for reelection. Specifically, an examination of four trait characteristics and two issue dimensions demonstrated the gender of the senator influenced citizens' evaluations for only one of these six concepts (i.e., health care). And when we examine people's likelihood of voting for their U.S. senator, the senator's gender fails to independently influence people's vote choice. In the end, then, the predictions of the strategic stereotype theory significantly and substantively shape the actions and attitudes of political elites (e.g., senators, candidates, reporters, editors), but gender stereotypes only minimally affect the attitudes of American citizens as they weigh decisions regarding the reelection of U.S. senators.

CHAPTER 8

The Changing Face of the U.S. Senate and Representational Messages

IN THIS FINAL CHAPTER, we review our findings on the relationship between gender and representational messages and place them in a broader context. We believe that our findings allow us to contribute to several concepts and debates in American politics, including how stereotypes held by citizens shape legislator's representational communications, how the media perpetuates stereotypes about women, and insights regarding the importance of descriptive representation.

ELITE COMMUNICATIONS AND REPRESENTATIVE DEMOCRACY

Communications flowing from legislators to citizens are dramatically understudied in the United States. Yet these messages play a fundamental role in shaping what citizens know about the backgrounds, personalities, and policy beliefs of their representatives. Buried in these messages are legislators' "description" and "interpretation" of their worldview and "justification(s)" for their behaviors (Fenno 1978, 136). One of the goals of this book is to prompt scholars, pundits, citizens, and journalists to systematically pay attention to messages emanating from members of the House and Senate. Today, it is infinitely easier for representatives to send messages to constituents and for researchers to analyze these messages. Thus, the messages provide a treasure trove of information regarding the quality of communications disseminated from Capitol Hill and aimed at citizens in districts and states.

We examined these communications using the U.S. senator's gender as a lens. We began by asking whether the gender of the senator influences the content and frequency of representational messages. The answer is an emphatic yes. The gender of the senator permeates all aspects of communications. Female senators are more likely than their male colleagues to highlight their political experience, discuss their committee work, and describe their leadership activities in the chamber. Furthermore, female senators are more likely than their male colleagues to talk about issues such as health care and education on their campaign websites, on their official websites, and in their press releases. And when talking about issues, female senators are more likely to take clear positions on issues. Finally, female senators, compared to their male colleagues, focus explicitly on traits like competence and leadership when discussing their personal attributes on their official and campaign websites and in their political advertisements.

Male senators, in contrast, are more likely than female senators to discuss their work on projects benefitting their states. Male senators also have a higher probability of highlighting family and state connections, as well as illustrating their care for their constituents. These messages are designed to enhance views of male senators as compassionate, empathetic, and connected to others. When men do focus on public policies, they are more likely than women to discuss foreign policy, the economy, and defense.

We develop a theory that marries two long-standing and classic theories of human behavior. First, the theory of rationality (e.g., Downs 1957), adopted by scholars interested in the actions of political elites, predicts that legislators will develop messages aimed at creating positive feelings among constituents in the hopes of securing reelection (e.g., Fenno 1978; Mayhew 1974; Jacobson and Kernell 1983). Second, gender-role theory explains that people have "shared expectations about appropriate qualities or behaviors" of men and women in society (Eagly 1987, 13) and these shared expectations will produce stereotypical views about male and female politicians. By merging these two theoretical strains, we develop a hybrid theory called the strategic stereotype theory. Our theory predicts that senators will attempt to maximize their chances of reelection by developing messages resonating with positive gender stereotypes while simultaneously revising negative gender stereotypes.

We think the strategic stereotype theory has reach and durability. Legislators develop representational messages by taking into account established and deep-rooted stereotypes held by citizens. Our theory, therefore, can be applied to a range of different actors and situations. We know, for example, that the American electorate collectively holds long-standing views, frequently guided and informed by existing stereotypes, based on race, ethnicity, political partisanship, age, social class, sexual preference, and religion, to name a few. And these stereotypes are intertwined with a range of public policies, such as affirmative action, social welfare, immigration, health care, civil liberties, among others. These programs cut across federal, state, and local governments, as well as over time. The strategic stereotype theory, then, can shed light on how different types of stereotypes shape representational communications about public policies at different levels of government.

The strategic stereotype theory can also be applied to new types of communications, such as Twitter and Facebook. Seventy-eight percent of all U.S. senators holding office in 2012 had a Facebook link on their official website, while 87% of all senators had a Twitter link on the main page of their official website. We expect the themes articulated on social-networking sites will mirror the themes senators emphasize in their press releases and on their official web pages. However, we encourage scholars to document the generalizability of our theory by looking at whether male and female senators highlight their stereotypical strengths on policy matters, while trying to revise stereotypical weaknesses regarding personal traits when communicating with constituents via social media.

The applicability of the theory has additional import because we find evidence that the variance in communications alters what people know about senators. Indeed, citizens are much more informed about female senators than their male colleagues. Furthermore, the importance of the gender of the senator in predicting levels of information remains influential in spite of stiff controls for respondents' party attachment, interest in politics, consumption of news, and sophistication about politics. This is especially true for female constituents. This finding resonates with recent research suggesting that women's interest in politics is piqued by the presence of female leaders. Women's involvement in the political system appears to be enhanced not only by the mere existence of female political leaders, but by the messages women deliver. Thus, remarkably, we are able to draw a straight line connecting communications sent by female senators to the attitudes and behaviors of female citizens. This finding speaks to the concerns of political philosophers and democratic practitioners who worry representational messages fall on deaf ears for the vast majority of citizens and will only be received by organized, experienced, and powerful interest and advocacy groups.

To be sure, citizens' information levels about legislators and their policies form the backbone of representative government. The variance in people's levels of knowledge, sophistication, and information is highly related to participation in democratic institutions. We contend that the link between representational communications, informed and shaped by the interaction of existing stereotypes with politicians' strategic behavior, provides a new avenue for coming to grips with the nature of our representative democracy.

INEQUITIES IN MEDIA TREATMENT OF FEMALE SENATORS

The power of the news media to capture and focus people's attention and to shape their thinking about issues, politicians, and events is well documented and has been growing rather than decreasing across the last half century (e.g., Kinder 2003). The role of the local media is particularly critical because it is one of only a few sources of political information regarding local politicians, local candidates, and local issues (Kahn and Kenney 1999). The singular influence of the news media in shaping citizens' beliefs and behaviors (Bartels 1993) makes the findings in this book particularly relevant and important. The upshot of our findings is the news media may act as an obstacle for women in elective office. We have shown that the news media do a better job covering male senators compared to their female counterparts. Male senators receive more coverage, are more likely to be quoted, and are more likely to be mentioned in headlines compared to female senators. Also, these patterns continue during campaigns for reelection where male senators continue to receive more coverage.

Perhaps even more problematic for female politicians, the news media is less likely to represent female senators' preferred messages in their coverage. For example, female senators are significantly more likely than male senators to focus on their experience and leadership credentials, but the news media cover these topics significantly less often for female senators. When senators are running for reelection, we find that reporters and editors continue to systematically misrepresent the messages of female senators.

These gender differences in news treatment are not new, of course. Scholars looking at presidential and statewide candidates have found that the news media more faithfully represent the messages of male candidates, compared to their female counterparts (e.g., Aday and Devitt 2001; Heldman, Carroll, and Olson 2005; Kahn 1996). However, some recent studies have suggested that some inequities in press treatment have diminished in recent years (e.g., Bystrom, Banwart, Kaid, and Robertson 2004; Smith 1997). Indeed, it is reasonable to expect that reporters and editors have begun to alter their coverage as more and more women run for highest levels of political office. Yet, the evidence presented in this book suggests that such sanguine conclusions are premature.

Furthermore, scholars who have begun to examine new media, including blogs and Internet news sites, suggest that gender inequities in coverage may be greater for Internet news, compared to traditional media (e.g., Lawrence and Rose 2010; Anderson 2011). Lawrence and Rose explained that Hillary Clinton, in her 2008 campaign for president, faced extensive and even offensive sexist rhetoric on the Internet. In particular, bloggers, online videos, and online commentary often made explicit sexual references to Hillary Clinton. Anderson also documents sexist coverage for Sarah Palin and Hillary Clinton during the 2008 campaign. For example, she cites an article on Salon.com that introduced a new political action committee called "Citizens United Not Timid," a registered 527 organization that was established to educate the public about "what Hillary Clinton really is" (Anderson 2011, 341).

To be sure, gender differences in media treatment are not restricted to the news; it is not a phenomenon reserved for political reporting. There appears to be a gender bias across the media industry. In television, for example, women continue to be underrepresented in primetime programming (e.g., Glascock 2001; Signorielli and Bacue 1999). Glascock (2001), in a study of almost 100 primetime fictional series on major network and cable stations in the late 1990s, finds that women are less likely to be major characters compared to men. In addition, female characters are more likely to be portrayed as mothers and wives and male characters are twice as likely to be bosses compared to female characters. Furthermore, Glascock reports a positive and significant correlation with the number of female executive producers and the prominence of female characters, suggesting that increasing the number of women behind the camera would improve women's representation in front of the camera.

Researchers have also documented the stereotypical treatment of women in product advertising. For example, in a recent study, Paek, Nelson, and Vilela (2011) find that women play a less prominent role in televised product commercials than men and they are much more likely to be presented as a "homemaker" or "housekeeper" (i.e., 32% for women vs. 1% for men). Mager and Helgeson (2011), looking at changes in magazine advertisements over the last 50 years, show that women continue to be portrayed as dependent and in need of men's protection in product advertisements in magazines. Furthermore, the authors show that the presentation of women as sex objects has actually increased in product commercials over the same 50-year period.

Women's stereotypical treatment has also been documented in major films, including action movies and G-rated movies aimed at children, where women are often displayed in traditional or subordinate roles (e.g., Gilpatric 2010; Smith, Pieper, Granados, and Choueiti 2010). Similarly, men outnumber women in music videos, with women more likely to be portrayed as sexual objects or as subordinate to men, while men are more likely to be portrayed as the aggressor (e.g., Turner 2011; Wallis 2011). In addition, video games underrepresent women by a ratio of seven to one, with women often being shown as sexual objects, and with 41% of the women characters being displayed in revealing clothing (Downs and Smith 2010).

In the end, the underrepresentation of women, as well as the stereotypical depiction of women, permeates all aspects of the media industry. Such widespread (mis)treatment of women may act as powerful socialization mechanism, perpetuating gender-role expectations in political and nonpolitical settings. The pervasiveness of stereotypical treatment of women in the media is an obstacle for women in public office and women striving for public office. While it is relatively straight forward to examine gender differences in press treatment, it is more difficult to propose effective remedies for change.

A simple step would be to increase the number of female sources in news stories. As we discussed earlier, women are less likely than men to be used as expert sources in the news (e.g., Liebler and Smith 1997), with women being used as sources less than 20% of the time in news stories (Media Report to Women 2010). More substantial changes require reprioritizing resources and personnel. For example, it may help to increase the number of female reporters covering female politicians in the local press. In our study, male reporters authored more than 60% of all the stories examined. And male reporters were just as likely to cover female senators as male senators (i.e., 61% for male senators and 63% for female senators). Female reporters may cover politics differently than their male colleagues. For instance, Sutcliffe, Lee, and Soderlund (2005) find that female reporters are more likely than male reporters to utilize female sources. In addition, female reporters may be responsive to the alternative agendas articulated by female senators. In Kahn's (1996) study of male and female candidates for statewide office in the 1980s and 1990s, she found that female reporters were more likely to focus on communal issues for female candidates for governor and senator, compared to male reporters. Female reporters, who share some of the same socialization experiences as female politicians, may cover female politicians differently than their male colleagues.

Perhaps even more importantly, increasing the number of women in leadership positions in news organizations may promote more equitable treatment of female politicians. Currently, female reporters are less frequently assigned to the political beats and more frequently report on "softer" news stories, such as health and human-interest stories (Desmond and Danilewicz 2010). In addition, women are less likely than men to hold management positions in news organizations, with women currently occupying about 20% of news director positions (Desmond and Danilewicz 2010). The lack of women in the upper echelon of news organizations may influence how female politicians are covered by these news organizations.

DESCRIPTIVE REPRESENTATION

As America's representative democracy evolved across the arc of U.S. history (e.g., expansion of the franchise, direct elections of U.S. senators, establishment of direct primaries, secret ballots), nagging questions persist regarding the inclusion of historically disadvantaged groups in legislative institutions (e.g., Guinier 1994). Universally disadvantaged by single-member, winner-take-all, plurality voting schemes, minority groups have had a very low probability of capturing legislative seats in contested elections. Recognizing this nearly ironclad "law" of representative democracies, many nations of the world have altered voting schemes to ensure or to increase the probability of minority group inclusion in legislative institutions (e.g., Kittilson 2008). The changing electoral laws have been aimed at improving legislative representation among racial and ethnic minority groups, women, and political parties (Jones 1998; Norris 1997; Rule 1994). The United States has not followed suit and the likelihood of altering voting practices by constitutional amendment is remote, especially in the near future.[1]

While women have been historically disadvantaged in Congress, women now constitute over 50% of the voting population (Abramson, Aldrich, and

Rhode 2012). Thus, improving women's representation in Congress can be accomplished without altering voting mechanisms anchored in the U.S. Constitution since 1789. And the number of women in Congress has been increasing in the last 30 years. As discussed in chapter 1, well over 100 million U.S. citizens are currently represented by women in the U.S. Senate. Today, women make up 20% of the senators in the U.S. Senate, a historic high.

FEMALE SENATORS PROMOTING POLICY MESSAGES

As more and more women begin to capture and hold seats in powerful legislative institutions like the U.S. Senate, opportunities emerge to explore some of the underlying assumptions for enhanced descriptive representation in Congress. At its core, descriptive representation assumes that citizens prefer to be represented by "individuals who in their own backgrounds mirror some of the more frequent experiences and outward manifestations of belonging to the group" (Mansbridge 1999, 628). In theory, then, female senators who "mirror" female constituents are much more likely to have lived similar lives, experienced similar triumphs and hardships, and developed similar attitudes about politics and public policy. Scholars for some time now have been compiling evidence, principally by examining roll-call votes in local, state, and national legislatures, demonstrating that female legislators are more likely than male legislators to vote for policies that have direct or indirect benefits for female citizens (e.g., Burrell 1994; Reingold 2008; Swers 1998). In addition, similar patterns hold for other aspects of the legislative process. For example, compared to male legislators, women are far more likely to focus on legislation aimed at women's interests when introducing bills (Swers 2002), during committee hearings (Arnold and King 2002), and in speeches on the floor of the U.S. House (Walsh 2002).

During the legislative process, then, female legislators pursue a distinct policy agenda. However, legislation begins with ideas and discussions about preferred public policies well before the actual introduction of a bill. The footprints of these discussions are often located in representational messages disseminated by senators to their constituents. Female senators articulate policy preferences that resonate with women by emphasizing two types of issues (1) established issues, like health care and education, that are preferred by women but do not routinely top the national agenda; and (2) emerging issues that are "not fully articulated" (Mansbridge 1999, 628) and "would be otherwise discounted" (Phillips 1995, 233) if women were not playing key roles in the legislative process. We found evidence that female senators emphasize both types of messages.

Regarding established issues, we document that men and women have distinct policy priorities. Resonating with their stereotypical strengths of compassion, empathy, and nurturance, female senators focus on issues in their press releases and websites where the overall goal is to assist and aid people. Male senators, on the other hand, focus on issues related to their stereotypical strength of competitiveness. Beyond promoting issues on the public agenda, we also find evidence that female senators provide leadership and "innovative thinking in context of uncrystallized" issues, trying to raise the public salience for new issues (Mansbridge 1999, 628). These are issues where the political parties and established politicians have failed to articulate a clear direction for public policy. A new issue uniquely relevant to female constituents where female senators took a leadership role is the issue of women's health. For example, female senators were active in discussing the need for (1) national standards for mammography clinics and equipment; (2) providing low-income women with breast- and cervical-cancer exams aimed at early detection; (3) providing Medicare coverage for bone-mass measurements, pap smears, and pelvic exams; (4) expanding insurance coverage so that new mothers can remain in the hospital 48 hours after childbirth; (5) increasing research for uterine fibroid research.

Female senators used their websites and press releases to open discussion and raise levels of awareness among politicians, journalists, and citizens about women's health as an important issue. As an illustration, here is a joint press release from 2006, cutting across partisan lines from Democratic Senator Debbie Stabenow from Michigan and Republican Senator Lisa Murkowski from Alaska.

On February 14, 2006, Senator Debbie Stabenow (D-MI) and Senator Lisa Murkowski (R-AK) introduced the Heart Disease Education, Analysis and Research, and Treatment (HEART) for Women Act. This bill would improve the prevention, diagnosis, and treatment of heart disease and stroke among women.

FACT: Heart disease and stroke actually kill more women each year than men.

FACT: Heart disease, stroke, and other cardiovascular diseases are the #1 killer in the United States and in Michigan.

FACT: Heart disease and stroke kill more women each year than the
        next 5 causes of death combined. In fact, cardiovascular disease
        kills nearly 12 times as many women as breast cancer.
FACT: In Michigan, 43% of all deaths in women are due to cardiovas-
        cular diseases.
FACT: 1 in 3 adult women has some form of cardiovascular disease.
FACT: Minority women, particularly African American, Hispanic and
        Native American women are at even greater risk from heart dis-
        ease and stroke.

More recently, in February 2012, a debate erupted surrounding President
Obama's commitment to insure contraceptive access for women as part of
health-care reform. During a U.S. House of Representative committee hear-
ing an all-male panel of House members invited only male witnesses to discuss the issue of birth control. Female Democratic senators blasted the all-
male panel in the press and on the floor of the U.S. Senate. Senator Barbara
Boxer said, "When I looked at this panel, obviously I was stunned. They are
so hostile to women's health that they didn't even think to have a person on
there who is female."[2] Four female senators—Senator Jeanne Shaheen, Senator Patty Murray, Senator Kirsten Gillibrand, and Senator Barbara Boxer, and
one male senator—Senator Chuck Schumer, stood up on the floor of the U.S.
Senate to express their outrage. Senator Shaheen explained in her statement,
"Time and time again, women have been silenced in this discussion, a discussion about our own very personal health care decisions . . . I think it is
critical to understand that the underlying issue here is about affordable access to contraception—something that is basic to women's health."[3]

Senator Murray articulated the special role of women when she said,
"The women of the Senate, the Democratic women, are here to say enough.
We are standing today and every day to fight for women and their right to
make their own basic health care decisions, not their employer, not an ex-
treme part of the Republican Party, not some men on a panel but themselves.
We will continue to do so, and I am proud to stand with the women of the
Senate to do just that." In a similar vein, Senator Gillibrand concluded her
speech on the floor of the U.S. Senate by saying, "we will stand here as often
as is necessary and draw a line in the sand that the women of the Senate will
continue to oppose these attacks on women's rights and women's health
care." At the end of the first decade of the 21st century, when more women
than men cast votes in senatorial elections, female senators are far more

likely than male senators to discuss issues unique to women's health care in their representational messages.

The arduous legislative process begins with back-and-forth discussions between legislators and citizens about the possibility of placing specific issues on the public agenda; something Phillips (1995) calls the "politics of ideas." In representative democracies, the presence of members from historically disadvantaged groups within legislative institutions sharply increases the likelihood that the focus of policy discussion will more broadly cover the range of society's ills (Dovi 2002; Phillips 1995). A legislative institution lacking female representatives "fails to grasp that rightful inclusions require that diversities within society have represented presence, embodied within representatives who bring distinctive perspectives into political institutions" (Urbinati and Warren 2008, 394). As Olympia Snowe pointed out in an interview, "I have always felt the special concern and the unique responsibility to single out those issues that are so important and critical to the future of women . . . It is not that male colleagues don't represent those issues; as a general population they do. But I think that women in Congress, in both the House and the Senate as well, will give special attention to those issues."[4] We provide evidence that "distinctive perspectives" are embedded in political communications flowing from senators to constituents, thus elevating the likelihood that a broader range of public policies will enter the legislative process.

FEMALE SENATORS PROMOTING FEELINGS OF RESPONSIVENESS

Members of historically disadvantaged groups develop feelings of mistrust toward political institutions generally and toward members of legislatures specifically (e.g., Gay 2002; Guinier 1994; Hibbing and Theiss-Morse 1995). Advocates of descriptive representation often argue that these feelings of mistrust can be attenuated by communications between minority legislators and constituents belonging to historically disadvantaged groups; what Mansbridge (1999, 628) refers to as "adequate communication in contexts of mistrust." Proponents of descriptive representation argue "adequate communication" can potentially move beyond promoting feelings of trust and begin to influence citizens' feelings of political responsiveness or "external efficacy" (Abramson, Aldrich, and Rohde 2012). Increasing people's belief that government is listening and responding to their needs and desires is an important characteristic of a healthy representative democracy.

168   THE CHANGING FACE OF REPRESENTATION

Mansbridge (1999, 64) hypothesizes, "Representatives and voters who share some version of a set of common experiences and the outward signs of having lived through those experiences can often read one another's signals relatively easily and engage in relative accurate forms of shorthand communication." We have demonstrated across the many pages of this book that female senators send quite different messages than male senators, communications likely to resonate more strongly with female constituents. Theoretically, then, when female constituents receive these messages from female senators, their feelings of government responsiveness may increase.

We can test this theoretical expectation by looking at whether male and female constituents' feelings of government responsiveness (i.e., external efficacy) vary with the gender of their senator. We have the requisite data in the campaign module ($n = 1,045$) of the Cooperative Congressional Election Study (CCES) to empirically test this question. In particular, we asked respondents a standard question used to tap feelings of external efficacy: "Public officials don't care much what people like me think" (Abramson, Aldrich, and Rhode 2012, 384). People who agree with this statement are considered low in terms of external efficacy, while respondents who disagree with the statement are believed to be higher in feelings of external efficacy.[5]

When we examine respondents' answers to this question, without considering the gender of the senator, we find that male and female respondents demonstrate similar levels of external efficacy.[6] However, when we consider the gender of the senator, our results change markedly. Female respondents living in states where a female senator is running for reelection indicate a significantly higher level of external efficacy than male respondents.[7] In contrast, the presence of a male senator is less consequential. For male and female respondents living in states with a male senator running for reelection, we find no significant gender difference in the respondents' level of external efficacy.[8] These results indicate that a female senator is perceived as uniquely powerful for female citizens, enhancing female citizens' feelings of government responsiveness. This finding resonates with the data presented in chapter 6, where we showed that women's knowledge about their senators increased significantly when they were asked to evaluate a female senator compared to a male senator. These two complementary findings provide strong evidence that women pay more attention to politics and they feel institutions are more responsive when they are represented by female senators.

Debates about the role of descriptive representation for historically disadvantaged groups will continue across the globe well into the 21st century (e.g., Hughes 2011; Urbinati and Warren 2008). However, in order to investigate the consequences of descriptive representation, it is necessary to examine how representatives with distinct backgrounds (i.e., women, minorities) communicate with their constituents. To be sure, we have provided considerable evidence showing that representational messages of female and male senators vary sharply from one another. Our findings indicate that female senators talk about alternative issues on the mainstream agenda, as well as promote new and emerging issues, such as women's health. In addition, our evidence indicates that the behavior of female senators influences how women view their government.

Democratic theorists, then, who argue that descriptive representation will yield a different kind of democracy among elites and citizens, are on solid empirical footing. This perspective is hardly new. John Adams, after crafting significant elements of the Massachusetts state constitution, wrote a pamphlet in the spring of 1776 in response to a number of colonists who were writing or preparing other state constitutions. Weary and cranky of repeating similar themes in various outlets, he wrote several key ideas in the pamphlet: "in constituting this representative assembly . . . it should be in miniature an exact portrait of the people at large. It should think, feel, reason, and act like them . . . It should be an equal representation, or, in other words, equal interests among the people should have equal interests in it." More than two centuries after Adams wrote these words, Mansbridge, too, returns to this time-honored theme: "the shared experience imperfectly captured by descriptive representation facilitates vertical communication between representatives and constituents" (Mansbridge 1999, 641). We demonstrate throughout this book that male and female senators communicate differently with their constituents, offer divergent representational messages, and validate the unique role women play in representational institutions.

APPENDIX A

Sample of Senators

TABLE A.1. Sample of Senators

Name of Senator	Class[a]	First Elected	ADA Score[b]
1. Murkowski, Lisa (R–AK)	III	2002	20
2. Stevens, Ted (R–AK)	II	1966	5
3. Lincoln, Blanche (D–AR)	III	1998	95
4. Pryor, Mark (D–AR)	II	2002	90
5. Boxer, Barbara (D–CA)	III	1992	100
6. Feinstein, Dianne (D–CA)	I	1992	95
7. Allard, Wayne (R–CO)	II	1992	0
8. Salazar, Ken (D–CO)	III	2004	100
9. Martinez, Mel (R–FL)	III	2004	5
10. Nelson, Bill (D–FL)	I	2000	55
11. Durbin, Richard (D–IL)	II	1996	100
12. Obama, Barack (D–IL)	III	2004	100
13. Landrieu, Mary (D–LA)	II	1996	95
14. Vitter, David (R–LA)	III	2004	15
15. Mikulski, Barbara (D–MD)	III	1986	90
16. Sarbanes, Paul (D–MD)	I	1976	100
17. Collins, Susan (R–ME)	II	1996	65
18. Snowe, Olympia (R–ME)	I	1994	65
19. Levin, Carl (D–MI)	II	1976	100
20. Stabenow, Debbie (D–MI)	I	2000	100
21. Burr, Richard (R–NC)	III	2004	5
22. Dole, Elizabeth (R–NC)	II	2002	5
23. Sununu, John (R–NH)	II	2002	10
24. Clinton, Hillary (D–NY)	I	2000	100
25. Schumer, Charles (D–NY)	III	1998	100
26. Smith, Gordon (R–OR)	II	1996	20
27. Wyden, Ron (D–OR)	III	1994	95
28. Chafee, Lincoln (R–RI)	I	1998	75
29. Cornyn, John (R–TX)	II	2000	10
30. Hutchison, Kay (R–TX)	I	1993	15
31. Cantwell, Maria (D–WA)	I	2000	95
32. Murray, Patty (D–WA)	III	1992	95

[a]Class I: 2006 election; Class II: 2008 election; Class III: 2010 election.
[b]ADA scores are for 2005.

APPENDIX B

Senator's Official Web Page Code Sheet

Senator Code   ____

Coder's Initials   ____

Date of Website   ____

Main Page

Images on front page? (1 = yes, 0 = no)   ____

Image of candidate? (1 = yes, 0 = no)   ____

Image of flag? (1 = yes, 0 = no)   ____

Other image? (1 = yes, 0 = no) (Specify)   ____

Press releases or news headlines on main page? (1 = yes, 0 = no)   ____

Video of senator available on main page? (1 = yes, 0 = no)   ____

Link to senator's blog? (1 = yes, 0 = no)   ____

Link to senator's podcast? (1 = yes, 0 = no)   ____

Link to photo album? (1 = yes, 0 = no)   ____

Link to legislation sponsored and cosponsored by senator?
    (1 = yes, 0 = no)   ____

Link to committee assignments? (1 = yes, 0 = no)   ____

Biography Page(s)

Is there a photo on the bio page? (1 = yes, 0 = no)   ____

(If yes) is the candidate pictured? (1 = yes, 0 = no)   ____

(If yes) is candidate dressed formally (1) or informally (0)?   ____

Family facts (number of paragraphs)   ____

Ties to state (number of paragraphs)   ____

Qualifications (life experience) (number of paragraphs)   ___
Qualifications (awards) (number of paragraphs)   ___
Group affiliations mentioned (number of paragraphs)   ___
Mention of national/international work   ___

Qualifications (education)   ___ (par)
(elementary or secondary schools = 1, high school = 2,   ___ (content)
junior college = 3, BA = 4, MA = 5, JD = 6, PhD = 7, MD = 8,   ___
honorary degree = 9, other = 10)   ___

Qualifications (work experience)   ___ (par)
(education = 1, law = 2, private business = 3, medicine = 4,   ___ (content)
government = 5, military = 6, media = 7, farming = 8,
other = 9)   ___

    ___

Qualifications (political experience)   ___ (par)
(number of terms in current office = 1, experience in   ___ (content)
another federal office = 2, experience at local (city) level   ___
politics = 3, experience in state level politics = 4, work for a   ___
political party or interest group = 5, community, school   ___
or neighborhood level politics (ex. school board) = 6,
congressional founder of organization, chairperson or
leader of a congressional committee or subcommittee = 7,
leader of congressional group or organization (other than
a committee) = 8, other = 9)

Mention of Committees, Subcommittee
Assignments & Caucus   ___ (par)
Participation   ___ (content)
(international relations, foreign policy = 1, military, defense,   ___
security = 2, economy, budget, taxes, business, misc.   ___
financial = 3, health care = 4, education = 5, poverty,   ___
welfare = 6, crime, drugs = 7, housing = 8, children,
families = 9, energy & environment = 10, jobs, employment,
wages = 11, Iraq = 12, war in Afghanistan = 13, terrorism = 14,
judiciary & law = 15, other = 16)

Mention of Legislative Accomplishments ___ (par)
(sponsored, cosponsored, supported, proposed,   ___ (content
pushed for legislation related to the following issue)   ___
areas) (education = 1, health care = 2, child & families = 3, ___
abortion = 4, right to die = 5, disaster relief = 6,
military/defense = 7, minimum wage = 8, gas prices = 9,
school prayer = 10, homeland security/terrorism = 11,
social security = 12, economic issues = 13, war in Iraq = 14,
war in Afghanistan = 15, immigration/English as an official
language = 16, gun control = 17, environment = 18,
affirmative action = 19, government ethics = 20, corporate
ethics = 21, business/economic/taxes issues = 22,
civil rights/discrimination = 23, jobs = 24, other = 25)

Mention of Caring for State   ___ (par)
(related to the following areas: poverty = 1,   ___ (content)
children and families = 2, business = 3, environment = 4,   ___
health care = 5, education = 6, race relations = 7,   ___
immigration = 8, law enforcement = 9, drugs/crime = 10,   ___
transit and infrastructure = 11, case work/gov't. benefits = 12, ___
homeland security = 13, economic development = 14,
military/local bases, troops = 15, misc. money brought back
to the district = 16, community building/development = 17,
other = 18)

<u>Top accomplishment mentioned</u> ("my biggest accomplishment is,"
"my top priority is," "most proud of")

                                                             ___ (par)
Issue = 1   ___ (content)
Project = 2
Other = 3 (specify)

If Issue, Use Chart Below

TABLE B.1. Top Accomplishment or Priority Issue on Senate Bio Page

Issue	No. of Paragraphs	Issue	No. of Paragraphs
Defense		Unemployment	
Foreign Aid		Taxes	
Homeland Security		Minimum Wage	
Terrorism		Environment	
War in Iraq		Hurricane Katrina	
Afghanistan		Abortion	
Iran		School Prayer	
North Korea		Civil Rights	
Israel/Palestine		Affirmative Action	
Treatment of Veterans		Human Rights/Torture	
Prescription Drugs		Government Spending	
Health Care/Health Insurance		Police Violence	
Child Care		English-Only	
AIDS		Immigration	
Social Security		Illegal Immigration	
Welfare/Food Stamps		Drugs	
Food Stamps		Crime	
Education		Poverty/Affordable Housing	
Jobs/Outsourcing		Gun Control	
Unemployment		Family Leave/Parental Rights	
Inflation		Death Penalty	
Business		Government Ethics	
Oil Prices		Consumer Credit	
Trade		Identity Theft	
Economy (general)		Corporate Scandal	
Budget		9/11 Relief/Rebuilding	
Farm		Consumer Protection	
Other (specify)		Other (specify)	

Personal Traits (bio page)

TABLE B.2. Personal Traits Noted on Senate Bio Page

Issue	No. of Paragraphs	Issue	No. of Paragraphs
Honest/Trustworthy		Hardworking	
Ambitious		Aggressive/"Fighter"	
Effective		Independent	
Ties to the State		Consistent, Stable	
Cares for State		Strong Leader	
Washington Ties		Professional Background	
Compassionate		"Humble Background"	
War Record		Elective Experience	
Intelligent		"Family Man/Woman"	
Advocate		Religious	
Knowledgeable		Accomplished	
Moral		Shrewd	
Military Career		"Self-Made Man/Woman"	
"Champion"		Competent	
Accomplished		Other (specify)	
Other (specify)			

Issue Mentions (bio page)

TABLE B.3. Issues Mentioned on Senate Bio Page

Issue	No. of Paragraphs	Issue	No. of Paragraphs
Defense		Unemployment	
Foreign Aid		Taxes	
Homeland Security		Minimum Wage	
Terrorism		Environment	
War in Iraq		Hurricane Katrina	
Afghanistan		Abortion	
Iran		School Prayer	
North Korea		Civil Rights	
Israel/Palestine		Affirmative Action	
Treatment of Veterans		Human Rights/Torture	
Prescription Drugs		Government Spending	
Health Care/Health Insurance		Police Violence	
Child Care		English-Only	
AIDS		Immigration	
Social Security		Illegal Immigration	
Welfare/Food Stamps		Drugs	
Food Stamps		Crime	
Education		Poverty/Affordable Housing	
Jobs/Outsourcing		Gun Control	
Unemployment		Family Leave/Parental Rights	
Inflation		Death Penalty	
Business		Government Ethics	
Oil Prices		Consumer Credit	
Trade		Identity Theft	
Economy (general)		Corporate Scandal	
Budget		9/11 Relief/Rebuilding	
Farm		Consumer Protection	
Other (specify)		Other (specify)	

APPENDIX C

Press Release Code Sheet

VARIABLE DESCRIPTION	CODE

Senator Code ___

Press Release Number (sequential) ___

Number of Paragraphs ___

Date of Press Release ___

Initials of Coder ___

Content of Press Release (# of paragraphs mentioning each)

    1 = Issues ___

    2 = Projects ___

    3 = Visits by Leaders ___

    4 = Symbolic (specify) ___

    5 = Other (specify) ___

Content of Press Release (mainly about) ___

    1 = Issues

    2 = Projects

    3 = Visits by Leaders

    4 = Symbolic (specify) ___

    5 = Other (specify) ___

Senator's Partisanship (1 = Yes, 0 = No) ___

Senator's Bipartisanship (1 = Yes, 0 = No) ___

Senator's Ideology   ___

    1 = Extremely Liberal
    2 = Liberal
    3 = Moderate
    4 = Conservative
    5 = Extremely Conservative

Endorsements of Senator

1 = President	5 = Celebrity ___
2 = National Office Holder—Elective	6 = Newspaper ___
3 = National Office Holder—	7 = Interest Group (specify) ___
Appointive	8 = Former Office Holder
4 = State Office Holder	9 = Other _____

Mention of Senator's Position	Number of Mentions
Leadership Position in the U.S. Senate	___
Committee Chair	___
Subcommittee Chair	___
Committee Member	___
Other _____	___

Mention of Senator's Bill Sponsorship/ Cosponsorship	Number of Mentions
	___
Mention of Bipartisan Cosponsorship (yes = 1, no = 0)	___

Mention of Federal Projects for State	Number of Mentions
Specify _____	___
Specify _____	___
Specify _____	___

Mention of Symbolic Actions	Number of Mentions
Specify _____	___
Specify _____	___
Specify _____	___

Traits (number of mentions of senator)

Honest	___	Ambitious	___
Trustworthy	___	Ties to the State	___
Elective Experience	___	Washington Ties (+)	___
Compassionate	___	War Record	___
Intelligent	___	Cares for State	___
Knowledgeable	___	Moral	___
Effective	___	Military Career	___
Hardworking	___	Aggressive	___
Independent	___	Consistent, Stable	___
Strong Leader	___	Professional Background	___
"Humble Background"	___	Long History in State	___
Other _____	___	Other _____	___

Issues

Responsibility (1 = take credit, 2 = blame someone else,
3 = deny responsibility, 0 = no mention)

	# Mentions	Position	Responsibility
Defense	___	___	___
Nuclear Nonproliferation	___	___	___
Terrorism	___	___	___
War in Iraq	___	___	___
Afghanistan	___	___	___
Iran	___	___	___
North Korea	___	___	___
Israel/Palestine	___	___	___
Homeland Security	___	___	___
Health (prescription drugs)	___	___	___
Elderly	___	___	___
Veterans	___	___	___
Welfare	___	___	___
Education	___	___	___
Illegal Drugs	___	___	___
Child Care	___	___	___

Business	___	___	___
Farm/Agriculture	___	___	___
Oil	___	___	___
Energy	___	___	___
Trade	___	___	___
Environment	___	___	___
Econ-general	___	___	___
Jobs	___	___	___
Taxes	___	___	___
Budget	___	___	___
Hurricane Katrina	___	___	___
Abortion	___	___	___
Civil Rights	___	___	___
Prayer in School	___	___	___
Gun Control	___	___	___
Death Penalty	___	___	___
Scandal	___	___	___
Big Gov't.	___	___	___
Immigration	___	___	___
Ethics	___	___	___
Lobby Reform/Transpar.	___	___	___
Judicial Nominations	___	___	___
Other_____	___	___	___

APPENDIX D

Newspaper Content Analysis Code Sheet

VARIABLE DESCRIPTION	CODE

Senator Code   ____

Article Number (sequential)   ____

Number of Paragraphs   ____

Date (month/day)   ____

Initials of Coder   ____

Type of Article

    1 = News Story   ____

    2 = Editorial/News Analysis

    3 = Other

Senator Mentioned in Headline

    1 = Yes; 0 = No   ____

Number of Paragraphs about Senator

      ____

Tone of Article about Senator

    1 = Positive; 2 = Negative; 3 = Mixed; 4 = Neutral;

    0 = Not about Senator   ____

Number of Quotes from Senator   ___

Number of Criticisms of Senator   ___

Content of News Article

    1 = Issues   ___
    2 = Projects   ___
    3 = Visits by Leaders   ___
    4 = Symbolic (specify) _____   ___
    5 = Other (specify) _____   ___
    6 = Election

Mention of Senator's Position	Number of Mentions
Leadership Position in the U.S Senate	___
Committee Chair	___
Subcommittee Chair	___
Committee Member	___
Other _____	___

Mention of Senator's Bill Sponsorship/ Cosponsorship	Number of Mentions
	___
Mention of Bipartisan Cosponsorship (yes = 1, no = 0)	___

Mention of Federal Projects for State	Number of Mentions
Specify _____	___
Specify _____	___
Specify _____	___

Mention of Symbolic Actions	Number of Mentions
Specify _____	___
Specify _____	___
Specify _____	___

Traits (number of mentions of senator)

Honest	___	Dishonest	___
Trustworthy	___	Untrustworthy	___
Elective Experience	___	Lacks Elective Experience	___
Compassionate	___	Insensitive	___
Intelligent	___	Unintelligent	___
Knowledgeable	___	Uninformed	___
Effective	___	Ineffective	___
Hardworking	___	Not Hardworking	___
Independent	___	Dependent	___
Strong Leader	___	Weak Leader	___
"Humble Background"	___	Privileged Background	___
Ambitious	___	Power-Hungry	___
Positive Ties to State	___	Negative Ties to State	___
Washington Ties (+)	___	Washington Ties (–)	___
War Record (+)	___	War Record (–)	___
Cares for State	___	Doesn't Care for State	___
Moral	___	Immoral	___
Military Career	___	Lack of Military Career	___
Aggressive	___	Passive	___
Consistent	___	Erratic	___
Professional Background	___	Lacks Prof. Background (–)	___
Long History in State	___	Short History in State	___
Other _____	___	Other _____	___

Issues

\# = Number of Mentions

Pos = explicit position on issue (1=yes, 0=no)

Resp = (1 = take credit, 2 = blame someone else, 3 = deny responsibility, 0 = no mention)

Val = valence (3 = positive, 2 = mixed, 1 = negative, 0 = neutral/no tone)

	\#	Pos	Resp	Val
Defense	___	___	___	___
Intelligence	___	___	___	___
Troops	___	___	___	___
Foreign Aid	___	___	___	___
Cent. America	___	___	___	___

Terrorism	—	—	—	—
War in Iraq	—	—	—	—
Afghanistan	—	—	—	—
Iran	—	—	—	—
North Korea	—	—	—	—
Israel/Palestine	—	—	—	—
Homeland Security	—	—	—	—
Nuclear Nonproliferation	—	—	—	—
Health Care	—	—	—	—
Elderly/Soc. Sec.	—	—	—	—
Veterans	—	—	—	—
Welfare	—	—	—	—
Education	—	—	—	—
Illegal Drugs	—	—	—	—
Child Care	—	—	—	—
Business	—	—	—	—
Oil/Gas Prices/Energy	—	—	—	—
Trade	—	—	—	—
Environment	—	—	—	—
Econ-general	—	—	—	—
Inflation	—	—	—	—
Jobs/Unemployment	—	—	—	—
Outsourcing	—	—	—	—
Taxes	—	—	—	—
Budget	—	—	—	—
Min. Wage	—	—	—	—
Farm	—	—	—	—
Stem Cell	—	—	—	—
Hurricane Katrina	—	—	—	—
Abortion	—	—	—	—
Civil Rights	—	—	—	—
Prayer in School	—	—	—	—

	#	Pos	Resp	Val
Gun Control	—	—	—	—
Death Penalty	—	—	—	—
School Vouchers	—	—	—	—
Scandal	—	—	—	—
Big Gov't.	—	—	—	—
Immigration	—	—	—	—
Gay Rights/Marriage	—	—	—	—
Judicial Nominations	—	—	—	—
Ethics	—	—	—	—
Lobby Reform/Transpar.	—	—	—	—
Civil Liberties	—	—	—	—
Other_____	—	—	—	—
Other_____	—	—	—	—
Other_____	—	—	—	—

Survey Questions from Cooperative Congressional Election Study (CCES/Common Content)

Approval of Senator

Do you approve or disapprove of the way <Senator's Name> is handling his/her job as U.S. Senator for <state>?

<1> Strongly approve
<2> Somewhat approve
<3> Somewhat disapprove
<4> Strongly disapprove
<5> Not sure

Party Identification of Senator

Do you happen to remember the party affiliation of <Senator's Name>?

<1> Democrat
<2> Republican
<3> Independent
<4> Don't know

Ideology of Senators

One way that people talk about politics in the United States is in terms of left, right, and center, or liberal, conservative, and moderate. We would like to know how you view the parties and candidates using these terms. The scale below represents the ideological spectrum from very liberal (o) to very conservative (100). The most centrist American is exactly at the middle (50).

Where would you place <Senator's Name>?
If you are not sure, or don't know, please check here ___.

<u>Roll Call Questions</u>

Late-Term Abortion Ban
First, we'd like to ask about a proposal in Congress to ban a type of late-term abortion sometimes called "partial-birth abortion." Some argue that late-term abortion is a barbaric procedure and should be banned. Others argue that late-term abortions are extremely uncommon and used only in exceptional circumstances best determined by a doctor, not the Congress. The proposed legislation could also be the opening to a broader ban on abortion.

How about <Senator's Name>? Do you think <he/she> voted for or against banning late-term abortion?

   <1> For (that is, to ban late-term abortion)
   <2> Against (that is, not to ban late-term abortion)
   <3> Don't Know

Funding for Stem Cell Research
Now we'd like to ask you about whether the federal government should fund stem cell research.

Some in Congress argue that this research may lead to cures for diseases and disabilities affecting large numbers of Americans, and should be funded. Others argue that a potential human life has to be destroyed in order to use these cells, and funding it would be unethical.

How about <Senator's Name>? Do you think <he/she> voted for or against funding the research?

   <1> For (that is, funding the research)
   <2> Against
   <3> Don't know

Phased Redeployment of U.S. Troops in Iraq

Congress also debated a proposal that the president begin phased redeployment of U.S. troops from Iraq starting this year and submit to Congress by the end of 2006 a plan with estimated dates for continued phased withdrawal.

Some politicians argue that setting out a plan to withdraw would make Iraqis take responsibility for their country and become more independent of the U.S. Others argue that it is too early to start withdrawing, and that doing so would make terrorists grow bolder.

How about <Senator's Name>? Do you think <he/she> voted for or against this plan?

   <1> For (setting a timetable to withdraw from Iraq)
   <2> Against
   <3> Don't know

Illegal Immigration

Another issue is illegal immigration. One plan considered by the Senate would offer illegal immigrants who already live in the U.S. more opportunities to become legal citizens.

Some politicians argue that people who have worked hard in jobs that the economy depends on should be offered the chance to live here legally. Other politicians argue that the plan is an amnesty that rewards people who have broken the law.

How about <Senator's Name>? Do you think <he/she> voted for or against this proposal?

   <1> For (offering illegal immigrants an opportunity to become citizens)
   <2> Against
   <3> Don't know

Raising the Minimum Wage
Congress considered a proposal to increase the federal minimum wage from
$5.15 to $6.25 within the next year and a half.

Some politicians argue that the wage should be increased because it hasn't
changed since 1997 and many workers still live in poverty. Other politicians
argue that raising the wage might force small businesses to cut jobs and
would hurt the economy.

How about <Senator's Name>? Do you think <he/she> voted for or against
increasing the minimum wage?

> <1> For (in favor of increasing the federal minimum wage)
> <2> Against
> <3> Don't know

Extension of Capital Gains Tax Cuts
We'd like to ask about cutting taxes on the money people make from selling
investments, also referred to as capital gains. This past year the Senate considered a bill to extend capital gains tax cuts passed in 2001.

Some politicians argue that these tax reductions make the economy strong
and encourage people to invest more. Others argue that the plan would
mostly benefit people who are already rich and that any tax cuts should be
shared more fairly among all taxpayers.

How about <Senator's Name>? Do you think <he/she> voted for or against
increasing these tax cuts?

> <1> For (that is to extend the capital gains tax cuts)
> <2> Against
> <3> Don't know

CAFTA
This year Congress also debated a new free trade agreement that reduces bar-
riers to trade between the U.S. and countries in Central America.

Some politicians argue that the agreement allows America to better compete in the global economy and would create more stable democracies in Central America. Other politicians argue that it helps businesses to move jobs abroad where labor is cheaper and does not protect American producers.

How about <Senator's Name>? Do you think <he/she> voted for or against the trade agreement?

    <1> For (that is, to ratify the trade agreement)
    <2> Against
    <3> Don't know

Party Identification of Respondent
Generally speaking, do you think of yourself as a Democrat, Republican, Independent or what?

[If Democrat or Republican], would you call yourself a strong [Democrat/Republican] or a not very strong [Democrat/Republican]? If Independent, do you think of yourself as closer to the Democratic or the Republican Party?

    <1> Strong Democrat
    <2> Weak Democrat
    <3> Democratic Leaner
    <4> Independent
    <5> Republican Leaner
    <6> Weak Republican
    <7> Strong Republican
    <8> Other
    <9> Don't know

Interest in Politics
How interested are you in politics and current affairs?

    <1> Very much interested
    <2> Somewhat interested
    <3> Not much interested

Pay Attention to the News
During the past week, how many times did you watch the national evening news?

    <1> Not at all (0 times)
    <2> Once or Twice (1–2 times)
    <3> A few times (3–4 times)
    <4> Almost every day (5–7 times)

APPENDIX F

Sample of Senators Running for Reelection

TABLE F.1. Sample of Senators Running for Reelection

Senator	State	Newspaper	Advertisements	Website
George Allen	VA	*Richmond Times-Dispatch*	Yes	Yes
Conrad Burns	MT	*Billings Gazette*	Yes	Yes
Robert Byrd	WV	*Charleston Gazette Daily*	Yes	Yes
Maria Cantwell	WA	*Seattle Times*	Yes	Yes
Lincoln Chafee	RI	*Providence Journal*	Yes	Yes
Hillary Clinton	NY	*New York Times*	No	Yes
Kent Conrad	ND	*Fargo Forum*	Yes	Yes
Mike DeWine	OH	*Plain Dealer*	Yes	Yes
John Ensign	NV	*Las Vegas Review Journal*	Yes	Yes
Dianne Feinstein	CA	*Los Angeles Times*	No	Yes
Orrin Hatch	UT	*Salt Lake Tribune*	Yes	Yes
Kay Bailey Hutchison	TX	*Houston Chronicle*	Yes	Yes
Jon Kyl	AZ	*Arizona Republic*	Yes	Yes
Robert Menendez	NJ	*Newark Star-Ledger*	Yes	Yes
Ben Nelson	NE	*Omaha World Herald*	Yes	Yes
Bill Nelson	FL	*St. Petersburg Times*	No	Yes
Rick Santorum	PN	*Philadelphia Inquirer*	Yes	Yes
Olympia Snowe	ME	*Bangor Daily News*	No	Yes
Debbie Stabenow	MI	*Detroit News*	Yes	Yes
Jim Talent	MO	*St. Louis Post Dispatch*	Yes	Yes
Craig Thomas	WY	*Casper Star-Tribune*	No	Yes

APPENDIX G

Political Advertising Code Sheet

VARIABLE DESCRIPTION	CODE
Researcher Code	___
Candidate Code	___
State Code	___
Ad Number (sequential)	___

Type of Candidate   ___

    1 = Incumbent
    2 = Challenger

Type of Ad

    1 = Positive Trait   10 = Endorsements   ___
    2 = Positive Issue   11 = Biography
    3 = Negative Trait   12 = Comparison: combination
    4 = Negative Issue   13 = Comparison: trait
    5 = Positive Combination   14 = Comparison: issue
    6 = Negative Combination   15 = Comparison: elective experience
    7 = Elective Experience   16 = Comparison: ideology
        (constituency/pork)   17 = Other _____
    8 = Positive Ideology
    9 = Negative Ideology

Traits of Candidate   Traits of Opponent

	Major	Minor		Major	Minor
Honest	___	___	Dishonest	___	___
Trustworthy	___	___	Untrustworthy	___	___
Compassionate	___	___	Insensitive	___	___
Intelligent	___	___	Unintelligent	___	___
Effective	___	___	Ineffective	___	___
Knowledgeable	___	___	Uninformed	___	___
Hardworking	___	___	Lazy	___	___
Independent	___	___	Dependent	___	___
Strong Leader	___	___	Weak Leader	___	___
Moral	___	___	Immoral	___	___
Consist., Stable	___	___	Erratic	___	___
Aggressive	___	___	Passive	___	___
Experienced	___	___	Inexperienced	___	___
Ambitious	___	___	Power-Hungry	___	___
Ties to State	___	___	No Ties to State	___	___
War Record	___	___	Lack War Record	___	___
Cares for State	___	___	No Care for State	___	___
Pos. Wash. Ties	___	___	Neg. Wash Ties	___	___
Voting Record +	___	___	Voting Record –	___	___
Special Life	___	___	(Un)common Man	___	___
Seniority	___	___	Special Interest Ties	___	___
Common Man	___	___	Other _____	___	___
Family	___	___	Other _____	___	___
Decisive	___	___	Other _____	___	___
For Middle Class	___	___			

Issues

= Number of Mentions

Pos = explicit position on issue *(1 = yes, 0 = no)

Resp = (1 = take credit, 2 = blame someone else, 3 = deny responsibility,
   0 = no mention)

Val = valence (1 = positive, 0 = neutral, –1=negative)

	Candidate				Opponent			
	#	Pos	Resp	Val	#	Pos	Resp	Val
Defense	—	—	—	—	—	—	—	—
Troops	—	—	—	—	—	—	—	—
Foreign Aid	—	—	—	—	—	—	—	—
Cent. America	—	—	—	—	—	—	—	—
Terrorism	—	—	—	—	—	—	—	—
War in Iraq	—	—	—	—	—	—	—	—
Afghanistan	—	—	—	—	—	—	—	—
Iran	—	—	—	—	—	—	—	—
North Korea	—	—	—	—	—	—	—	—
Israel/Palestine	—	—	—	—	—	—	—	—
Homeland Security	—	—	—	—	—	—	—	—
Health Care	—	—	—	—	—	—	—	—
Elderly/Soc. Sec.	—	—	—	—	—	—	—	—
Welfare	—	—	—	—	—	—	—	—
Education	—	—	—	—	—	—	—	—
Prescription Drugs	—	—	—	—	—	—	—	—
Child Care	—	—	—	—	—	—	—	—
Business	—	—	—	—	—	—	—	—
Oil/Gas Prices/Energy	—	—	—	—	—	—	—	—
Trade	—	—	—	—	—	—	—	—
Environment	—	—	—	—	—	—	—	—
Econ-general	—	—	—	—	—	—	—	—
Inflation	—	—	—	—	—	—	—	—
Unemployment	—	—	—	—	—	—	—	—
Jobs	—	—	—	—	—	—	—	—
Outsourcing	—	—	—	—	—	—	—	—
Taxes	—	—	—	—	—	—	—	—
Budget	—	—	—	—	—	—	—	—
Min. Wage	—	—	—	—	—	—	—	—
Stem Cell	—	—	—	—	—	—	—	—
Hurricane Katrina	—	—	—	—	—	—	—	—
Abortion	—	—	—	—	—	—	—	—
Civil Rights	—	—	—	—	—	—	—	—
Prayer in School	—	—	—	—	—	—	—	—

Gun Control   —   —   —   —   —   —   —   —

Death Penalty   —   —   —   —   —   —   —   —

School Vouchers   —   —   —   —   —   —   —   —

Scandal   —   —   —   —   —   —   —   —

Big Gov't.   —   —   —   —   —   —   —   —

Immigration   —   —   —   —   —   —   —   —

Ethics   —   —   —   —   —   —   —   —

Other____   —   —   —   —   —   —   —   —

Other____   —   —   —   —   —   —   —   —

Other____   —   —   —   —   —   —   —   —

APPENDIX H

Campaign News Content Analysis Code Sheet

VARIABLE DESCRIPTION   CODE

Newspaper Code   ＿

Date (month/day/year)   ＿

Article Number (sequential)   ＿

Location of Article (page number)   ＿

Location of Article (section)   ＿

Length of Article (number of paragraphs)   ＿

Type of Article

    1 = News Story   4 = News Analysis   ＿

    2 = Column   5 = Other, Specify _____

    3 = Editorial

Candidate Mentioned in Headline   ＿

    1 = Only Incumbent

    2 = Only Challenger

    3 = Both Candidates

    4 = Neither Candidate

Number of Paragraphs

    About Incumbent   ＿

    About Challenger   ＿

Tone of Headline: Incumbent

    1 = Positive   ___
    2 = Negative
    3 = Mixture
    4 = Indifferent/Neutral
    0 = Not about Candidate

Tone of Headline: Challenger

    1 = Positive   ___
    2 = Negative
    3 = Mixture
    4 = Indifferent/Neutral
    0 = Not about Candidate

Tone of Article: Incumbent

    1 = Positive   ___
    2 = Negative
    3 = Mixture
    4 = Indifferent/Neutral
    0 = Not About Candidate

Tone of Article: Challenger

    1 = Positive   ___
    2 = Negative
    3 = Mixture
    4 = Indifferent/Neutral
    0 = Not about Candidate

Criticisms of Incumbent   Source ___   Number ___

    1 = By Opponent   Source ___
    2 = By Other Source   Source ___
    3 = Unattributed
    0 = Not Criticized

Criticisms of Challenger   Source ___   Number ___

    1 = By Opponent   Source ___
    2 = By Other Source   Source ___
    3 = Unattributed
    0 = Not Criticized

Traits of Incumbent	Major	Minor	Traits of Challenger	Major	Minor
Honest	___	___	Dishonest	___	___
Trustworthy	___	___	Untrustworthy	___	___
Compassionate	___	___	Insensitive	___	___
Intelligent	___	___	Unintelligent	___	___
Effective	___	___	Ineffective	___	___
Knowledgeable	___	___	Uninformed	___	___
Hardworking	___	___	Lazy	___	___
Independent	___	___	Dependent	___	___
Strong Leader	___	___	Weak Leader	___	___
Moral	___	___	Immoral	___	___
Consist., Stable	___	___	Erratic	___	___
Aggressive	___	___	Passive	___	___
Experienced	___	___	Inexperienced	___	___
Ambitious	___	___	Power-Hungry	___	___
Ties to State	___	___	No Ties to State	___	___
War Record	___	___	Lack War Record	___	___
Cares for State	___	___	No Care for State	___	___
Pos. Wash. Ties	___	___	Neg. Wash. Ties	___	___
Voting Record +	___	___	Voting Record –	___	___
Special Life	___	___	(Un)common Man	___	___
Seniority	___	___	Special Interest Ties	___	___
Common Man	___	___	Other _____	___	___
Family	___	___	Other _____	___	___
Decisive	___	___	Other _____	___	___
For Middle Class	___	___			
Other _____	___	___			
Other _____	___	___			
Other _____	___	___			

Issues

\# = Number of Mentions

Pos = explicit position on issue (1 = yes, 0 = no)

Resp = (1 = take credit, 2 = blame someone else, 3 = deny responsibility, 0 = no mention)

Val = valence (1 = positive, 0 = neutral, –1=negative)

	Candidate				Opponent			
	#	Pos	Resp	Val	#	Pos	Resp	Val
Defense	___	___	___	___	___	___	___	___
Troops	___	___	___	___	___	___	___	___
Foreign Aid	___	___	___	___	___	___	___	___
Cent. America	___	___	___	___	___	___	___	___
Terrorism	___	___	___	___	___	___	___	___
War in Iraq	___	___	___	___	___	___	___	___
Afghanistan	___	___	___	___	___	___	___	___
Iran	___	___	___	___	___	___	___	___
North Korea	___	___	___	___	___	___	___	___
Israel/Palestine	___	___	___	___	___	___	___	___
Homeland Security	___	___	___	___	___	___	___	___
Health Care	___	___	___	___	___	___	___	___
Elderly/Soc. Sec.	___	___	___	___	___	___	___	___
Welfare	___	___	___	___	___	___	___	___
Education	___	___	___	___	___	___	___	___
Prescription Drugs	___	___	___	___	___	___	___	___
Child Care	___	___	___	___	___	___	___	___
Business	___	___	___	___	___	___	___	___
Oil/Gas Prices/Energy	___	___	___	___	___	___	___	___
Trade	___	___	___	___	___	___	___	___
Environment	___	___	___	___	___	___	___	___
Econ-general	___	___	___	___	___	___	___	___
Inflation	___	___	___	___	___	___	___	___
Unemployment	___	___	___	___	___	___	___	___
Jobs	___	___	___	___	___	___	___	___
Outsourcing	___	___	___	___	___	___	___	___
Taxes	___	___	___	___	___	___	___	___
Budget	___	___	___	___	___	___	___	___
Min. Wage	___	___	___	___	___	___	___	___

Stem Cell   —   —   —   —   —   —   —   —
Hurricane Katrina   —   —   —   —   —   —   —   —
Abortion   —   —   —   —   —   —   —   —
Civil Rights   —   —   —   —   —   —   —   —
Prayer in School   —   —   —   —   —   —   —   —
Gun Control   —   —   —   —   —   —   —   —
Death Penalty   —   —   —   —   —   —   —   —
School Vouchers   —   —   —   —   —   —   —   —
Scandal   —   —   —   —   —   —   —   —
Big Gov't.   —   —   —   —   —   —   —   —
Immigration   —   —   —   —   —   —   —   —
Ethics   —   —   —   —   —   —   —   —
Other_____   —   —   —   —   —   —   —   —
Other_____   —   —   —   —   —   —   —   —
Other_____   —   —   —   —   —   —   —   —

Survey Questions from Cooperative Congressional Election Study (CCES/Individual Module)

Personality Trait Assessments

In your opinion, does the phrase DISHONEST describe [Senate Incumbent Up for Reelection—Insert Name] extremely well, quite well, not too well or not well at all?

> Extremely Well
> Quite Well
> Not Too Well
> Not Well at All
> Don't Know

In your opinion, does the phrase REALLY CARES ABOUT PEOPLE LIKE YOU describe [Senate Incumbent Up for Reelection—Insert Name] extremely well, quite well, not too well or not well at all?

> Extremely Well
> Quite Well
> Not Too Well
> Not Well at All
> Don't Know

In your opinion, does the phrase INEXPERIENCED describe [Senate Incumbent Up for Reelection—Insert Name] extremely well, quite well, not too well or not well at all?

Extremely Well
Quite Well
Not Too Well
Not Well at All
Don't Know

In your opinion, does the phrase PROVIDES STRONG LEADERSHIP describe [Senate Incumbent Up for Reelection—Insert Name] extremely well, quite well, not too well or not well at all?

Extremely Well
Quite Well
Not Too Well
Not Well at All
Don't Know

Issue Competence Questions

What is your best guess about [senate incumbent up for reelection—insert name]'s competence in dealing with health care issues?

Very Competent
Competent
Somewhat Competent
Somewhat Incompetent
Incompetent
Very Incompetent
Don't Know

What is your best guess about [senate incumbent up for reelection—insert name]'s competence in dealing with economic issues?

Competent
Somewhat Competent
Somewhat Incompetent
Incompetent
Very Incompetent
Don't Know

Candidate Favorability Scales

Using a scale from 1 to 10, where 10 means you feel very favorable toward the person and 1 means you feel very unfavorable toward the person, where would you rank [senate incumbent up for reelection—insert name] on this scale? Please give a number between 1 and 10.

1
2
3
4
5
6
7
8
9
10
Don't Know

Party Proximity

In general, do you think of yourself as a Democrat, a Republican or Independent?

If Democrat or Republican, how strongly do you feel about your party?

If Independent, do you lean toward one of the parties? If so, which one?

Ideological Proximity

One way that people talk about politics in the United States is in terms of liberal, conservative, and moderate. We would like to know how you view the parties and candidates using these terms. The scale below represents the ideological spectrum from very liberal to very conservative.

Where would you place yourself on this line?

Where would you place the incumbent senator?

Iraq Proximity

Some politicians argue that setting out a plan to withdraw would make Iraqis take responsibility for their country and become more independent of the U.S. Others argue that it is too early to start withdrawing, and that doing so would make terrorists grow bolder. What do you think? If you were faced with this decision, would you vote for or against a plan to start withdrawing troops this year?

How about the incumbent senator? Do you think [he/she] voted for or against this plan?

How about the challenger? If [he/she] were faced with this decision, do you think [senate challenger—insert name] would vote for or against a plan to start withdrawing troops this year?

Sociotropic Assessments
Would you say that OVER THE PAST YEAR the nation's economy has gotten worse, stayed about the same, or gotten better?

Much better
Better
About Same
Worse
Much Worse
Not Sure

Job Approval of President Bush
Do you approve or disapprove of the way George W. Bush is handling his job as president?

Strongly approve
Somewhat approve
Somewhat disapprove
Strongly disapprove
Not sure

Notes

Chapter 1

1. The interview with Olympia Snowe was conducted by the Center for American Women and Politics (CAWP) during the 103rd Congress.
2. http://healthcarereform.procon.org/view.resource.php?resourceID=003712.
3. She won her fourth term to the U.S. Senate in November 2010, capturing over 60% of the vote.
4. These press releases were posted on Senator Mikulski's website between November 19 and December 3, 2009. http://www.mikulski.senate.gov/media/pressrelease/12-03-2009.cfm.
5. http://www.usatoday.com/news/washington/2009-12-03-senate-healthcare_N.htm.
6. http://www.mikulski.senate.gov/media/pressrelease/12-03-2009.cfm.
7. One extolled the virtues of the Patient Protection and Affordable Care Act, the name of the health-care-reform bill in the Senate.
8. Schiller (2000), in her book *Partner and Rivals: Representation in U.S. Senate Delegations,* argues that the dual representation in the Senate forces senators of the same state to emphasize different priorities since they are competing for the attention of the state media and the attention of constituents. Schiller relies on newspaper accounts to identify the senators' priorities. Grimmer (2010) argues that news accounts are a "polluted measure" of senators' expressed preferences since the content of news stories are influenced by the editorial decisions of the newspaper. Grimmer reexamines Schiller's thesis by examining over 24,000 press releases for senators serving in the U.S. Senate in 2007. Unlike Schiller, Grimmer finds that senators who represent the same state have expressed agendas that are *more similar* than senators who represent different states. Grimmer argues that this similarity may occur because senators of the same state may rely on similar groups as part of their "reelection" constituents or senators may multiply the effectiveness of their own communication by working with the other senator from their state.

9. The Reid Health Care Bill was the name of the health-care legislation in the Senate, bearing the name of the Democratic Majority Leader, Harry Reid.

10. http://www.youtube.com/watch?v=PQTr3pTJIzg.

11. http://www.cbsnews.com/8301-503544_162-20000981-503544.html.

12. The four senators have prepared dozens of press releases expressing their views on health care, as well as posting statements on their webpages. In addition, they have canvassed their states talking to citizens about their positions, holding town-hall meetings, making public speeches, and orchestrating press conferences.

13. http://hutchison.senate.gov/?p=press_release&id=679.

14. In this book, we focus on the U.S. Senate. The U.S. Senate is a vital partner with the U.S. House of Representatives for the passage of legislation in the U.S. bicameral system. In addition, the Senate, because of its various powers related to international affairs (e.g., confirmation powers for U.S. ambassadors, approval of treaties negotiated by the president), is an important institution for understanding the United States' role in international relations. Compared to the U.S. House, senators have longer terms in office and the vast majority of senators represent much larger constituencies. In chapter 2, we detail the unique virtues of studying the U.S. Senate as compared to the U.S. House. Finally, we focus on one house of the national legislature, as compared to state legislatures, because of the prominent role communication plays in developing relationships with constituents across the national stage. To be sure, we encourage the examination of all communications that constitute the nature of representation in large and small legislative bodies in the U.S. and around the world.

15. U.S. Census Bureau, July 2009 estimates.

16. To be sure, a significant number of scholars have examined communications flowing from constituents to representatives in order to determine if and how legislators locate the individual and aggregate policy preferences of citizens (e.g., Dahl 1956; Miller and Stokes 1963; Pitkin 1967; Eulau and Walke 1978; Page and Shapiro 1983; Stimson, Mackuen, and Erikson 1995).

17. Students of representation refer to these activities as substantive representation, allocation responsiveness, and symbolic representation.

18. Eulau and Karps (1978) identify service responsiveness as an aspect of representation. While we agree that service responsiveness is an aspect of the representational relationship (e.g., Fenno 1978; Fiorina 1977), service responsiveness concerns *non-legislative* services (e.g., case work) that a representative performs for individuals in the state. We do not focus on this particular aspect of representation here. A key reason is that general communications to constituents do not involve specific casework. Rather, these communications tend to be more specific and personal (e.g., a letter to a constituent, locating a citizen's lost Social Security check, assisting a veteran with medical benefits).

19. Local newspaper coverage focuses more extensively on coverage of U.S. senators than local television stations or national news outlets (e.g., Arnold 2004; Fowler, Goldstein, Hale, and Kaplan 2007; Kahn and Kenney 1999).

20. Tim Arango, "Fall in Newspaper Sales Accelerates to Pass 7%," *New York Times,* April 27, 2009.

21. Hayes (2011) notes that gender stereotypes and party stereotypes overlap. Women and Democrats are viewed as more compassionate, and men and Republicans are considered stronger leaders.

22. In contrast, Congress also develops and implements "regulatory" and "redistributive" programs where specific individuals or groups are assisted at the expense of others (Weingast 1994). For example, redistributive programs include Food Stamps or Aid to Families with Dependent Children. Or certain environmental regulations on industries place burdens on producers, for example. A key issue with regulatory and redistributive policies is that they are not as popular with citizens as distributive programs. Thus, very few senators focus their communications on these kinds of programs.

23. Anzia and Berry (2011), looking at men and women in the U.S. House of Representatives from 1984 to 2004, find that women bring more federal spending home, compared to their male counterparts. However, we do not know whether women are more likely than men to advertise their success in bringing federal money back to their districts.

24. However, some research suggests that gender differences in the quantity of news coverage may be fading (e.g., Bystrom, Banwart, Kaid, and Robertson 2004; Jalalzai 2006).

25. However, Fowler and Lawless (2009), looking at gubernatorial campaigns between 1990 and 1997, find that women candidates for governor received less coverage of "female" issues compared to male candidates.

26. Scholars looking at campaign coverage in statewide races find that news coverage reinforces "gendered" traits, with women candidates receiving more attention to communal traits like warmth and compassion, while male candidates receive more media attention for their experience and competence (e.g., Bystrom, Banwart, Kaid, and Robertson 2004; Kahn 1996).

Chapter 2

1. Senator Felton served only one day.

2. Senator Caraway was subsequently elected to a second term and served in the U.S. Senate from 1931 to 1945.

3. In 2006, the 14 women senators represented about 119 million citizens in the U.S. Senate. 2006 Census figures are from "Vintage 2006: State Tables," available at http://www.census.gov/popest/data/historical/2000s/vintage_2006/.

4. We examined the senators' issue pages, as well as the front page and the biography page on senators' websites. However, senators varied in their reliance on issue pages, making it more difficult to make conclusions about issue emphasis on these pages.

5. Cohen's kappa is a chance-corrected measure of inter-rater reliability that

assumes two raters, *n* cases, and *m* mutually exclusive and exhaustive nominal categories (see Rourke, Anderson, Garrison, and Archer 2000).

6. To avoid any periodicity problems, we sampled every odd day in the first month (e.g., January) and then every even day the following month.

7. The 2006 official senator websites can be located at http://ia410331. us.archive.org/congress109th/.

8. We did not measure service responsiveness since the discussion of case work did not appear in the senator's press releases.

9. While we only looked at one newspaper per state, research suggests that coverage patterns across newspapers in a state are similar in content, amount, placement, and tone (Kahn and Kenney 1999).

10. Once coding began, team meetings were held every week to review the progress of the coders. Reliability checks were again performed, comparing one of the author's coding of the news articles with the coding by the research assistants. Cohen's kappa produced a reliability score of .91 ($p < .001$).

11. For more detail about the 2006 CCES see Ansolabehere 2007.

12. We would like to thank Jamie Druckman for allowing us to use his campaign website data.

13. See Druckman, Kifer, Parkin (2009) for more details about the coding of the campaign websites and how reliability was assessed.

14. The number of advertisements aired by these safe incumbents may have been extremely limited or nonexistent (Goldstein and Freedman 2002; Sides 2006).

15. We use the same coding procedure for the political advertising content analysis as we did in the content analysis of the governing messages. One of the authors conducted the reliability checks, comparing the author's coding of the advertisements with the coding by the research assistants. Cohen's kappa was used to assess intercoder reliability with a resulting score of .91 ($p < .001$).

16. We use the same coding procedure here as we did in the content analysis of news coverage during the governing period. Ten research assistants helped code the news coverage. Intercoder reliability, using Cohen's kappa, was assessed producing a score of .88 ($p < .01$).

17. See Appendix I for the exact question wording for survey questions included in our module.

Chapter 3

1. The senators' official websites are located at http://www.senate.gov/general/contact_information/senators_cfm.cfm.

2. As discussed in chapter 2, the senator's official website was examined at least once for each of the 32 senators. For 19 of the 32 senators, we examined their official websites twice: once in February and once in September. Overall, 27 of the 32 websites were examined in February and 24 of the 32 websites were examined in September, for a total of 51 websites.

3. While women are somewhat more likely to display links to podcasts and to feature a legislative link, these differences fail to reach statistical significance when we control for the seniority and party of the senator, as well as whether the senator is up for reelection.

4. While senators' websites contain numerous pages (e.g., issue pages, news room, services for constituents), the biography page is available for every senator in our sample.

5. All examples of U.S. senators' official websites in 2006 can be located at: http://www.webharvest.gov/collections/congress109th/senate_members_al pha.html.

6. The difference between men and women senator's discussion of legislative accomplishments is statistically significant at $p < .10$. However, when we conduct a multivariate analysis, controlling for the senator's party, seniority, and placement in the election cycle, the gender of the senator fails to reach standard levels of statistical significance.

7. This difference is statistically significant ($t = 2.77$, $p < .01$).

8. We rely on negative binomial regression since the distribution of the dependent variables are not normally distributing, violating an assumption of OLS regression.

9. Throughout this book, we use the following terms interchangeably: "female" traits and "communal" traits, "male" traits, and "agentic" traits.

10. This difference is statistically significant (F = 6.838, $p < .05$).

11. We rely on logistic regression since the dependent variable is dichotomous: mentioning an issue as a top accomplishment or not.

12. Throughout this book, "communal" issues and "female" issues are used interchangeably as are "competitive" issues and "male" issues.

13. We also looked at whether committee assignments were related to a senator's emphasis on competitive and communal issues since committee assignments often drive legislative priorities (see Hall 1996; Schiller 1995). Of the 20 standing committees in the U.S. Senate, more than half are easily classified as dealing with competitive issues (e.g., Appropriations, Armed Services, Budget, Foreign Relations, Finance), while several cover both competitive and communal issues (e.g., Agriculture, Nutrition, and Forestry; Banking, Housing, and Urban Affairs). Given the large number of committees focused on competitive issues, all the senators in the sample sat on at least one of these committees. However, not all senators sat on a committee devoted to communal issues (e.g., Health, Education, Labor, and Pensions). Therefore, we looked at whether senators sitting on committees devoted to communal issues were more likely to mention these types of issues on their websites. However, committee assignment failed to significantly influence the senator's likelihood of mentioning communal issues on their websites. Similarly, senators sitting on communal committees were not significantly less likely to focus on competitive issues.

14. The only exception to the pattern is North Carolina, where Elizabeth Dole spent more time on "male" issues, compared to Richard Burr.

15. See   http://webharvest.gov/congress109th/20061114005829/http://mi
kulski.senate.gov/.

16. See   http://webharvest.gov/congress109th/20061114004546/http://sar
banes.senate.gov/.

Chapter 4

1. http://www.gillibrand.senate.gov/newsroom/press/release/gillibrand-sen
ate-democratic-women-call-on-boehner-to-abandon-pledge-to-continue-con
traception-fight.

2. http://schumer.senate.gov/Newsroom/record.cfm?id=336252.

3. For more details about our sampling and coding procedures, see chapter 2.

4. We rely on logistic regression because we are examining the probability of
mentioning competitive issues (1 = mentioning these issues, 0 = not mentioning
these issues) or communal issues in the senators' press releases.

5. This difference is statistically significant ($F = 7.31, p < .01$).

6. As we did in chapter 3, we looked at whether committee assignments were
related to a senator's emphasis on issues. In particular, we looked at whether senators sitting on committees devoted to communal issues were more likely to
mention these types of issues in their press releases. However, committee assignment failed to significantly influence the senator's likelihood of mentioning
communal issues. Similarly, senators sitting on communal committees were not
less likely to focus on competitive issues.

7. The seven pairs of senators are: (1) Lisa Murkoski (R-AK) and Ted Stevens
(R-AK), (2) Blanche Lincoln (D-AR) and Mark Pryor (D-AR), (3) Barbara Mikulski
(D-MD) and Paul Sarbanes (D-MD), (4) Debbie Stabenow (D-MI) and Carl Levin
(D-MI), (5) Elizabeth Dole (R-NC) and Richard Burr (R-NC), (6) Hillary Clinton
(D-NY) and Charles Schumer (D-NY), (7) Kay Bailey Hutchison (R-TX) and John
Cornyn (R-TX).

8. As with web pages, the senators of North Carolina do not follow the general pattern: Elizabeth Dole is less likely to discuss "female" issues, when compared to Richard Burr.

9. If we examine the proportion of paragraphs focusing on competitive and
communal issues, we find the same pattern. The proportion of paragraphs devoted to communal issues, relative to competitive issues, is greater for women
senators than male senators. For example, Senator Debbie Stabenow of Michigan
talks about communal issues 51% of the time, while Senator Carl Levin discusses
these same issues only 34% of the time.

10. The gender difference in allocation emphasis is statistically significant ($F = 24.157, p < .01$). All statistical tests are two-tailed tests, unless otherwise specified.

11. Since we are examining count data (i.e., the number of times a senator
mentions federal projects in his or her press releases), we rely on negative binomial regression, since the data are not normally distributed around the mean.

12. Some researchers have found that female state legislators believe they de-

vote more time than men to keeping in touch with constituents and helping constituents with their problems (e.g., Carey, Niemi, and Powell 1998; Richardson and Freeman 1995). However, Reingold (2000) finds few gender differences in perceived constituency service efforts.

13. The gender difference in symbolic emphasis reaches statistically significance (F = 2.152, p < .10, one-tailed test).

14. The binomial regression coefficient for gender in the model predicting the number of references to the senator's symbolic activities is –.12 with a standard error of .22. The control variables included in the multivariate model are the party of the senator, proximity to an election, seniority of the senator, and the number of total paragraphs in the press releases.

15. This difference is statistically significant (F = 9.42, p < .05).

16. This difference is statistically significant (F = 7.30, p < .05).

17. As in our earlier analysis, we rely on negative binomial regression since we are examining count data here (i.e., the number of times a senator takes a clear position in his or her press releases).

18. Dolan and Kropf (2004), looking at newsletters of members of Congress, find male legislators are more likely to claim credit on "male" issues (e.g., defense), while women legislators are more likely to claim credit on "female" issues (e.g., health care).

19. Since we are examining count data here (i.e., the number of times a senator claims credit in his or her press releases), we rely on negative binomial regression since the data are not normally distributed around the mean.

20. The dependent variable is 1 if the senator claims credit in the press release and 0 if the senator does not claim credit. Given the binary dependent variable, we rely on logistic regression in this analysis.

Chapter 5

1. The article was published on August 23, 2010, in the *New York Times,* http://www.nytimes.com/2010/08/24/nyregion/24bigcity.html.

2. This column was published on December 2, 2009, in the *Boston Globe,* http://www.boston.com/news/local/breaking_news/2009/12/beam_on_poli tic_10.html.

3. This article was published on June 7, 2003, in the *New York Times,* http://www.nytimes.com/2003/06/07/us/working-mothers-swaying-senate-debate-as-senators.html?scp=1&sq=sheryl+gay+stolberg+%22blanche+lincoln%22+frist+&st=nyt.

4. However, some researchers have found less substantial gender differences in the quantity of news coverage (e.g., Bystrom, Banwart, Kaid, and Robertson 2004; Fowler and Lawless 2009; Jalalzai 2006).

5. This difference is statistically significant at p < .01 (F = 8.4).

6. This difference is statistically significant at p < .01 (F = 10.32).

7. In our analysis, we log the number of press releases, as well as the size of the

newspaper, to base 10 because of outliers in the dataset (i.e., a few senators with a very large number of press releases and a few newspapers with very large circulation sizes).

8. We rely on logistic regression here since the dependent variable is dichotomous (i.e., the senator was mentioned in the headline or not).

9. In this analysis, we rely on negative binomial regression since the distribution of the dependent variables are not normally distributing, violating an assumption of OLS regression.

10. Lawrence and Rose conclude that the negative focus on her personal traits and background was more pronounced on the internet than on cable and network television.

11. The gender difference in the number of criticisms is statistically significant at $p < .01$ (F = 7.39).

12. The gender difference in coverage of positive traits is statistically significant at $p < .10$ (F = 3.17) and the gender differences in coverage of favorable policy outcomes is statistically significant at $p < .01$ (F = 13.63).

13. In this analysis, we rely on negative binomial regression since the distribution of the dependent variables are not normally distributing, violating an assumption of OLS regression.

14. We rely on logit regression here since the dependent variable is dichotomous (i.e., the senator was credited for a positive policy outcome in the article or not).

15. We recoded the trait measure to –1 to 1 because the majority of original trait scores clustered by –1 and 1. Because the dependent variable in this analysis is ordinal, we rely on logistic ordinal regression.

16. The gender difference in issue coverage is statistically significant (F = 11.00, $p < .01$). The gender difference in trait coverage is not statistically significant (F = 2.11, n.s.).

17. In this analysis, we rely on negative binomial regression since the distribution of the dependent variables are not normally distributing, violating an assumption of OLS regression.

18. This difference is statistically significant (F = 2.31, $p < .10$) with a one-way test.

19. We rely on logit regression here since the dependent variable is dichotomous (i.e., competitive issues or communal issues are mentioned in the article or not).

20. This difference is statistically significant ($t = 6.62, p < .01$).

21. The gender difference in news emphasis on issue positions is statistically significant (F = 12.96, $p < .01$) as is the gender difference in news emphasis on leadership positions (F = 21.22, $p < .01$).

22. The gender difference in news emphasis on symbolic responsiveness is statistically significant (F = 17.88, $p < .01$) as is the gender difference in news emphasis on allocation responsiveness (F = 7.19, $p < .01$).

23. In calculating the probabilities, we keep all interval level variables (i.e., se-

niority, log of circulation size, log of press releases) at their mean and each nominal variable at its mode (i.e., Democrat for party of the senator, Upcoming Election for Election Year). We rely on the technique described by King (1989).

Chapter 6

1. http://pewresearch.org/pubs/770/iraq-war-five-year-anniversary.

2. The *New York Times* article can be found at http://query.nytimes.com/gst/fullpage.html? res=9D03E0DF1630F930A15755C0A9609C8B63&scp=2&sq=Iraq+War+Levin+Amendment&st=nyt&pagewanted=print.

3. For each question, a respondent is given a score of 1 if the respondent answers the question and the respondent is given a score of 0 if the respondent does not answer the question. After creating the binary variable (answered = 1; not answered = 0) for each of the three questions, the three variables are summed, producing a three-point index.

4. In the information environment index, we create a standardized measure of news coverage and a standardized measure of issue paragraphs in the senator's press releases. We sum these two measures, creating an index ranging from two to eight, where two indicates that the amount of news coverage was two standard deviations below the mean and the amount of issue attention in the press releases was two standard deviations below the mean. A score of eight, in contrast, indicates that the amount of news coverage was two standard deviations above the mean and the amount of issue attention in the press releases was two standard deviations above the mean. We did not assess the independent impact of news coverage and press releases on people's level of knowledge because the two indicators were highly correlated, creating multicollinearity problems. Creating a combined index of the information environment also makes theoretical sense since people are not exposed to news coverage and press releases in isolation. We explored alternative operationalizations of the information environment index (e.g., examining the number of overall paragraphs—not issue paragraphs—in the press releases). However, the adopted operationalization of the information environment was superior in terms of construct validity.

5. We also examined whether the party of the senator and the seniority of the senator influenced citizens' knowledge of senators, but neither variable is influential; therefore, we do not include these variables in the present analysis.

6. The political interest question and the question assessing attention to news were not asked of all the respondents. Therefore, the number of respondents included in our analysis drops to about 5,400 respondents. We re-ran each of the models in this chapter without political interest and attention to news and the substantive findings do not change (although the importance of political sophistication and education because more powerful). However, because of the importance of political interest and attention to news for understanding political knowledge levels, we include these variables in each of the models.

7. In the analysis in this chapter, we rely on a more stringent measure of sta-

tistical significance ($p < .05$) since we have a large sample of respondents (at least 4,000 respondents in each of the analysis).

8. Senator Hillary Clinton, one of the "Senator 2" senators, is probably more widely known than the typical senator because of her prior position as First Lady. In each of the models in this chapter, we have included a dummy variable for Hillary Clinton to make sure her inclusion is not inflating the importance of the gender of the senator. In the analysis in table 6.1, the dummy variable for Hillary Clinton fails to reach statistical significance and the coefficient for the gender of the senator is essentially unchanged (.59, with a standard error of .07).

9. The series of questions began with the following preface: "As you know, Senators and Representatives in Washington regularly have to decide how to vote on issues affecting the country. We'd like to ask you how you would vote on some of these same issues as well as how you think your representative voted." See appendix E for complete question wording for each of the ballot questions.

10. We reran the analysis in table 6.2 with a dummy variable for Hillary Clinton in the equation predicting respondents' ability to answer roll-call questions about "Senator 2." The dummy variable is significant (.47, with a standard error of .15). However, the gender of the senator remains sizeable and statistically significant (.30, with a standard error of .08).

11. In the analysis in table 6.3, the dummy variable for Hillary Clinton fails to reach statistical significance and the coefficient for the gender of the senator is essentially unchanged (.63, with a standard error of .08).

12. In calculating these probabilities, we vary the gender of the senator and hold all of the remaining variables in the model at their means.

13. Looking at ADA scores, no senator in our sample has a 50 (moderate) score on the ADA roll call index.

14. That is, 53% of the respondents correctly place the senior senator and 56% of respondents correctly place the junior senator on the ideological scale.

15. We reran the analysis in table 6.4 with a dummy variable for Hillary Clinton in the equation predicting respondents' ability to correctly identify the senator's ideology for "Senator 2." The dummy variable is significant (.83, with a standard error of .15). However, the gender of the senator remains sizeable and statistically significant (.34, with a standard error of .08).

16. We reran the analysis in table 6.5 with a dummy variable for Hillary Clinton in the equation predicting respondents' knowledge of senators' roll-call votes for "Senator 2." The dummy variable is significant (.41, with a standard error of .12). However, the coefficient for gender of the senator barely budges and remains highly significant (.66, with a standard error of .06).

17. In both figure 6.2 and figure 6.3, we calculate point estimates for Senator 1 only.

Chapter 7

1. http://www.gallup.com/poll/116677/presidential-approval-ratings-gal lup-historical-statistics-trends.aspx.

2. David W. Moore, "Three Years of War Have Eroded Public Support," March 17, 2006, www.gallup.com/poll/21952/.

3. Michael Bouchard spent less than $6 million ($5,763,160), http://www.na tionaljournal.com/almanac/person/debbie-stabenow-mi/.

4. http://www.opensecrets.org/races/election.php?state=MI&cycle=2006.

5. http://democraticspace.com/usa/2006/senate/MI/20061102-detroit-free-press.pdf.

6. http://www.opensecrets.org/races/summary.php?cycle=2006&id=NJS1.

7. http://maristpoll.marist.edu/new-jersey-campaign-2006-final-poll/.

8. In 2006, 23 male senators ran for reelection, while 4 senators retired. Appendix F includes a list of the senators included in the campaign sample.

9. See chapter 2 for more details about the campaign website data set and the political advertising data set. Advertisements were unavailable for five of the senators.

10. See chapter 2 for more details about the survey questions and the sampling of respondents.

11. In our examination of campaign messages, we focus exclusively on issues and personal traits. These types of messages dominate campaign communications (Kahn and Kenney 1999). We do not examine symbolic and allocation messages, often found in representational messages, as they simply do not appear with any regularity in campaign messages.

12. When examining personal traits, we look at campaign advertising instead of campaign websites because we do not have explicit measures of personal traits from the campaign websites.

13. The bivariate relationship between the gender of the senator and the reliance on agentic traits is significant ($F = 35.01, p < .01$).

14. We rely on logit regression since the dependent variable in the model is binary (i.e., are agentic traits mentioned in the advertisement or not).

15. Men and women senators do not differ in their mentions of communal traits in their advertisements, according to bivariate and multivariate results.

16. We chose to examine the biography section of the website for issue discussion because all senators presented issue information in this section of their website. In comparison, less than two-thirds of senators mentioned issues on the front page of their campaign website and not all senators included an issue page on their campaign website. Nevertheless, the gender differences in issue emphasis are persistent whether we examine (1) the biography page, (2) the issue page, or (3) the front page of the campaign website.

17. We conduct a multivariate analysis examining the number of competitive issues on the senator's biography page, controlling for party, seniority, competition, and the opponent's emphasis on competitive issues on challenger's main campaign webpage. We find the coefficient for gender of the senator is negatively signed, although not statistically significant. We also conduct a multivariate analysis examining the number of communal issues on the senator's biography page, controlling for party, seniority, competition, and the opponent's emphasis on communal issues on challenger's main campaign webpage. Consistent with

the bivariate results, we find the coefficient for gender of the senator is positively signed, although not statistically significant.

18. The differences between men and women senators' emphases on issues is statistically significant at the $p < .05$ level for the campaign advertising data, according to the difference in proportions test. We conduct a multivariate analysis examining the proportion of issue discussion focusing on communal issues, relative to competitive issues (e.g., the number of communal issues mentioned divided by the total number of competitive and communal issues mentioned). Again, we control for party, seniority, competition, and the opponent's emphasis on communal issues in their advertisements. We find that the coefficient for gender of the senator is positive, but not statistically significant.

19. We look at campaign websites instead of political advertisements because we have campaign website data for all incumbents running for reelection.

20. Articles average about one paragraph about issues (i.e., .87 paragraphs) with coverage of competitive issues averaging about a half of paragraph (i.e., .40 paragraphs) per article, while coverage of communal issues is less common, averaging about .17 paragraphs per article.

21. We find the same pattern when we look at coverage of communal issues, like health care and the environment. When men senators discuss these issues on their campaign webpage, they have a .08 probability of receiving coverage for these policy matters. In contrast, when they steer clear of these issue domains, the probability that they will receive press attention for these issues drops to nearly 0 (i.e., a probability of .02). For women senators, the difference in the probability of garnering coverage for communal issues changes from a probability of .01 when women senators do not emphasize these issues to a probability of .04 when they emphasize these policy matters on their campaign websites.

22. We look at campaign advertising instead of campaign websites because we do not have explicit measures of personal traits from the campaign websites. Also, since we do not have campaign advertisements for all senate incumbents, we restrict our analysis of campaign news to the 16 incumbents where advertising data is available.

23. The difference between the news coverage focus on agentic traits and the focus on agentic traits in the senators' advertisements is statistically significant for women senators ($p < .05$), according to the difference in proportions test.

24. As we did in table 7.2, we estimate a multiplicative model to see if women senators are significantly less capable than male senators at garnering coverage for their preferred traits messages. We focus on agentic traits since male traits receive more attention in the press and because women senators focus heavily on agentic traits in their political advertisements. The results of the multiplicative analysis demonstrate that women are significantly less effective than male senators at garnering news attention for agentic traits when they emphasize these personality characteristics in their advertisements. The interaction coefficient (advertising emphasis on agentic traits * gender of senator) is negative and statis-

tically significant at $p < .10$ (unstandardized regression coefficient is –2.3, with a standard error of 1.3).

25. We rely on the issue competence measure developed and employed by political scientists studying gender stereotypes (e.g., Sapiro 1981/82). The exact question wording for the survey questions is presented in appendix I.

26. We consider vulnerable senators to be appointed senators and senators involved in scandals. Senators who were appointed, rather than elected, are Lincoln Chafee of Rhode Island and Robert Menendez of New Jersey, and senators involved in scandals are George Allen of Virginia, Conrad Burns of Montana, Jim Talent of Missouri, and Robert Byrd of West Virginia. In identifying vulnerable senators, we adopt the procedure outlined by Abramowitz and Segal (1992). Vulnerable senators are coded 1, while other senators are code 0. We examined whether the vulnerability of the senator influenced the senators' controlled communications or news coverage in the senator's state, but vulnerability failed to have a consistent and significant effect.

27. 24% of the senators mentioned the economy on the front page of their campaign website and 19% of the senators mentioned health care on the front page of their campaign website.

28. To measure party proximity, we rely on a seven-point party identification measure and give respondents the highest score (3) if they are a strong partisan and share the party of the incumbent. Respondents who are strong partisans and share the party of the challenger are given the lowest score (–3). Independents and people identifying with a third party are placed at the middle of the scale (0). To measure ideological proximity, we rely on the respondent's self-placement on a 100-point ideological scale and the respondent's placement of the incumbent and challenger on the same ideological scale. We recode the 100-point scales into 5 points (0–20 = 1, 21–40 = 2, 41–60 = 3, 61–80 = 4, 81–100 = 5). Then, we calculate (1) the absolute value of the difference between the respondent's ideological self-placement and respondent's placement of the incumbent's ideology, and (2) the absolute value of the difference between the respondent's ideological self-placement and the respondent's placement of the challenger's ideology. Finally, we subtract the respondent's closeness to the incumbent from the respondent's closeness to the challenger. The resulting ideological proximity score ranges from 4 (the respondent and incumbent share the same location on the ideological scale) to –4 (the respondent and the challenger share the same location on the ideological scale).

29. We also examined whether the challenger's emphasis on health care or the economy of the front page of the challenger's campaign website influenced people's assessments of the senator's ability to deal with economic and health issues. However, the measure of the challenger's campaign message was far from statistically significant. Finally, we looked at whether the tone of the campaign (i.e., the challenger criticized the senator on the front page of the challenger's campaign website, the proportion of critical paragraphs in the news) influenced citizens'

issue assessments, but neither variable achieved statistical significance in either model in table 7.3.

30. We also developed a measure of the content of trait discussion in the candidates' political advertisements. As discussed earlier, we have no explicit measure of traits from the senators' campaign webpages. For each trait dimension (i.e., honesty, experience, leadership, empathy), we calculated the number of positive mentions (e.g., about the senator's honesty) about the senator's traits in the senator's own commercials and the number of negative mentions (e.g., about the senator's dishonesty) about the senator's traits in the challenger's commercials. We subtracted the challenger's negative mentions from the senator's positive dimensions for each trait dimension, creating a measure assessing the tone of trait discussion in the candidates' commercials. However, since commercials are only available for a subset of the 21 senators, we restrict our analysis to 16 senators where advertising data is available. When we examine the impact of advertising trait content on citizens' assessments of the candidates' personality, the advertising variable fails to reach statistical significance in any of the models estimated. Given the necessity of excluding five senators (and three women senators) from our sample when including the advertising variable, we drop the advertising variable from the following analysis. Excluding the advertising variable from the models does not change the substantive results of the model.

31. The vote choice question was asked after the election in the post-election survey. We only include respondents who indicate voting in the election. By relying on two waves of interviews, we diminish the possibility of reciprocal causality between the attitudinal assessments and the vote choice measure (Markus 1982).

32. In other words, we include the dependent variables from table 7.3 and table 7.4 as independent variables in table 7.6.

33. Respondents who held the same position as their incumbent senator of the issue of Iraq were given the highest score (+1), while respondents who differed with their incumbent senator on the issue of Iraq were given the lowest score (−1), and respondents who had no position on Iraq were placed at 0. In particular, respondents were asked whether they would be for or against a plan to withdraw troops from Iraq in the next year. See appendix I for the exact question wording.

34. The significance of sociotropic assessments of the economy on evaluations of candidates has been documented at the presidential and sub-presidential level (e.g., Hetherington 1996; Kinder and Kiewiet 1981). Respondents who believed the economy was getting much better received the highest score (+2), while respondents who believed the economy was getting much worse received the lowest score (−2). We also looked at whether assessments of the state economy were influential and whether tying the Republican incumbent to the state of the national (or state) economy mattered. These alternative economic measures did not significantly influence voting decisions ($p < .10$).

35. Respondents who strongly approved of Bush's handling of his job as president and were living in states where Republican incumbents were running for reelection were given the highest score (4), respondents who somewhat approved

of Bush's handling of his job and were living in states where Republican incumbents were running for reelection were given a 3, respondents who somewhat disapproved of Bush's handling of his job and were living in states where Republican incumbents were running for reelection were given a 2, respondents who strongly disapproved of Bush's handling of his job and were living in states where Republican incumbents were running for reelection were given a 1. We used the same logic in coding responses from respondents living in states with Democratic incumbents (e.g., respondents who strongly disapproved of Bush's handling of his job and were living in states where Democratic incumbents were running for reelection were given the highest score, 4).

36. We rely on logistic regression since the dependent variable is binary (1 = vote for incumbent, 0 = do not vote for incumbent).

37. We also analyze a more parsimonious model predicting voting for the incumbent senator where we exclude measures of the campaign and measures of candidate characteristics, except for the gender of the senator. The gender of the senator continues to be inconsequential. We examine whether certain respondents—women—are more likely to support a woman senator at the polls. To examine this "affinity effect," we reestimate the model in table 7.6, including a multiplicative term where we interact the gender of the respondent with the gender of the senator. The interaction term does not achieve statistical significance. The logit coefficient is 2.0 with a standard error of 1.24. The "affinity effect" is not significant in the models predicting trait assessments (i.e., table 7.4) or issue evaluations (i.e., table 7.3).

Chapter 8

1. One exception is a series of decisions by the U.S. Supreme Court encouraging the creation of minority-majority congressional districts (for a summary, see Jacobson 2009).

2. http://thehill.com/blogs/floor-action/house/211399-female-democratic-senators-blast-all-male-gop-led-birth-control-panel.

3. Quotes from the floor speeches are taken from the 2012 *Congressional Record,* vol. 158, p. S882, www.gpo.gov.

4. The interview with Olympia Snowe was conducted by the Center for American Women and Politics (CAWP) during the 103rd Congress.

5. Respondents could answer the question on a scale ranging from one to four, where one represents "strongly agree" and four represents "strongly disagree."

6. The F-statistic is .21, indicating no significant gender differences in the respondents' level of external efficacy.

7. The F-statistic is 6.26 and statistically significant at $p < .02$.

8. The F-statistic was 2.16, failing to reach standard levels of statistical significance. When we look at female respondents' level of political efficacy when they are residing in a state with a male senator running for reelection versus a female

senator, we find that female respondents' report significantly higher levels of political efficacy when they are living in states with a female senator seeking reelection ($F = 6.54$, $p < .02$). In contrast, when we look at male respondents' level of political efficacy in states with male versus female incumbents running for reelection, we find no significant differences in male respondents' level of political efficacy ($F = 2.37$, $p = .12$).

References

Abbe, Owen G., Jay Goodiffe, Paul S. Herrnson, and Kelly D. Patterson. 2003. "Agenda Setting in Congressional Elections: The Impact of Issues and Campaigns on Voting Behavior." *Political Research Quarterly* 56 (4): 419–30.

Abramowitz, Alan I. 1975. "Name Familiarity, Reputation, and the Incumbency Effect in a Congressional Election." *Western Political Science Quarterly* 28 (4): 668–84.

Abramowitz, Alan I. 2006. "National Conditions, Strategic Politicians, and U.S. Congressional Elections: Using the Generic Vote to Forecast the 2006 House and Senate Elections." *PS: Political Science and Politics* 39 (4): 863–66.

Abramowitz, Alan I., and Jeffrey A. Segal. 1990. "Beyond Willie Horton and the Pledge of Allegiance: National Issues in the 1988 Elections." *Legislative Studies Quarterly* 15 (4): 565–80.

Abramowitz, Alan I., and Jeffrey A. Segal. 1992. *Senate Elections.* Ann Arbor: University of Michigan Press.

Abramson, Paul R., John H. Aldrich, and David W. Rohde. 2012. *Change and Continuity in the 2008 and 2010 Elections.* Washington, DC: CQ Press.

Aday, Sean, and James Devitt. 2001. "Style over Substance: Newspaper Coverage of Elizabeth Dole's Presidential Bid." *Journal of Press/Politics* 6 (2): 52–73.

Adler, E. Scott, Chariti E. Gent, and Cary B. Overmeyer. 1998. "The Home Style Homepage: Legislator Use of the World Wide Web for Constituency Contact." *Legislative Studies Quarterly* 23 (4): 585–98.

Alexander, Deborah, and Kristi Andersen. 1993. "Gender as a Factor in the Attribution of Leadership Traits." *Political Research Quarterly* 46 (3): 527–45.

Alpert, Bruce. 2006. "La. Delegation against Pullout—Only One Backs Demos' Request." *New Orleans Times-Picayune,* August 3.

Anderson, Karrin Vasby. 2011. "'Rhymes with Blunt': Pornification and U.S. Political Culture." *Rhetoric and Public Affairs* 14 (2): 327–68.

Ansolabehere, Stephen. 2007. "Access versus Integrity in Voter Identification Requirements." Paper presented at the New York University Law School's Election Law Symposium for the Annual Survey of American Law, New York.

Ansolabehere, Stephen, and Philip E. Jones. 2010. "Constituents' Responses to

Congressional Roll-call Voting." *American Journal of Political Science* 54 (3): 583–97.

Armstrong, Rob. 2004: *Covering Politics: a Handbook for Journalists.* Ames, IA: Blackwell.

Arnold, Douglas R. 1992. *The Logic of Congressional Action.* New Haven: Yale University Press.

Arnold, Douglas R. 2004. *Congress, the Press, and Political Accountability.* Princeton: Princeton University Press.

Arnold, Laura W., and Barbara M. King. 2002. "Women, Committees, and Institutional Change in the Senate." In *Women Transforming Congress,* edited by Cindy Simon Rosenthal. Norman: University of Oklahoma Press.

Atkeson, Lonna R. 2003. "Not All Cues are Created Equal: The Conditional Impact of Female Candidates on Political Engagement."*Journal of Politics* 65 (4): 1040–61.

Atkeson, Lonna R., and Timothy B. Krebs. 2008. "Press Coverage of Mayoral Candidates—The Role of Gender in News Reporting and Campaign Issue Speech." *Political Research Quarterly* 61 (2): 239–52.

Bargh, John A. 1984. "Automatic and Conscious Processing of Social Information." In *The Handbook of Social Cognition,* edited by Robert S. Wyer Jr. and Thomas K. Srull. Hillsdale, NJ: Erlbaum.

Barnett, Jim. 2006. "Wyden Says It's 'Crunch Time' for Baghdad." *Portland (OR) Oregonian,* March 8.

Bartels, Larry M. 1993. "Messages Received." *American Political Science Review* 87 (2): 267–85.

Bartels, Larry M. 2002. "The Impact of Candidate Traits in American Presidential Elections." In *Leaders' Personalities and the Outcomes of Democratic Elections,* edited by Anthony King. Oxford: Oxford University Press.

Bartels, Larry M. 2010. "The Study of Electoral Behavior." In *The Oxford Handbook of American Elections and Political Behavior,* edited by Jan E. Leighley. New York: Oxford University Press.

Beyer, Sylvia. 1990. "Gender Differences in the Accuracy of Self-Evaluations of Performance." *Journal of Personality and Social Psychology* 59 (5): 960–70.

Bickers, Kenneth N., Diana Evans, Robert M. Stein, and Robert D. Wrinkle. 2007. "The Electoral Effect of Credit Claiming for Pork Barrel Projects in Congress." Paper presented at the Workshop on Elections and Distribution, Yale University, October 26–27.

Bodenhausen, Galen V., and Robert S. Wyer Jr. 1985. "Effects of Stereotypes on Decision Making and Information-Processing Strategies." *Journal of Personality and Social Psychology* 48 (2): 267–82.

Boles, Janet. 2001. "Local Elected Women and Policy-Making: Movement Delegates or Feminist Trustees?" In *The Impact of Women in Public Office,* edited by Susan J. Carroll. Bloomington: Indiana University Press.

Braden, Maria. 1996. *Women Politicians in the Media.* Lexington: University Press of Kentucky.

Brians, Craig L., and Martin P. Wattenberg. 1996. "Campaign Issue Knowledge and Salience: Comparing Reception from TV Commercials, TV News, and Newspapers." *American Journal of Political Science* 40 (1): 172–93.

Broverman, Inge K., Susan Raymond Vogel, Donald M. Broverman, Frank E. Clarkson, and Paul S. Rosenkrantz. 1972. "Sex Role Stereotypes: A Current Appraisal." *Journal of Social Issues* 28 (2): 59–78.

Burgess, Diana, and Eugene Borgida. 1999. "Who Women Are, Who Women Should Be: Descriptive and Prescriptive Gender Stereotyping in Sex Discrimination." *Psychology, Public Policy, and Law* 5 (3): 665–92.

Burns, Nancy, Kay L. Schlozman, and Sidney Verba. 2001. *The Private Roots of Public Action: Gender, Equality, and Political Participation.* Cambridge, MA: Harvard University Press.

Burrell, Barbara. 1994. *A Woman's Place Is in the House: Campaigning for Congress in the Feminist Era.* Ann Arbor: University of Michigan Press.

Bystrom, Dianne G. 2006. "Advertising, Web Sites, and Media Coverage: Gender and Communication along the Campaign Trail." In *Gender and Elections: Shaping the Future of American Politics,* edited by Susan J. Carroll and Richard L. Fox. Cambridge: Cambridge University Press.

Bystrom, Dianne G., Mary C. Banwart, Lynda L. Kaid, and Terry A. Robertson. 2004. *Gender and Candidate Communication.* New York: Routledge.

Campbell, Angus, Philip E. Converse, Warren E. Miller, and Donald Stokes. 1960. *The American Voter.* New York: Wiley.

Campbell, David E., and Christina Wolbrecht. 2006. "See Jane Run: Women Politicians as Role Models for Adolescents." *Journal of Politics* 68 (2): 233–47.

Cann, Arnie, and William D. Siegfried. 1990. "Gender Stereotypes and Dimensions of Effective Leader Behavior." *Sex Roles* 23 (7/8): 413–19.

Carey, John M., Richard G. Niemi, and Lynda Powell. 1998. "Are Women State Legislators Different?" In *Women and Elective Office: Past, Present, and Future,* edited by Sue Thomas and Clyde Wilcox. New York: Oxford University Press.

Carroll, Susan J. 2002. "Representing Women: Congresswomen's Perceptions of Their Representational Roles." In *Women Transforming Congress,* edited by Cindy Simon Rosenthal. Norman: University of Oklahoma Press.

Carroll, Susan J. 2009. "Reflections on Gender and Hillary Clinton's Presidential Campaign: The Good, the Bad, and the Misogynic." *Politics and Gender* 5 (1): 1–20.

Carroll, Susan J., and Ronnee Schreiber. 1997. "Media Coverage of Women in the 103rd Congress." In *Women, Media, and Politics,* edited by Pippa Norris. New York: Oxford University Press.

CAWP. 2010. Women in Elective Office Face Sheet. Center for American Women and Politics, Eagleton Institute. Rutgers University. http://www.cawp.rut gers.edu/fast_facts/levels_of_office/documents/elective.pdf.

Chaffee, Steven H., and Stacey F. Kanihan. 1997. "Learning from Politics from the Mass Media." *Political Communication* 14 (4): 421–27.

Cialdini, Robert B., and Melanie R. Trost. 1998. "Social Influence: Social Norms,

Conformity, and Compliance." In *The Handbook of Social Psychology,* 4th ed., edited by Daniel T. Gilbert, Susan T. Fiske, and Gardner Lindzey. Boston: McGraw-Hill.

Clarke, Peter, and Susan H. Evans. 1983. *Covering Campaigns: Journalism in Congressional Elections.* Palo Alto: Stanford University Press.

Clarke, Peter, and Eric Fredin. 1978. "Newspapers, Television and Political Reasoning." *Public Opinion Quarterly* 42 (2): 143–60.

Collie, Melissa P. 1988. "Universalism and the Parties in the U.S. House of Representatives, 1921–80." *American Journal of Political Science* 32 (4): 865–83.

Converse, Philip. 1964. "The Nature of Belief Systems in Mass Publics." In *Ideology and Discontent,* edited by David Apter. New York: Free Press.

Cook, Fay L. 1990. "Congress and the Public: Convergent and Divergent Opinions on Social Security." In *Social Security and the Budget,* edited by Henry Aaron. Lanham, MD: University Press of America.

Cook, Timothy. 1989. *Making Laws and Making News: Media Strategies in the U.S. House of Representatives.* Washington, DC: Brookings Institution.

Cook Political Report. 2006. Washington, DC: Cook Political Report. http://cookpolitical.com.

Converse, Philip E. 1970. "Attitudes and Non-attitudes: Continuation of a Dialogue." In *A Quantitative Analysis of Social Problems,* edited by Edward R. Tufte. Reading, MA: Addison-Wesley.

Cox, Gary. 2007. "Swing Voters, Core Voters and Distributive Politics." Paper presented at the Workshop on Elections and Distribution, Yale University, October 26–27.

Cox, Gary W., and Mathew D. McCubbins. 1993. *Legislative Leviathan: Party Government in the House.* Berkeley: University of California Press.

Dabelko, Kirsten L., and Paul S. Herrnson. 1997. "Women's and Men's Campaigns for the U.S. House of Representatives." *Political Research Quarterly* 50 (1): 121–35.

Dahl, Robert A. 1956. *A Preface to Democratic Theory.* Chicago: University of Chicago Press.

Dahl, Robert A. 1971. *Polyarchy.* New Haven: Yale University Press.

Dahl, Robert A. 1989. *Democracy and Its Critics.* New Haven: Yale University Press.

Dasgupta, Nilanjana, and Shaki Asgari. 2004. "Seeing Is Believing: Exposure to Counter Stereotypic Women Leaders and Its Effect on the Malleability of Automatic Gender Stereotyping." *Journal of Experimental Social Psychology* 40 (5): 642–58.

Deaux, Kay, and Marianne LaFrance. 1998. "Gender." In *The Handbook of Social Psychology,* 4th ed., edited by Susan T. Fiske, Daniel T. Gilbert, and Gardner Lindzey. New York: McGraw-Hill.

Deaux, Kay, and Laurie L. Lewis. 1983. "Components of Gender Stereotypes." *Psychological Documents* 13, 25 (Ms. No. 2583).

Delli Carpini, Michael X., and Scott Keeter. 1993. "Measuring Political Knowledge: Putting First Things First." *American Journal of Political Science* 37 (4): 1179–1206.

Devitt, James. 1999. "Framing Gender on the Campaign Trail: Women's Executive Leadership and the Press." Report to the Women's Leadership Fund. http://198.65.255.167/v2/researchandreports/framinggender/Framing_Gender_Report.pdf.

Diamond, Irene. 1977. *Sex Roles in the State House.* New Haven: Yale University Press.

Dixit, Avinash, and John Londregan. 1996. "The Determinants of Success of Special Interests in Redistributive Politics." *Journal of Politics* 58 (4): 1132–55.

Dodson, Debra L., and Susan J. Carroll. 1991. *Reshaping the Agenda: Women in State Legislatures.* New Brunswick, NJ: Center for the American Woman and Politics.

Dolan, Julie, and Jonathan Kropf. 2004. "Credit Claiming from the U.S. House: Gendered Communications Styles?" *Harvard International Journal of Press/Politics* 9 (1): 41–59.

Dolan, Kathleen. 2005. "Do Women Candidates Play to Gender Stereotypes? Do Men Candidates Play to Women? Candidate Sex and Issues Priorities on Campaign Websites." *Political Research Quarterly* 58 (1): 31–44.

Dolan, Kathleen. 2011. "Do Women and Men Know Different Things? Measuring Gender Differences in Political Knowledge." *Journal of Politics* 73 (1): 97–107.

Dovi, Suzanne. 2002. "Preferable Descriptive Representatives: Will Just Any Woman, Black or Latino Do?" *American Political Science Review* 96 (4): 729–43.

Dow, Jay. 2009. "Gender Differences in Political Knowledge: Distinguishing Characteristics-Based and Returns-Based Differences." *Political Behavior* 31 (11): 117–36.

Downs, Anthony. 1957. *An Economic Theory of Democracy.* New York: Harper & Row.

Downs, Edward, and Stacy L. Smith. 2010. "Keeping abreast of Hypersexuality: A Video Game Character Content Analysis." *Sex Roles* 62 (11/12): 721–33.

Druckman, James N. 2004. "Priming the Vote: Campaign Effects in a U.S. Senate Election." *Political Psychology* 25 (4): 577–94.

Druckman, James. 2005. "Media Matter: How Newspapers and Television News Cover Campaigns and Influence Voters." *Political Communication* 22 (4): 463–81.

Druckman, James N., Martin J. Kifer, and Michael Parkin. 2007. "The Technological Development of Candidate Web Sites: How and Why Candidates Use Web Innovations." *Social Science Computer Review* 25 (4): 425–42.

Druckman, James N., Martin J. Kifer, and Michael Parkin. 2009. "Campaign Communications in U.S. Congressional Elections." *American Political Science Review* 103 (3): 343–66.

Eagly, Alice H. 1987. *Sex Differences in Social Behavior: A Social-Role Interpretation.* Hillsdale, NJ: Erlbaum.

Eagly, Alice H., and Steven J. Karau. 2002. "Role Congruity Theory of Prejudice Toward Female Leaders." *Psychological Review* 109 (3): 573–98.

Eagly, Alice H., Wendy Wood, and Amanda B. Diekman. 2000. "Social Role Theory of Sex Differences and Similarities: A Current Appraisal." In *The Developmental Social Psychology of Gender,* edited by Thomas B. Eckes and Hanns M. Trautner. Mahwah, NJ: Erlbaum.

Epstein, Michael, Richard G. Niemi, and Lynda W. Powell. 2005. "Do Women and Men State Legislators Differ?" In *Women and Elective Office: Past, Present, and Future,* 2nd ed., edited by Sue Thomas and Clyde Wilcox. New York: Oxford University Press.

Erbring, Lutz, Edie N. Goldenberg, and Arthur H. Miller. 1980. "Front-Page News and Real-World Cues: A New Look at Agenda Setting by the Media." *American Journal of Political Science* 24 (1): 16–49.

Eulau, Heinz, and Paul Karps. 1977. "The Puzzle of Representation: Specifying Components of Responsiveness." *Legislative Studies Quarterly* 2 (3): 233–55.

Eulau, Heinz, and Paul Karps. 1978. "The Puzzle of Representation: Specifying Components of Responsiveness." In *The Politics of Representation,* edited by Heinz Eulau and John Wahlke. Thousand Oaks, CA: Sage.

Eulau, Heinz, and John Wahlke. 1978. *The Politics of Representation: Continuities in Theory and Research.* Thousand Oaks, CA: Sage.

Falk, Erika. 2008. "Cutting Women Out: The Media's Bias against Female Presidential Candidates." *Boise Weekly,* March 5. http://www.boiseweekly.com/boise/cutting-women-out/Content?oid=935838.

Falk, Erika. 2010. *Women for President: Media Bias in Eight Campaigns.* Urbana: University of Illinois Press.

Falk, Erika, and Kate Kenski. 2006. "Issue Saliency and Gender Stereotypes: Support for Women as Presidents in Times of War and Terrorism." *Social Science Quarterly* 87 (1): 1–18.

Feather, Norman T. 1969. "Attribution of Responsibility and Valence of Success and Failure in Relation to Initial Confidence and Task Performance." *Journal of Personality and Social Psychology* 13 (2): 129–44.

Fenno, Richard F., Jr. 1978. *Home Style: House Members in Their Districts.* Boston: Little, Brown.

Fenno, Richard F., Jr. 1986. "Adjusting to the U.S. Senate." In *Congress and Policy Change,* edited by Gerald C. Wright, Leroy N. Rieselbach, and Lawrence C. Dodd. New York: Agathon.

Fenno, Richard F., Jr. 1996. *Senators on the Campaign Trail: The Politics of Representation.* Norman: University of Oklahoma Press.

Fenno, Richard F., Jr. 1998. "Introduction." In *Explorations in the Evolution of Congress,* edited by H. Douglas Price. Berkeley: IGS Press.

Ferejohn, John. 1974. *Pork Barrel Politics.* Palo Alto: Stanford University Press.

Fiorina, Morris P. 1977. *Congress-Keystone of the Washington Establishment.* New Haven: Yale University Press.

Fiorina, Morris P. 1981. *Retrospective Voting in American National Elections.* New Haven: Yale University Press.

Fiske, Alan P., Nick Haslam, and Susan T. Fiske. 1991. "Confusing One Person with Another: What Errors Reveal About the Elementary Forms of Social Relations." *Journal of Personality and Social Psychology* 60 (5): 656–74.

Fiske, Susan T., Richard R. Lau, and Richard A. Smith. 1990. "On the Varieties and Utilities of Political Expertise." *Social Cognition* 8 (1): 31–48.

Fiske, Susan T., and Steven L. Neuberg. 1990. "A Continuum of Impression Formation, from Category-based to Individuating Processes: Influences of Information and Motivation on Attention and Interpretation." In *Advances in Experimental Social Psychology,* edited by Mark P. Zanna. New York: Academic Press.

Fowler, Erika F., Kenneth M. Goldstein, Matthew Hale, and Martin Kaplan. 2007. "Does Local News Measure Up?" *Stanford Law and Policy Review* 18 (2): 410–31.

Fridkin, Kim L., Jill Carle, and Gina S. Woodall. 2011. "The Vice-Presidency as the New Glass Ceiling: An Examination of Sarah Palin's Media Coverage." In *Women and the Executive Branch,* edited by Melody Rose. Boulder: Lynne Rienner.

Fridkin, Kim L., and Patrick J. Kenney. 2007. "The Role of Candidate Traits in U.S. Senate Campaigns." Paper presented at the annual meeting of the American Political Science Association, Chicago.

Fridkin, Kim L., and Patrick J. Kenney. 2009. "The Role of Gender Stereotypes in U.S. Senate Campaigns." *Politics & Gender* 5 (3): 301–24.

Fridkin, Kim L., and Patrick J. Kenney. 2011. "The Role of Candidate Traits in Campaigns." *Journal of Politics* 73 (1): 61–73.

Fridkin, Kim L., and Gina Woodall. 2005. "Different Portraits, Different Leaders? Gender Differences in US Senators' Presentation of Self." In *Women and Elective Office: Past, Present, and Future,* 2nd ed., edited by Sue Thomas and Clyde Wilcox. New York: Oxford University Press.

Funk, Carolyn L. 1996. "Understanding Trait Inferences in Candidate Images." In *Research in Micropolitics: Vol. 4, Rethinking Rationality,* edited by Michael X. Delli Carpini, Leonie Huddy, and Robert Y. Shapiro. Greenwich, CT: JAI.

Funk, Carolyn L. 1999. "Bringing the Candidate into Models of Candidate Evaluation." *Journal of Politics* 61 (3): 700–720.

Gaffney, Amber M., and Danielle L. Blaylock. 2010. "Hillary Clinton's Race: Did She Match the Presidential Prototype?" *Advancing Women in Leadership Journal* 30 (6): 1–15.

Galston, William A. 2001. "Political Knowledge, Political Engagement, and Civic Education." *Annual Review Political Science* 4 (1): 217–34.

Gay, Claudine. 2002. "Spirals of Trust? The Effect of Descriptive Representation on the Relationship between Citizens and Their Governments." *American Journal of Political Science* 95 (4): 585–602.

Gerrity, Jessica C., Tracy Osborn, and Jeanette M. Mendez. 2007. "Women and Representation: A Different View of the District?" *Politics and Gender* 3 (2): 179–200.

Gershon, Sarah A. 2008. "Communicating Female and Minority Interests Online: A Study of Web Members of Congress Site Issue Discussion among Female, Latino, and African American." *International Journal of Press/Politics* 13 (2): 120–33.

Gilpatric, Katy. 2010. "Violent Female Action Characters in Contemporary American Cinema." *Sex Roles* 62 (11/12): 734–46.

Glascock, Jack. 2001. "Gender Roles on Prime-time Network Television: Demographics and Behaviors." *Journal of Broadcasting and Electronic Media* 45 (4): 656–69.

Glick, Peter, Korin Wilk, and Michele Perreault. 1995. "Images of Occupations: Components of Gender and Status in Occupational Stereotypes." *Sex Roles* 32 (9/10): 564–82.

Goldenberg, Edie N., and Michael W. Traugott. 1984. *Campaigning for Congress.* Washington, DC: Congressional Quarterly Press.

Goldstein, Kenneth, and Joel Rivlin. 2005. "Political Advertising in the 2002 Elections Revisited." The Wisconsin Advertising Project, the Department of Political Science at the University of Wisconsin-Madison. http://wiscadpro ject.wisc.edu/publications.php#pieces.

Graber, Doris A. 1993. *Mass Media and American Politics,* 4th ed. Washington, DC: Congressional Quarterly Press.

Graber, Doris A. 2009. *Mass Media and American Politics,* 8th ed. Washington, DC: CQ Press.

Grimmer, Justin. 2010. "A Bayesian Hierarchical Topic Model for Political Texts: Measuring Expressed Agendas in Senate Press Releases." *Political Analysis* 18 (1): 1–35.

Grose, Christian R., and Suzanne Globetti. 2007. "Valence Voters: Images, Issues, and Citizen Vote Choice in U.S. Senate Elections." Paper presented at the annual meeting of the Midwest Political Science Association, Chicago.

Guadagno, Rosanna E., and Robert B. Cialdini. 2007. "Gender Differences in Impression Management in Organizations: A Qualitative Review." *Sex Roles* 56 (7/8): 483–94.

Guinier, Lani. 1994. *The Tyranny of the Majority: Fundamental Fairness in Representative Democracy.* New York: Free Press.

Gulati, Girish J. 2004. "Revisiting the Link between Electoral Competition and Policy Extremism in the U.S. Congress." *American Politics Research* 32 (5): 495–520.

Hall, Richard L. 1996. *Participation in Congress.* New Haven: Yale University Press.

Hansen, Susan B. 1997. "Talking about Politics: Gender and Contextual Effects on Political Proselytizing." *Journal of Politics* 59 (1): 73–103.

Harris, John F., and Beth Frerking. 2008. "Clinton Aides: Palin Treatment Sexist." *Politico,* December 8. http://www.politico.com/news/stories/0908/13129.html.

Hastie, Reid. 1981. "Schematic Principles in Human Memory." In *Social Cognition: The Ontario Symposium,* edited by Edward T. Higgins, C. Peter Herman, and Mark P. Zanna. Hillsdale, NJ: Erlbaum.

Hastie, Reid, and Purohit A Kumar. 1979. "Person Memory: Personality Traits as Organizing Principles in Memory for Behaviors." *Journal of Personality and Social Psychology* 37 (1): 25–38.

Hayes, Danny. 2005. "Candidate Qualities through a Partisan Lens: A Theory of Trait Ownership." *American Journal of Political Science* 49 (4): 908–23.

Hayes, Danny. 2010. "Trait Voting in U.S. Senate Elections." *American Politics Research* 38 (6): 1102–29.

Heatherington, Laurie, Andrea B. Burns, and Timothy B. Gustafson. 1998. "When Another Stumbles: Gender and Self-Presentation to Vulnerable Others." *Sex Roles* 38 (11/12): 889–913.

Heilman, Madeline, and Tyler G. Okimoto. 2007. "Why are Women Penalized for Success at Male Tasks? The Implied Communality Deficit." *Journal of Applied Psychology* 92 (1): 81–92.

Heldman, Caroline, Sue Carroll, and Stephanie Olson. 2005. "She Brought Only a Skirt: Print Media Coverage of Elizabeth Dole's Bid for the Presidential Nomination." *Political Communication* 22 (3): 315–35.

Heldman, Caroline, Sarah Oliver, and Meredith Conroy. 2009. "From Ferraro to Palin: Sexism in Media Coverage of Vice Presidential Candidates." Paper presented at the American Political Science Association conference, Ontario, Canada.

Herrnson, Paul S. 1995. *Congressional Elections: Campaigning at Home and in Washington,* 4th ed. Washington, DC: CQ Press.

Herrnson, Paul S., J. Celeste Lay, and Atiya K. Stokes. 2003. "Women Running 'as Women': Candidate Gender, Campaign Issues, and Voter-Targeting Strategies." *Journal of Politics* 65 (1): 244–55.

Hetherington, Marc J. 1996. "The Media's Role in Forming Voters' National Economic Evaluations in 1992." *American Journal of Political Science* 40 (2): 372–95.

Hibbing, John R., and Elizabeth Theiss-Morse. 1995. *Congress as Public Enemy: Public Attitudes Toward American Political Institutions.* New York: Cambridge University Press.

Hill, Seth J., James Lo, Lynn Vavreck, and John Zaller. 2007. "The Opt-In Internet Panel: Survey Mode, Sampling Methodology and the Implications for Political Research." Unpublished paper, Department of Political Science, UCLA. http://www.sethjhill.com/mode.htm. Accessed September 11, 2011.

Hoffman, Lindsay H. 2006. "Is Internet Content Different After All? A Content Analysis of Mobilizing Information in Online and Print Newspapers." *Journalism and Mass Communication Quarterly* 83 (1): 53–76.

Huddy, Leonie, and Teresa Capelos. 2002. "Gender Stereotyping and Candidate Evaluation: Good News and Bad News for Women Politicians." In *The Social Psychology of Politics,* edited by Victor C. Ottati, R. Scott Tindale, John Edwards, Fred B. Bryant, Linda Heath, Daniel C. O'Connell, Yolanda Suarez-Balcazar, and Emil Posavac. New York: Kluwer Academic Press.

Huddy, Leonie, and Nayda Terkildsen. 1993. "Gender Stereotypes and the Perception of Male and Female Candidates." *American Journal of Political Science* 37 (1): 119–47.

Hughes, Melanie M. 2011. "Intersectionality, Quotas, and Minority Women's Political Representation Worldwide." *American Political Science Review* 105 (3): 1–17.

Hunt, Reed R. 1995. "The Subtlety of Distinctiveness: What von Restorff Really Did." *Psychonomic Bulletin and Review* 2 (1): 105–12.

Iyengar, Shanto, and Donald Kinder. 1987. *News That Matters.* Chicago: University of Chicago Press.

Jacobson, Gary C. 2009. *The Politics of Congressional Elections,* 7th ed. New York: Addison-Wesley Educational.

Jacobson, Gary C., and Samuel Kernell. 1983. *Strategy and Choice in Congressional Elections,* 2nd ed. New Haven: Yale University Press.

Jalalzai, Farida. 2006. "Women Candidates and the Media: 1992–2000 Elections." *Politics and Policy* 34 (3): 606–33.

Johnson, Dennis. 2004. *Congress Online: Bridging the Gap between Citizens and their Representatives.* New York: Routledge.

Johnson, Stefanie K., Susan E. Murphy, Selamawit Zewdie, and Rebecca J.Reichard. 2008. "The Strong Sensitive Type: Effects of Gender Stereotypes and Leadership Prototypes on the Evaluation of Male and Female Leaders." *Organizational Behavior and Human Decision Processes* 106 (1): 39–60.

Jones, Mark P. 1998. "Gender Quotas, Electoral Laws, and the Election of Women. Lessons from the Argentine Provinces." *Comparative Political Studies* 31 (1): 3–21.

Junn, Jane. 1991. "Participation and Political Knowledge." In *Political Participation and American Democracy,* edited by William Crotty. New York: Greenwood Press.

Kahn, Kim Fridkin. 1993. "Incumbency and the News Media in U.S. Senate Elections: An Experimental Investigation." *Political Research Quarterly* 46 (4): 715–40.

Kahn, Kim Fridkin. 1996. *The Political Consequences of Being a Woman: How Stereotypes Influence the Conduct and Consequences of Political Campaigns.* New York: Columbia University Press.

Kahn, Kim Fridkin, and Patrick J. Kenney. 1999. *The Spectacle of U.S. Senate Campaigns.* Princeton: Princeton University Press.

Kaniss, Phyllis. 1991. *Making Local News.* Chicago: University of Chicago Press.

Karp, Jeffrey A., and Susan A. Banducci. 2008. "When Politics Is Not Just a Man's Game: Women's Representation and Political Engagement." *Electoral Studies* 27 (1): 105–15.

Kenski, Kate, and Kathleen Hall Jamieson. 2000. "Do Men Know More About Politics Than Women?" In *Everything You Think You Know about Politics and Why You're Wrong,* edited by Kathleen Hall Jamieson. New York: Basic Books, New Republic Books.

Kinder, Donald R. 1986. "Presidential Character Revisted." In *Political Cognition: The 19th Annual Carnegie Symposium on Cognition,* edited by Richard R. Lau and David O. Sears. Hillsdale, NJ: Erlbaum.

Kinder, Donald R. 2003. "Communication and Politics in the Age of Information." In *The Oxford Handbook of Political Psychology,* edited by David O. Sears, Leonie Huddy, and Robert Jervis. New York: Oxford University Press.

Kinder, Donald R., and D. Roderick Kiewiet. 1981. "Sociotropic Politics: The American Case." *British Journal of Political Science* 11 (2): 129–61.

Kinder, Donald R., Mark D. Peters, Robert P. Abelson, and Susan T. Fiske. 1980. "Presidential Prototypes." *Political Behavior* 2 (4): 315–37.

King, Gary. 1989. *Unifying Political Methodology: The Likelihood Theory of Statistical Inference.* Cambridge: Cambridge University Press.

Kite, Mary E., Kay Deaux, Elizabeth L. Haines. 2008. "Gender Stereotypes." In *The Psychology of Women: A Handbook of Issues and Theories,* edited by Florence L. Denmark and Michele A. Paludi. Westport, CT: Praeger.

Kittilson, Miki C. 2008. "Representing Women: The Adoption of Family Leave Policies in Comparative Perspective." *Journal of Politics* 70 (2): 323–34.

Koch, Jeffrey W. 1997. "Candidate Gender and Women's Psychological Engagement in Politics." *American Politics Quarterly* 25 (1): 118–33.

Koch, Jeffrey W. 2000. "Do Citizens Apply Gender Stereotypes to Infer Candidates' Ideological Orientations?" *Journal of Politics* 62 (2): 414–29.

Krasno, Jonathan. 1997. *Challengers, Competition, and Reelection: Comparing Senate and House Elections.* New Haven: Yale University Press.

Lammers, Joris, Ernestine H. Gordijn, and Sabine Otten. 2009. "Iron Ladies, Men of Steel: The Effects of Gender Stereotyping on the Perception of Male and Female Candidates Are Moderated by Prototypicality." *European Journal of Social Psychology* 39 (2): 86–195.

Larson, Mary S. 2001. "Interactions, Activities and Gender in Children's Television Commercials: A Content Analysis." *Journal of Broadcasting and Electronic Media* 45 (1): 41–56.

Lawless, Jennifer L. 2004. "Women, War, and Winning Elections: Gender Stereotyping in the Post-September 11th Era." *Political Research Quarterly* 57 (3): 479–90.

Lawrence, Regina G., and Melody Rose. 2009. *Hillary Clinton's Run for the White House: Media, Gender Strategy, and Campaign Politics.* Boulder: Lynne Rienner.

Leary, Mary Ellen. 1977. *Phantom Politics: Campaigning in California.* Washington, DC: Public Affairs Press.

Lee, Suk-Jae, Brian M. Quigley, Mitchell S. Nesler, Amy B. Corbett, and James T. Tedeschi. 1999. "Development of a Self-Presentation Tactics Scale." *Personality and Individual Differences* 26 (4): 701–22.

Lewis-Beck, Michael S. 1980. *Applied Regression: An Introduction.* Thousand Oaks, CA: Sage.

Liebler, Carol M., and Susan J. Smith. 1997. "Tracking Gender Differences: A Comparative Analysis of Network Correspondents and Their Sources." *Journal of Broadcasting and Electronic Media* 41 (1): 58–68.

Lipinski, Daniel. 2001. "The Effect of Messages Communicated by Members of Congress: The Impact of Publicizing Votes." *Legislative Studies Quarterly* 26 (1): 81–100.

Lipinski, Daniel, and Gregory Neddenriep. 2004. "Using 'New' Media to get 'Old' Media Coverage: How Members of Congress Utilize Their Web Sites to Court Journalists." *Harvard International Journal of Press/Politics* 9 (1): 7–21.

Lippmann, Walter. 1925. *The Phantom Public.* New York: Harcourt, Brace.

Lodge, Milton, Kathleen M. McGraw, and Patrick Stroh. 1989. "An Impression-

Driven Model of Candidate Evaluation." *American Political Science Review* 83 (2): 399–419.

Lodge, Milton, Marco R. Steenbergen, and Shawn Brau. 1995. "The Responsive Voter: Campaign Information and the Dynamics of Candidate Evaluation." *American Political Science Review* 89 (2): 309–26.

Lord, Robert G., Douglas J. Brown, and Jennifer L. Harvey. 2001. "System Constraints on Leadership Perceptions, Behavior and Influence: An Example of Connectionist-Level Processes." In *The Blackwell Handbook of Social Psychology: Group Processes,* edited by Michael A. Hogg and Scott Tindale. Oxford: Blackwell.

Lord, Robert G., Christy L. de Vader, and George M. Alliger. 1986. "A Meta-Analysis of the Relation between Personality Traits and Leadership Perceptions: An Application of Validity Generalization Procedures." *Journal of Applied Psychology* 71 (3): 402–10.

Lord, Robert G., and Karen Maher. 1991. *Leadership and Information Processing.* New York: Routledge.

Lowi, Theodore J. 1964. "American Business, Public Policy, Case Studies, and Political Theory." *World Politics* 16 (4): 677–715.

Macrae, C. Neil, Miles Hewstone, and Riana J. Griffiths. 1993. "Processing Load and Memory for Stereotype-based Information." *European Journal of Social Psychology* 23 (1): 77–87.

Mager, John, and James G. Helgeson. 2011. "Fifty Years of Advertising Images: Some Changing Perspectives on Role Portrayals along with Enduring Consistencies." *Sex Roles* 64 (3/4): 238–52.

Maier, Scott R. 2010. "Newspapers Offer More News Than Do Major Online Sites." *Newspaper Research Journal* 31 (1): 6–19.

Manin, Bernhard, Adam Przeworski, and Susan C. Stokes. 1999. "Introduction." In *Democracy, Accountability, and Representation,* edited by Adam Przeworski, Susan C. Stokes, and Bernhard Manin. Cambridge: Cambridge University Press.

Manning, Jennifer, Colleen Shogan, and Susan Smelcer. 2011. "Women in the United States Congress: 1917–2011." *Congressional Research Service Report for Congress.* http://www.fas.org/sgp/crs/misc/RL30261.pdf. Accessed September 11, 2011.

Mansbridge, Jane. 1999. "Should Blacks Represent Blacks and Women Represent Women? A Contingent 'Yes'." *Journal of Politics* 61 (3): 628–57.

Markus, Gregory B. 1982. "Political Attitudes During an Election Year: A Report on the 1980 NES Panel Study." *American Political Science Review* 76 (3): 538–60.

Martin, Joanne, and Debra E. Meyerson. 1998. "Women and Power: Conformity, Resistance, and Disorganized Coaction." In *Power and Influence in Organizations,* edited by Roderick Kramer and Margaret A. Neale. Thousand Oaks, CA: Sage.

Matland, Richard E. 1994. "Putting Scandinavian Equality to the Test: An Experimental Evaluation of Gender Stereotyping of Political Candidates in a Sample of Norwegian Voters." *British Journal of Political Science* 24 (2): 273–92.

Mayer, William G. 1993. "Trends in Media Usage." *Public Opinion Quarterly* 57 (4): 593–611.

Mayhew, David. 1974. *Congress: The Electoral Connection.* New Haven: Yale University Press.

McCombs, Maxwell E. 1993. "The Evolution of Agenda-setting Research: Twenty-Five Years in the Marketplace of Ideas." *Journal of Communication* 43 (1): 58–67.

McDermott, Monika L. 1997. "Voting Cues in Low-Information Elections: Candidate Gender as Social Information Variable in Contemporary United States Elections." *American Journal of Political Science* 41 (1): 270–83.

McDermott, Monika L. 1998. "Race and Gender Cues in Low-Information Elections." *Political Research Quarterly* 51 (4): 895–918.

McGraw, Kathleen M. 2003. "Political Impressions." In *Political Psychology,* edited by David O. Sears, Leonie Huddy, and Robert Jervis. Oxford: Oxford University Press.

Media Report to Women. 2010. http://www.mediareporttowomen.com/statistics.htm. Accessed October 20, 2011.

Mikulski, Barbara, Kay Bailey Hutchison, Dianne Feinstein, Barbara Boxer, Patty Murray, Olympia Snowe, Susan Collins, Mary Landrieu, Blanche L. Lincoln, and Catherine Whitney. 2000. *Nine and Counting: The Women of the Senate.* New York: William Morrow.

Miller, Warren E. 1991. "Party Identification, Realignment, and Party Voting: Back to Basics." *American Political Science Review* 85 (2): 557–68.

Miller, Warren E., and Donald E. Stokes. 1963. "Constituency Influence in Congress." *American Political Science Review* 57 (1): 45–56.

Mondak, Jeffery J., and Mary R. Anderson. 2004. "The Knowledge Gap: A Reexamination of Gender-Based Differences in Political Knowledge." *Journal of Politics* 66 (2): 492–512.

Neuendorf, Kimberly A. 2002. *The Content Analysis Guidebook.* Thousand Oaks, CA: Sage.

Nesbitt, Jim. 2006. "Lawmakers Find Facts are Fluid on Encyclopedia Site." *Raleigh (NC) News & Observer,* February 3.

Niven, David. 2005. "Gender Bias? Media Coverage of Women and Men in Congress." In *Gender and American Politics: Women, Men, and the Political Process,* edited by Sue Tolleson-Rinehart and Jyl Josephson. New York: M. E. Sharpe.

Niven, David, and Jeremy Zilber. 2001a. "Do Women and Men in Congress Cultivate Different Images? Evidence from Congressional Websites." *Political Communication* 18 (4): 395–405.

Niven, David, and Jeremy Zilber. 2001b. "How Does She Have Time for Kids and Congress? Views on Gender and Media Coverage from House Offices." In *Women and Congress: Running, Winning and Ruling,* edited by Karen O'Connor. New York: Haworth Press.

Norris, Pippa. 1997. *Passages to Power.* Cambridge: Cambridge University Press.

Paek, Hye-Jin, Michelle R. Nelson, and Alexandra M. Vilela. 2011. "Examination of Gender-Role Portrayals in Television Advertising Across Seven Countries." *Sex Roles* 64 (3/4): 192–207.

Page, Benjamin I., and Robert Y. Shapiro. 1983. "Effects of Public Opinion on Policy." *American Political Science Review* 77 (1): 175–90.

Paletz, David L., and Robert M. Entman. 1981. *Media, Power, Politics.* New York: Free Press.

Palfrey, Thomas R., and Keith T. Poole. 1987. "The Relationship between Information, Ideology, and Voting Behavior." *American Journal of Political Science* 31 (3): 511–30.

Petrocik, John R. 1996. "Issue Ownership in Presidential Elections, with a 1980 Case Study." *American Journal of Political Science* 40 (3): 825–50.

Petrocik, John R., William L. Benoit, and Glenn J. Hansen. 2003/2004. "Issue Ownership and Presidential Campaigning, 1952–2000." *Political Science Quarterly* 118 (4): 599–626.

Phillips, Anne. 1995. *The Politics of Presence.* Oxford: Clarendon Press.

Phillips, Anne. 1998. *Feminism and Politics.* Oxford: Oxford University Press.

Pierce, Patrick A. 1993. "Political Sophistication and the Use of Candidate Traits in Candidate Evaluation." *Political Psychology* 14 (1): 21–35.

Pitkin, Hanna F. 1967. *The Concept of Representation.* Berkeley: University of California Press.

Poole, Keith T., and L. Harmon Zeigler. 1985. *Women, Public Opinion, and Politics: The Changing Political Attitudes of American Women.* New York: Longman.

Project for Excellence in Journalism. 2005. *The State of the News 2005.* Washington, DC: Project for Excellence in Journalism. www.stateofthenewsmedia. org.

Project for Excellence in Journalism. 2006. *The State of the News Media 2006.* Washington, DC: Project for Excellence in Journalism. www.stateofthenewsmedia.org.

Project for Excellence in Journalism. 2010. *The State of the News Media: An Annual Report on American Journalism.* Washington, DC: Project for Excellence in Journalism. www.stateofthenewsmedia.org.

Puopolo, Sonia T. 2001. "The Web and U.S. Senatorial Campaigns 2000." *American Behavioral Scientist* 44 (12): 2030–47.

Rahn, Wendy M. 1993. "The Role of Partisan Stereotypes in Information Processing about Political Candidates." *American Journal of Political Science* 37 (2): 472–96.

Reingold, Beth. 2000. *Representing Women: Sex, Gender, and Legislative Behavior in Arizona and California.* Chapel Hill: University of North Carolina Press.

Reingold, Beth. 2008. "Women as Office Holders: Linking Descriptive and Substantive Representation." In *Political Women and American Democracy,* edited by Christina Wolbrecht, Karen Beckwith, and Lisa Baldez. New York: Cambridge University Press.

Richardson, Lilliard E., Jr., and Patricia K. Freeman. 1995. "Gender Differences in Constituency Service Among State Legislators." *Political Research Quarterly* 48 (1): 169–79.

Rodgers, Shelly, Esther Thorson, and Michael Antecol. 2001. "'Reality' in the *St. Louis Post-Dispatch.*" *Newspaper Research Journal* 21 (3): 51–68.

Rosenwasser, Shirley M., and Norma G. Dean. 1989. "Gender Role and Political Office: Effects of Perceived Masculinity/Femininity of Candidate and Political Office." *Psychology of Women Quarterly* 13 (1): 77–85.

Rosenwasser, Shirley M., and Jana Seale. 1988. "Attitudes toward a Hypothetical Male or Female Presidential Candidate." *Political Psychology* 9 (4): 591–98.

Rourke, Liam, Terry Anderson, Randy Garrison, and Walter Archer. 2000. "Methodological Issues in the Content Analysis of Computer Conference Transcripts." *International Journal of Artificial Intelligence in Education* 12:8–22.

Ruble, Thomas L. 1983. "Sex Stereotypes: Issues of Change in the 1970s." *Sex Roles* 9 (3): 397–402.

Rule, Wilma. 1994. "Parliament of, by, and for the People: Except for Women?" In *Electoral Systems in Comparative Perspective,* edited by Wilma Rule and Joseph F. Zimmerman. London: Greenwood Press.

Ruskin, Liz. 2006. "Alaska Lawmakers Got Cash from Abramoff Clients; Stevens Has Donated the Contributions He Received to Charity." *Anchorage Daily News,* January 5.

Sapiro, Virginia. 1981/1982. "If US Senator Baker Were a Woman: An Experimental Study of Candidate Images." *Political Psychology* 3 (1/2): 61–83.

Sapiro, Virginia. 1982. "Private Costs of Public Commitments or Public Costs of Private Commitments? Family Roles versus Political Ambition." *American Journal of Political Science* 26 (2): 265–79.

Schaffner, Brian F. 2006. "Local News Coverage and the Incumbency Advantage in the U.S. House." *Legislative Studies Quarterly* 31 (4): 491–511.

Schaffner, Brian F., and Patrick J. Sellers. 2003. "The Structural Determinants of Local Congressional News Coverage." *Political Communication* 20 (1): 41–57.

Scheufele, Dietram A., and Matthew C. Nisbet. 2002. "Being a Citizen Online— New Opportunities and Dead Ends." *Harvard International Journal of Press/ Politics* 7 (3): 55–75.

Schiller, Wendy J. 1995. "Senators as Political Entrepreneurs: Using Bill Sponsorship to Shape Legislative Agendas." *American Journal of Political Science* 39 (1): 186–203.

Schiller, Wendy J. 2000. *Partners and Rivals: Representation in U.S. Senate Delegations.* Princeton: Princeton University Press.

Schumaker, Paul, and Nancy E. Burns. 1988. "Gender Cleavages and the Resolution of Local Policy Issues." *American Journal of Political Science* 32 (4): 1070–95.

Schwindt-Bayer, Leslie A., and William Mishler. 2005. "An Integrated Model of Women's Representation." *Journal of Politics* 67 (2): 407–28.

Scott, Kristyn A., and Douglas D. Brown. 2006. "Female First, Leader Second? Gender Bias in the Encoding of Leadership Behavior." *Organizational Behavior and Human Decision Processes* 101 (2): 230–42.

Shepsle, Kenneth A. 1972. "The Strategy of Ambiguity: Uncertainty and Electoral Competition." *American Political Science Review* 66 (2): 555–68.

Signorielli, Nancy, and Aaron Bacue. 1999. "Recognition and Respect: A Content Analysis of Prime-time Television Characters across Three Decades." *Sex Roles* 40 (7/8): 527–44.

Smith, Kevin B. 1997. "When All's Fair: Signs of Parity in Media Coverage of Female Candidates." *Political Communication* 14:71–82.

Smith, Stacy L., Katherine M. Pieper, Amy Granados, and Marc Choueiti. 2010. "Assessing Gender-Related Portrayals in Top-Grossing G-Rated Films." *Sex Roles* 62 (11/12): 774–86.

Spence, Janet T., and Robert L. Helmreich. 1978. *Masculinity and Femininity: Their Psychological Dimensions, Correlates, and Antecedents.* Austin: University of Texas Press.

Srull, Thomas K., and Robert S. Wyer. 1989. "Person Memory and Judgment." *Psychological Review* 96 (1): 58–83.

Stangor, Charles, Laure Lynch, Changming Duan, and Beth Glass. 1992. "Categorization of Individuals on the Basis of Multiple Social Features." *Journal of Personality and Social Psychology* 62 (2): 207–18.

Stimson, James A., Michael B. MacKuen, and Robert S. Erikson. 1995. "Dynamic Representation." *American Political Science Review* 89 (3): 543–65.

Stokes, Susan C. 2005. "Perverse Accountability: A Formal Model of Machine Politics with Evidence from Argentina." *American Political Science Review* 99 (3): 315–25.

Stolle, Dietlind, and Elisabeth Gidengil. 2010. "What Do Women Really Know? A Gendered Analysis of Varieties of Political Knowledge." *Perspectives on Politics* 8 (1): 93–109.

Strutton, David, Lou E. Pelton, and James R. Lumpkin. 1995. "Personality Characteristics and Salespeople's Choice of Coping Strategies." *Journal of the Academy of Marketing Science* 23 (2): 132–40.

Sutcliffe, John B., Martha F. Lee, and Walter C. Soderlund. 2005. "Women and Crisis Reporting: Television News Coverage of Political Crises in the Caribbean." *Harvard International Journal of Press/Politics* 10 (3): 99–124.

Swers, Michele L. 1998. "Are Congresswomen More Likely to Vote for Women's than Their Male Colleagues?" *Legislative Studies Quarterly* 23 (3): 435–48.

Swers, Michelle L. 2002. *The Difference Women Make: The Policy Impact of Women in Congress.* Chicago: University of Chicago Press.

Tewksbury, David, and Scott L. Althaus. 2000. "Differences in Knowledge Acquisition among Readers of the Paper and Online Versions of a National Newspaper." *Journalism and Mass Communication Quarterly* 77 (3): 457–79.

Thomas, Sue. 1991. "The Impact of Women on State Legislative Policies." *Journal of Politics* 53 (4): 958–76.

Turner, Jacob S. 2011. "Sex and the Spectacle of Music Videos: An Examination of the Portrayal of Race and Sexuality in Music Videos." *Sex Roles* 64 (3/4): 173–91.

Urbinati, Nadia, and Mark E. Warren. 2008. "The Concept of Representation in Contemporary Democratic Theory." *Annual Review of Political Science* 11:387–412.

U.S. Census Bureau. 2009. "Cumulative Estimates of Resident Population Change for the United States, Regions, States and Puerto Rico and Region and State Rankings." December. http://www.census.gov/popest/states/NST-pop-chg.html.

Verba, Sidney, Nancy Burns, and Kay Lehman Schlozman. 1997. "Knowing and Caring about Politics: Gender and Political Engagement." *Journal of Politics* 59 (4): 1051–72.

Vinson, Danielle C. 2003. *Through Local Eyes: Local Media Coverage of Congress and Its Members.* Cresskill, NJ: Hampton Press.

Wahlke, John C. 1971. "Policy Demands and System Support: The Role of the Represented." *British Journal of Political Science* 1 (3): 271–90.

Wallis, Cara. 2011. "Performing Gender: A Content Analysis of Gender Display in Music Videos." *Sex Roles* 64 (3/4): 160–72.

Walsh, Katherine C. 2002. "Enlarging Representation: Women Bringing Marginalized Perspectives to Floor Debate in the House of Representatives." In *Women Transforming Congress,* edited by Cindy S. Rosenthal. Norman: University of Oklahoma Press.

Weingast, Barry R. 1994. "Reflections on Distributive Politics and Universalism." *Political Research Quarterly* 47 (2): 319–27.

Welch, Susan. 1985. "Are Women More Liberal than Men in the U.S. Congress?" *Legislative Studies Quarterly* 10 (1): 125–34.

Westlye, Mark. 1991. *Senate Elections and Campaign Intensity.* Baltimore: Johns Hopkins University Press.

Williams, John E., Robert C. Satterwhite, and Deborah L. Best. 1999. "Pancultural Gender Stereotypes Revisited: The Five Factor Model." *Sex Roles* 40 (7/8): 513–25.

Wood, Wendy, and Alice H. Eagly. 2002. "A Cross-Cultural Analysis of the Behavior of Women and Men: Implications for the Origins of Sex Differences." *Psychological Bulletin* 128 (5): 699–727.

Woods, Harriet. 2000. *Stepping Up To Power: The Political Journey of American Women.* Boulder: Westview Press.

Wright, Gerald C., Jr., and Mark B. Berkman. 1986. "Candidates and Policy in U.S. Senate Elections." *American Political Science Review* 80 (2): 567–90.

Xenos, Michael A., and Kirsten A. Foot. 2005. "Politics as Usual, or Politics Unusual? Position Taking and Dialogue on Campaign Websites in the 2002 US Elections." *Journal of Communication* 55 (1): 169–85.

Yiannakis, Diana E. 1982. "House Members' Communication Styles: Newsletters and Press Releases." *Journal of Politics* 44 (4): 1049–71.

Zaller, John R. 1992. *The Nature and Origins of Mass Opinion.* Cambridge: Cambridge University Press.

Zhao, Xinshu, and Steven H. Chaffee. 1995. "Campaign Advertisements versus Television News as Sources of Political Issue Information." *Public Opinion Quarterly* 59 (1): 41–56.

Zoch, Lynn M., and Judy V. Turk. 1998. "Women Making News: Gender as a Variable in Source Selection and Use." *Journalism & Mass Communication Quarterly* 75 (4): 762–75.

Index

Adams, John, 169
advertising, representational messaging
    and, 13, 14–15, 23, 25. *See also* political
    advertisements
agentic v. communal traits, 211*n*9
    and gender-role theory, 15–17, 21, 23, 25–
        27
    leadership prototypes and, 21, 24, 84–85
    in news coverage, 23–25, 79, 84–85, 97,
        98–100, 98 (*fig.*), 99 (*table*), 102–4, 103
        (*table*), 107, 140, 141 (*fig.*), 144–45, 144
        (*fig.*), 218*nn*23, 24, 209*n*26
    on official websites, 47, 48–49, 52–54, 53
        (*table*), 54 (*table*), 56–57, 61, 102, 135,
        141 (*fig.*), 211*nn*7, 8
    in political advertisements, 137 (*fig.*),
        138, 138 (*table*), 144–45, 144 (*fig.*),
        217*nn*13–15, 218*nn*23, 24
    in press releases, 65, 68, 73, 74, 76
    in reelection campaigns, 135, 136–38, 137
        (*fig.*), 138 (*table*), 140, 141 (*fig.*), 144,
        144 (*fig.*), 146, 155, 217*nn*12–15, 218*n*23,
        220*n*30
    and representational messaging, 16–28
    See also communal v. competitive issues
Allard, Wayne, 171 (*table*)
Allen, George, 39, 193 (*table*), 219*n*26
allocation responsiveness
    and credit claiming, 78, 79 (*table*)
    in news coverage, 104–5, 105 (*fig.*), 106–
        7, 106 (*table*), 108, 214*n*22
    in press releases, 25, 27, 34, 67, 68, 72, 73
        (*table*), 79, 104, 106, 106 (*table*),
        212*nn*10, 11
    in representational messaging, 8–9, 12,
        22–23, 209*nn*22, 23, 212*n*10
Ashdown, Pete, 39

biography pages, website. *See* websites, of-
    ficial
Boehner, John, 63
Bouchard, Michael, 133–34, 217*n*3
Boxer, Barbara, 32, 53, 166, 171 (*table*)
Braun, Carol Moseley, 81–82
Brown, Sherrod, 39
Burns, Conrad, 39, 193 (*table*), 219*n*26
Burr, Richard, 36, 58, 171 (*table*), 211*n*14,
    212*n*7, 212*n*8
Bush, George W., 71, 96, 109, 133, 135, 152,
    153, 155, 220*n*35
Byrd, Robert, 193 (*table*), 219*n*26

campaigns. *See* reelection campaigns
Cantwell, Maria, 81, 171 (*table*), 193 (*table*)
Caraway, Hattie, 31, 209*n*2
Cardin, Ben, 2, 3, 5–6, 208*n*12
Chafee, Lincoln, 48, 171 (*table*), 193 (*table*),
    219*n*26
Charen, Mona, 48
citizen knowledge and assessment of sena-
    tors
    and accuracy of perceptions, 110, 120–
        21, 122–26, 125 (*table*), 127 (*table*), 128,
        129–30, 129 (*fig.*)
    citizen characteristics in measuring,
        115–16, 117 (*table*), 118, 119, 119 (*table*),
        121 (*table*), 123 (*table*), 124–25, 125 (*ta-
        ble*), 127 (*table*), 130, 159, 160, 215*nn*6,
        7, 216*n*8
    and "descriptive" representation, 131
    gender gap in, 11, 28, 110–14, 120, 122,
        124, 125–26, 128, 127 (*table*), 128 (*fig.*),
        129 (*fig.*), 130, 131
    and gender stereotypes, 10, 26–27, 41,
        110–11